PLEASE ENJOY YOUR HAPPINESS

PAUL BRINKLEY-ROGERS

TOUCHSTONE

New York   London   Toronto   Sydney   New Delhi

Touchstone
An Imprint of Simon & Schuster, Inc.
1230 Avenue of the Americas
New York, NY 10020

Copyright © 2016 by Paul Brinkley-Rogers
Originally published in 2016 in Great Britain by Pan Macmillan

"Sonnet XVII" from *100 Love Sonnets: Cien sonetos de amor* by Pablo Neruda, translated by Stephen Tapscott, on page 355, is reproduced by permission of the University of Texas Press. Copyright © Pablo Neruda 1959 and Fundación Pablo Neruda, Copyright © 1986 by the University of Texas Press.

First Touchstone hardcover edition August 2016

TOUCHSTONE and colophon are registered trademarks of Simon & Schuster, Inc.

For information about special discounts for bulk purchases, please contact Simon & Schuster Special Sales at 1-866-506-1949 or business@simonandschuster.com.

The Simon & Schuster Speakers Bureau can bring authors to your live event. For more information or to book an event, contact the Simon & Schuster Speakers Bureau at 866-248-3049 or visit our website at www.simonspeakers.com.

Interior design by Kyle Kabel

Manufactured in the United States of America

10 9 8 7 6 5 4 3 2 1

ISBN 978-1-5011-5125-5
ISBN 978-1-5011-5127-9 (ebook)

This story is dedicated to those Japanese women from all walks of life who with grace, warmth, and kindness helped Japan rise to new greatness after the disaster of World War II.

CONTENTS

CONTENTS

PLEASE
ENJOY YOUR
HAPPINESS

PROLOGUE

In the private world of a sweetheart I once had there was a secret valley, much like Shangri-La. She told me that in that valley her family lived happily and all her lost friends waited for her, their faces happy. Her youthful secrets were there, locked in the ice and snow that ringed her paradise. This imaginary valley was not in Tibet. It was not in Japan. It was somewhere in vast landlocked Manchuria in northern China. It was there that Kaji Yukiko was born. She knew she would never see it again.

Yukiko was almost a woman when she fled from Harbin, a sophisticated city of Manchuria. Japan surrendered in September 1945, its puppet state in Manchuria was abandoned, and massive Soviet forces moved in, together with vengeful Chinese guerrillas, forcing the 1.7 million Japanese colonists there to flee for their lives. Repatriated, after many hardships, back to Japan, Yukiko became the ultimate outsider in a homeland she did not know. Tall, beautiful, poised, ferociously curious, gifted in languages including Russian, Mandarin, Japanese, and English, she became a plaything of Hiroshima criminals and wealthy businessmen. But, finally, one terrible day, she ran away. In her chest of drawers, on top of her favorite books

1

of poetry, she kept a short sword—a *tanto shira*—wrapped in deep violet silk, for the inevitable day the gangsters came for her.

Her past was catching up with her when I met her. She had created a new private world around her interests in literature and music. But she desperately needed someone to confide in, someone to love. She had lost everyone and everything she loved. For her, love had no future.

I was an outsider too: a young English kid who had enlisted in the US Navy. I was nineteen. The year was 1959. Yukiko was thirty-one when she picked me out of the crowd of sailors in the White Rose, the bar in the seaport of Yokosuka where she worked. She walked up to me with a tired smile and said, "Hello." I was so inexperienced and tongue-tied I did not know what to say. I was focused completely on how near she was to me and how her eyes were focused only on me. I still remember the mix of fragrance and heat, and it still has the same effect on my aging body as it did then when I was young.

"What is that book in your hand?" she asked, in the sort of delicately phrased English that foreigners sometimes speak, unaware that they are putting native speakers to shame.

"It is poetry," I said, my face red.

"And who is that poet?"

"I don't know if you know him. It is Dylan Thomas, the favorite of many young men."

She looked at me quickly and in disbelief, not as if I were a fool, or clever, but as if I were a blank sheet of paper on which she could write. "Oh yes," she said brightly. "Mr. Dylan Thomas. The wild man. The free man. I envy him. He once wrote to a woman, 'Poetry may not appeal to the intelligent mind more than to the unintelligent.' Isn't that wonderful! Yes. Let's go! Let's talk about that."

I looked around the bar. There were about thirty sailors like me, dressed in their white summer uniforms, some drunk, some loud, some sitting cheek to cheek with girls in bright glittery gowns. I could not imagine a discussion like this one was really happening. It was like some kind of dream. And yet here was this intimidating woman, dressed entirely in black, asking me, "How old are you?" and saying, when I answered, "Come with me, sailor boy. Come on!"

She told me I was without a doubt the first man in the history of the US Navy who dared to enter a Japanese country-and-western bar with a book of poetry in his hands.

"You may need a friend," she said. "Sailors do not read verse. Someone might pick a fight with you because you carry that book. You are not normal," she added, in a kindly manner.

Thus began an unfinished romance that was also a friend-ship. It started right there, in a darkened corner booth uphol-stered in black vinyl as if it were the backseat in a teenager's Chevy. As I have grown into my seventies, I have come to accept that this romance is still going on. Even now it haunts me. It survives, bobbing up and down on the surface of my life, which has had its share of disappointments. At times it becomes spectral, and now it is compelling me to write about what happened in the middle months of 1959. I hear that voice again, full of excitement and anticipation: "Come on! Come on!"

But this is not a ghost story. This is a story about a real young man—myself—and a real woman. It was Yukiko who stripped illusions from the realities of life and showed me what it takes to be a man. It was her "duty," she said, to educate me in poetry, writing, language, and opera, and to familiarize me with films from the golden age of Japanese cinema and those moody songs about broken hearts known as *enka*. Her actions allowed me to appreciate the importance of loyalty, honor, respect, and courage.

She urged me to live life without regret: to live a life without love if need be.

She predicted with a great deal of conviction in her long letters that I would become a writer and said she knew she would read about me someday. She spent hours typing those letters as if they were manuscripts, infusing them with poetry from forgotten ages and those tough *enka* lyrics—about hopeless love, two-timing men, abandoned women, drunken nights, lost innocence, futile longing—that might as well have been written about her own struggle to survive.

She told me she would always remember what we had shared together after I sailed away forever. That inevitable day was coming. I could not stay. If I had jumped ship, I would have ended up in jail. She asked me many, many times to promise that I would never forget her. She asked for that in her letters. She asked me in person, staring at me with an intensity that I, a mere boy, did not understand but that I appreciate now. I have not forgotten her.

Sometime in 2012, I found her letters in the poetry section of my personal library, tucked into a thick volume of notebooks written by Gerard Manley Hopkins. One letter was handwritten with a fountain pen in the cursive script of disciplined penmanship taught in classrooms long ago. The other letters were typed.

As soon as my fingers touched the paper the letters were written on I realized what they were. I stepped back from the shelves and propped up the pillows on my battleship-grey couch, which is a wonderful place to read and nap. I read the letters one by one, slowly, in chronological order. I have ten of them. There were more, but somewhere in my long life the rest disappeared, although I do have the notes I made about them when I was correcting Yukiko's use of English at her request. I read the letters again, and then to my surprise I started sobbing. It was almost like having a broken heart, except that I was thrilled and happy and, strangely, also a little chagrined. I realized that I had been so young when she wrote to me that I had not appreciated how much effort she had made, often with the use of her hefty *Sanseido's Japanese-English Dictionary*, to lay bare her heart on the softness of this paper made from the leaves of mulberry trees.

I read the letters yet again, this time out loud. I could hear the sound of her voice speaking to me through the static noise of half a century of life that included three broken marriages and all the anguish that went with them, but also the joys of fatherhood, living a full life, and professional success. I have had relationships with several remarkable women during those years. But in that moment it dawned on me that none of those relationships was as compelling and challenging as the one I had with Kaji Yukiko.

The chapters are, in effect, one long letter to this woman who so profoundly influenced my life. Her friendship was a gift to a very young man who would like in somber old age to say thank you.

Chapter 1

ONE FINE DAY

The months and days are the travelers of eternity.
The years that come and go are also voyagers.

—Bashō Matsuo*

Kaji Yukiko! I have your letters. I found them again after all
these years. One is written, so neatly, so carefully, in blue
ink. You typed the others on your Smith Corona portable.
The paper is still creamy white and soft, as if it were made of
silk. When I read your letters this afternoon, it was as if you
were still speaking to me. I could hear your voice—strong,
determined, willful, elegant. You can tell from the tenor of my
voice, I think, how emotional that moment was for me. You
once said, when I was nineteen, that you read each of your
letters out loud before you put it in the mail, so that when I
opened the envelope I would hear the sound of your voice.
"I will be a bird, sitting in a tree," you said. "If you keep my
letters and read them again, you will hear me singing." That

---

* From *Oku no hosomichi* (*Narrow Road to the Interior*), by Bashō Matsuo,
1644–1694. Bashō believed that art could create an awareness that permitted
seeing and communicating the elusive essence of experience.

was in April 1959 in the seaport of Yokosuka, Japan. The long rainy season was beginning. It is now 2014 and the year is coming to an end. It is Christmas and, as usual, I am alone. Your letters are spread out on my bed.

I have read them all again, closely. They demand to be read closely because there is not much time left. I am seventy-five now. You—if you still live—are at least eighty-six. I can hear your voice clearly but have been struggling to recall exactly how you looked when we knew each other more than half a century ago. It has been at least twenty-five years since the last black-and-white photograph I had of you was destroyed when my damned roof in Bisbee, Arizona, started leaking. All I can visualize now are the hard outlines of your face, as if it had been chiseled out of stone and never loved. The jet-black hair down to your shoulders, with your fringe cut straight over your fierce eyes. How serious you were.

I remember that you were born in the depths of winter in Harbin, China. Your name, Yukiko, means Snow Child. When World War II was ending and the Soviets stormed into the Japanese colony in cold northern China, your family fled south to try to find a ship that would take you to safety in Japan. Your eyes were full of tears when you told me in the White Rose that your father had been killed and your brothers died, and then it was just you and your mother trying to escape.

It was dark in that bar, where we often met when my ship, the USS *Shangri-La*, was in port. In the gloom, you were a tall, thin shadow, like you are now when I imagine you. You thought it was so funny that I was a sailor on an attack aircraft carrier loaded with nuclear weapons but named after a mythical paradise. I remember you pulled out a dictionary and you found the word *irony* and you said, "When I am old, I am going to remember this very funny thing."

Maybe you are with your grandchildren now, your back bent, on your knees, the children demanding. Have you told them that for a few months you knew a young sailor who helped you with your English, who captured your heart and to whom you read poetry? I think probably not. You may still be the shy though assertive one. Are you an orderly, obedient Japanese? Now I am the one who is laughing! There is simply no way you could ever be submissive or just a face in the crowd. You were the woman who discussed the poet Bashō Matsuo with me soon after we met on April 15, 1959. You waved dismissively in my face when I talked naively about Jack Kerouac. You were the woman who insisted that the haiku was preferable, very much so, to *On the Road*'s stream of consciousness.

"Haiku are shorter than short," you said in your careful English, "but the content is profound. A good haiku is like a single snowdrop peeping through the ice. *On the Road* goes on forever. It is like an airplane crash."

You didn't like Johnny Cash and his version of "Hillbilly Heaven" either, and I don't blame you, because that is what they played so loudly at the White Rose when the sailors came to drag you out to the dance floor. You would stagger back to the booth where I sat, muttering, "Gershwin . . . Miles . . . Are they just a dream?"

I do not have copies of the letters I sent to you. But I do have the poetry I wrote at your urging, which I included with every letter I mailed to you. It is probably better that I do not have my letters. What did I know about love and longing when I was nineteen? Japanese women often said with a giggle that I looked like Anthony Perkins. "Oh no, Paul-san," you said. "You look like me: a refugee." And there was some accuracy in that, because I was an immigrant kid on a four-year US Navy enlistment who was not yet an American citizen. I was only two years off the boat from Europe. I was a stranger in a strange land made even stranger by the shock of sudden immersion in things Japanese. The more that interest grew, the less I liked certain things about the United States. Ice-cold Coca-Cola—that was fine. Segregation. Guns. Ignorance. Intolerance. It didn't take much for a kid like me, who carried a thirty-five-cent paperback copy of James Michener's *Sayonara* in his kit bag, to realize that I would be a rebel and a ronin (masterless samurai) all my life, no matter where I was. You told me that. You also predicted in your letters that I would become a writer, all of which happened, although I suppose you do not know that.

I still have that copy of *Sayonara*. It was printed on cheap paper, so its pages are yellowing. We talked about the story for hours, and I told you how Lieutenant Commander Charlie L. Peeples, the Protestant chaplain on my ship, did his best to warn the entire crew of 3,448 men that getting involved with a Japanese woman, and especially attempting to marry one, was against "command policy," pretty much the way it was in *Sayonara*. You and I had to sneak into those sections of Yokosuka that were off-limits to navy personnel just to have an undisturbed conversation and sip coffee. Do you remember how angry I was, and how much I hated everything I thought was unjust and unfair? You were so worried. You didn't want us to end up like the American officer and the Japanese actress, unhappy and torn apart by the rules. Here is that copy of *Sayonara* with the naked geisha on it, which we passed from hand to hand many times when we talked about that love story. The cover is coming loose. I treated that book as a talisman. It went with me to Vietnam and Cambodia in the war years. For me, the story still rings true. I read the book in Saigon and Phnom Penh. During my long career as a journalist, it went with me to Manila, to Cuba, to China, to Argentina. I know how to lose myself in impossible love. You taught me that.

I have started to dream in Japanese again since rediscovering your letters. Why am I dreaming that way? Sometimes I do not exactly know. But I did begin thinking about Japan again with emotion for the first time in many years in 2011, during the disaster of the Tōhoku earthquake, when I spent long hours on my couch watching live video feeds from NHK (Nippon Hōsō Kyōkai, Japan's equivalent of the BBC) on my laptop computer. I was an emotional shipwreck. And then again I was overwhelmed by nostalgia after I bought opera tickets in 2012 for *Madama Butterfly*. And there was that April evening in 1996 here in Arizona when I encountered the gentle Oe Kenzaburō, the 1994 Nobel laureate, drinking tea in a hotel bar and staring out the picture window at a big pile of rocks through his antique spectacles with perfectly round lenses. He told me, at the end of a long conversation about love and longing in which your name came up, "Don't fail to write about this lovely woman before you die or you will regret it when you are in Heaven." It is only now, after reading your letters, that I realize how much you cared about me. Maybe age has made me wiser, more appreciative, and wistful. I grew up, finally, I suppose, and now I am an old man looking back, far back, to that brief time in my life when we were more than friends. Sometimes you are talking to me in my dreams. I am lost in Tokyo or some other city. I am looking for a train to take me to Kyoto, but I can't find the train station. You are speaking Japanese, and I am struggling to understand you. How strange that in my brain there is a reservoir of fluent Japanese! You might be interested to know that when I went to university I majored in Japanese language and history, and that I lived and worked in Tokyo in the 1970s. I was an idiot in my youth. I made no real effort to look for you. It is only now, after my marriages, that I appreciate who you were and what you did for me. You told me over and over again, "Go to university." You demanded it! You told me to write poetry. You demanded it! Write for newspapers. Write for magazines. Write books. "Write! Write! Write!" you said. I was reeling, not comprehending, astonished at what you were telling me. You imagined reading what I had published. You saw something in me that I could not begin to see in myself.

Here is the first of your letters, written soon after the *Shangri-La* left Yokosuka, as it often did after ten or fifteen days in port, to patrol the South China Sea. It was delivered to the ship by mail plane. The *Shangri-La* would sail away for two or three weeks, and then it would be back again. We were together, and I would go. We were together, and I would go. From April until the last day of summer in September, I was always arriving and leaving. You were always there, waiting on your hilltop, hiding from crows and other malevolent creatures until you could jump down the 101 steps and dash through the wet streets lit by the neon lights of nightclubs so you could greet me.

Dear Paul,

Just I came back home now. Nobody stay, so make me feel better. It is only one day since we parted. I did not want to work. I did not know how hard it is to work until I finished tonight. I request the studio to print a photograph of myself today. So I'll get it tomorrow then send you that photo with this letter. Please look at the woman you see in the photo and smile just a bit because I want to see your smile in my dreams.

Well, first of all, what pleases me is the fact that you have never given to me decadent impressions from a moral or ethical sense. I can't explain this very well. I hope sincerely that you understand. But I think that we had spend time for a right and lovely time. You were just you, and I was just me, and I knew we could not become lovers. The beautiful and important thing is that we both found that we loved showing respect. In that way we loved each other. We respect each other and then we surround this respect with the kind of longing that a poet would call "ardent." Is that the correct word? I think so, because I am an older woman and the word ardent means a lot to me. Because I am an older woman I can say to you with so much happiness, but maybe with some tears, that even if I cannot meet you again I will never regret that I spent my time with you.

It was for me not the sad, bitter Wakare mo tanoshi [Even Parting Is Enjoyable, the 1947 film by Naruse Mikio about women struggling with the chaos of postwar Japan] but some day our experience will become a very nice memory for us. You were so considerate to me. You were always kind to such a selfish woman as I am. I never forget you. How happy I was, except for my sorrow coming or parting. I was filled in everything by only your being with me and our conversations. Every moment of mine was filled and when we were together even if we did not say anything, we understood each other. And, after you left, my feeling of existence lessened so I could not write you last night even though I wanted to so much.

This morning I sent off your ship from my mountain. When I went to the top and at 15 minutes to 8:00 already sailors formed a line on the deck. When I had heard the whistle, I wish I could use magic to make stop the ship. But . . . just at 8:00 o'clock the Shangri-La started to take you away from me. Then when the ship became just a form, I came down from the mountain before my eyes become as hazy as the mist hanging over the ocean. Those were my maiden eyes.

Well, I hope you are thinking of me and write to me. I'm looking forward to hearing from you. Please take care of yourself and remember me to be your friend. I'll write you again. I hope you understand this broken English and please after correcting this letter, send a copy back to me to study.

Still my cold is sukoshi [just a little] but soon all right, so don't worry about that.

Love,

Yukiko

P.S.

I send you the words Respect. Sincerity. Gratitude.

I remember those long nights at the White Rose when we talked politics. I said some of the crew thought I was a Communist and that my commanding officer told me—when I did not buy the official doctrine that "Red China" was America's enemy—"Rogers! The US Navy doesn't pay you to think!" Or those afternoons we sat talking in the Mozart coffee shop, and the delicate sound of the piano in the wet heat of the summer impelled you to touch my hand, as if I were a child or maybe as if we were both children, across the white tablecloth? "This makes me think of my father," you said. "He played piano for me when I was a little girl.

Sad. So sad were those years." Then there was the day you invited me to climb the hill to your apartment. You lit a stick of incense and said a Buddhist prayer. You were upset when I asked you why you were praying. I looked out your window, through the rain, at my ship far off in the bay, and for no apparent reason the tears welled up in both our eyes, and I held you tight, and you told me, "Paul. Never let me go!" I still shiver when I remember that moment. I was just a boy. I held you for a while and then I let you go, and I said, "I'll never forget you. Never!" You looked embarrassed. Or was that look something else?

That was much later in the summer, just two days before the *Shangri-La* left Yokosuka forever on September 22. I had to return to the ship. You gave me your umbrella. You didn't want me to get wet. I wanted to kiss you, but I couldn't because I knew, and you knew, that it was all going to end. My youngster's heart could not cope with the parting, so I was impatient and I offered up only an abrupt good-bye. As I was going down the steps I turned to look. You were staring at me. I could not see the expression on your face through the glass. I saw just your outline, which is all that I can see now, after all these years. If you could have been at the opera with me last year, you would have understood why in my seventies I am filled with longing—for what, I do not know. You would have understood why when Butterfly sang "*Un bel dì*" (One Fine Day) I immediately thought of you on the mountain watching my ship leave, waiting for its return. Maybe you are buried on the mountain. Maybe not. But here are Puccini's lyrics to the most wonderful aria about lost love ever written. Men and women—even hardened and bitter men and women—sob when the abandoned Butterfly, who has never given up hope, begins singing:

> One fine day, we will see
> A thread of smoke arising on the sea
> Over the far horizon
> And then the ship appearing
> Then the trim white vessel
> Glides into the harbor
> Thundering its salute.
> Do you see? Now he is coming
> I do not go to meet him. Not I.
> I stay upon the brow of the hill
> And wait there
> And wait for a long time
> But I never weary of the long waiting.
>
> From out of the crowded city
> There is a man coming in the distance,
> Climbing the hill.
> Who is it? Who is it? *Chi sarà? chi sarà?*
> *E come sarà giunto Che dirà? che dirà?*
> He will call "Butterfly" from the distance.
> I, without answering
> Stay hidden
> A little to tease him,
> A little, so as not to die.
> [. . .]
> One fine day you will find me
> A thread of smoke arising on the sea

In the far horizon
And then the ship appearing.
This will all come to pass as I tell you
Banish your idle fears
For he will return.
I know with total faith, I know he will return.

Chapter 2

THE TORMENT

A thin mist veils the moon and the flowers.
Now is a good time to meet you.
My stockinged feet walk on the steps.
I carry my embroidered slippers in my hand.
To the south of the painted hall,
I tremble a short while in your arms,
"It is not easy for me to come out.
Will you make the best of it?"

—Li Yu, from "A Meeting,"
tenth century, published in
Poems of Solitude

There was that moment at that small, shabby hotel, on a dirt side road leading nowhere, when I found you lying on the floor, your wrists slashed, dark red blood everywhere. They told me at the White Rose that you had gone there because you were "unhappy." I thought I would go there to cheer you up. When I saw you with your eyes closed and with dried blood caked on your arms, I thought you were dead. The room reeked with the dangerous smell of blood. The young hotel clerk was shaking. She was horrified. She rushed out after saying she was going to call the police. I knelt down, not knowing what to do. So I touched your cheek. It was cold, but you stirred. Your eyes opened and you looked up at me with a strange sweet smile on your face. "I don't want to die," you whispered. "I don't want to cause you big trouble."

And then you fainted, and I tore the bed sheet and tied your wrists to try to stop the bleeding and the next thing I knew the police were ordering me roughly in Japanese to back away. I had never known such fear. I was going to collapse myself, but then a police lieutenant wearing a tan raincoat and black beret, with one of those extraordinarily potent Peace cigarettes in his mouth, came through the door and told me in excellent English, "Let me take care of this. You probably should go. You don't want to get mixed up in this. Go back to your ship. I promise you we will take care of her."

I looked at you. You were limp, lying with your legs apart, your arms straight out, as if you had been crucified. I could not see whether you were breathing. You were so unearthly pale that you looked as if you had been dug out of a snowdrift. You were wearing a simple white dress, a string of red plastic beads round your neck, and bright red lipstick. It was as if I had interrupted you in the middle of an elaborate ritual.

I had that image of you in my mind as I wandered through the alleys where lives were being lived as they were in those days: The women splashing water on the sidewalks to keep down dust. The delicious onion and shrimp vapors coming from fried rice cooking in big steel pans that always made me instantly hungry. Happy children in their navy-blue-and-white uniforms coming home from classes with black leather schoolbags on their backs. I could hear the melancholy sounds of an *enka* coming from one house and I guessed at that moment it was a woman singing about a lost love or a life not worth living and I wondered whether that was why you had tried to kill yourself. There was still blood on my hands. There was a tap running, and a woman watched curiously as she saw me washing the blood away. She came up to me, and I could see that she was worried I had been injured. I did not know enough Japanese then to explain what had happened, so I thanked her and sat on the curb while she patted me on the back as if I were a baby. It took a while for me to put everything in perspective and calm down enough so that I could continue walking to the main gate of the navy base. I did not want to talk to anyone about what had happened. I lay down on my bunk, shut my eyes, and saw that image of you that I could not erase from my mind. One of many thoughts filled me with terror: Was I the reason you had cut your wrists?

In the morning, I went back to the White Rose, not knowing whether I would be welcome. The *mamasan* (woman manager) was sitting inside by the door, which was decorated with little mementos of love tacked up by the girls (we always called them "girls" and they in return called us "boys") who worked there as hostesses. She wore a kind of white apron over a simple blouse and the baggy *mompe* pants farmworkers wear. She also wore geta, the wooden sandals that make a reassuring *clip-clop, clip-clop* in the alleys on dark nights when hardly anything is visible. The girls working in the bar always called her, respectfully, Mama. That was her role, and she was good at it. I never knew her name. I asked once. She shook her head. That's why I always called her Mama. Her authority was absolute in the White Rose; she treated all of us—hostesses and sailors—with firm and resolute affection, as if we were all toddlers.

A Japanese bar hostess is not a prostitute, Mama told me when we first met. A hostess pours drinks, cracks jokes, makes conversation, rubs sore backs, and expresses sympathy for things that ail men's minds. Some guys had also pinned photos of themselves on the door with messages such as, "See you next time, Michiko. I love you!" or "Sonny loves Reiko," showing a sailor with a big lipstick kiss on his face put there by the woman of his dreams. The girls had left small objects around the doorway, like the votive offerings deposited by the Catholic faithful praying for sick relatives and children. There were ribbons and tortoiseshell hair clips. There were handkerchiefs with messages on them in Japanese, which of course I could not read then, but I knew the meaning of the red hearts alongside the kanji characters written in ballpoint pen.

Mama looked up at me sadly. I thought she was going to tell me that you were dead. She gripped my arm so I could not move and she said, loudly, "I'm sorry!" You once told me in jest, I think, that the Japanese could be "distressingly polite." A half dozen of the hostesses ran up to us. They wore cocktail dresses as if they were waiting to be taken to the Ritz. Several of them had been crying, and their mascara was running. They clasped handkerchiefs to their faces. They put their arms round me. "Thank you so much," one of them finally blurted. I guess I knew then that you were alive.

Reiko, a sturdy, red-cheeked farm girl from Aomori in northern Japan, spoke some English. She was able to tell me that you were in the hospital and had been given blood transfusions and that you had been able to send them a message saying, "Anthony Perkins found me."

"How do you say that?" Reiko asked earnestly. "Should I call that 'rescue'? Did you rescue her? You are a good boy! Very good boy! We love you!" The girls started laughing, and a couple of them ruffled my hair. And then Reiko said, "Go to the hospital, please. Quickly! Urgently! You need talk to Yuki-chan."

I was beginning to discover that all these women had secrets. Some of these secrets I learned over time. Every time the *Shangri-La* steamed out of port I knew more of them.

In those days the enemy was "Red China." The *Shangri-La* was, according to US Navy nomenclature, an "attack aircraft carrier"; publicity about the ship called it a "Man o' War with Men of Peace." But it was home base to several squadrons of jet and propeller attack aircraft, and in its bowels were nuclear weapons in a locked-down area guarded by the ship's Marine Corps detachment. We would go charging up and down the Sea of Japan and the South China Sea like a bull chasing machos in the narrow streets of Pamplona. Once, somewhere down toward the Philippines, the *Shangri-La* shuddered and blew its whistle furiously as it tried to put on the brakes. I rushed up on deck. A gloriously antique white four-masted schooner straight out of a Joseph Conrad novel was crossing our path. Its decks were loaded with green bananas, breadfruit, and wooden crates. I could read the ship's name through the patina of rust on its bow: *The Torment*. The crew was straining to get more speed out of the sails. *The Torment* leaned over into the arc of pure white spray it made in the emerald sea. Its safety, its destiny, depended on its skipper, a white-haired man at the wheel wearing a white shirt unbuttoned to the waist. He was laughing—or maybe cursing—as the vast bulk of the *Shangri-La* cast a shadow over him. He did not look back as he steered *The Torment* to safety.

We seamen, by the way, called our vessel the "Shitty Shang." Every day we were fed "shit on a shingle," shredded chipped beef in a milky sauce on black toast, the whole thing loaded with saltpeter or other chemicals to smother our libido, or so the story went. I envied the skipper of *The Torment* at that moment and every man aboard her being tossed about in our wake.

Another time we came across a single palm tree fastened to a tiny white coral speck of an island no bigger, it seemed to me, than a soccer field. The sea was like glass, and the island seemed to be floating on it, while the palm tree with its coconuts swayed as if it were an island girl delighting in our presence. The next time we came that way, the palm tree and its island were gone. I asked about that. Someone told me our aircraft had bombed it into oblivion.

The girls at the White Rose and the dozens of other saloons in Yokosuka had their secrets. We sailors had secrets too, but ours were bright and funny and full of bravado. We would never admit we were lonely. Never. We were certain we were not lonely. But the truth was that every time we arrived in Yokosuka we went looking for the girls we knew. On the fringes of the streets with bars were a few whorehouses for sailors who wanted sex but did not want company, those who could not handle tears of joy, or holding hands, or slow dancing. Hostesses at bars like the White Rose often had secrets that were nightmares of desperation. This was less than fifteen years after the end of World War II. Many women had lost husbands, sweethearts, brothers, sisters, parents, and friends. Millions of homes had been destroyed in US firebombing runs directed not at military or industrial targets but at the civilian population. You told me once that people with connections to Hiroshima and Nagasaki often had extreme personalities, even if they were not in those cities when the atom bombs tumbled out of the sky. And families like yours that had settled as colonists in northern China when imperial Japan seized territory there also were shattered, almost as if they had been A-bomb survivors, by the violence they experienced trying to escape from Manchuria when the Soviets attacked. Whole settler villages were exterminated. You told me an especially horrifying story about a heavily built Russian woman soldier in leather boots who killed a huddled group of Japanese mothers and their children with her machine gun, which you called "a mandolin." Parents abandoned their children or pleaded with Chinese families to take them. Women whose men were killed often were raped or offered themselves as wives to Chinese farmers. Japanese records suggest that more than thirty thousand civilians perished and another thirty thousand were never accounted for in the month of August 1945 alone. The bulk of the exodus continued until late 1946, dwindling to a trickle of people in 1948. Those who made it back to Japan, you said, were often treated as if they were foreigners because they had been born in a foreign land.

Yes, you had secrets, the first of which I heard when I walked into your hospital room and saw you lying in a wrought-iron bed. Someone had placed a single white gladiolus flower in a chipped glass vase on the table by the window.

We did not say anything for several minutes. There was a lot of sunlight coming through the window, and it blinded me until I found a corner of the room where I could see you better. Your eyes were following me around the room—that I knew. Everything in the room was white, including your face, but the pupils of your eyes were as black as the seeds of a longan tree. Finally you said, in a kind of English that sounded as if it had been rehearsed, "Paul. I am a very bad woman. Can you forgive me?"

What a big question that was to put to a kid right out of high school. You addressed me as if I were an adult.

"Yes! Yes!" I exclaimed, without understanding what I should forgive. I was just so happy that you were not dead and that my life as a man with you as my guide would not come to an end because you were gone. You were sitting up straight in that metal bed. I put my arms round you. You were rigid. "I am so sorry," you said, again and again, and for one strange moment I thought you thought I was going to hit you.

"I have to tell you a story," you said. I think that instant was the dawn of my lifelong fascination with the stories that burden every human being, regardless of nationality or culture. Those stories—mixtures of memories and forgetfulness and of fantasy and dread—are the stuff of fretful dreams until peace comes with death. Up until this moment you were Yukiko, the strong woman with a fragile beauty who talked to me about poetry and politics, who guided me like an angel to the door of all the arts. You swung that door wide and said, "Enter," knowing that I would be captivated. You sensed that in me. I had not been to college yet. That would not happen until after my four years in the navy. You could mold me and shape me and introduce me to all those hints of Japan's two-thousand-year-old culture and history I picked out every day in your grimy port city and at the Mozart café. There also was "our" bookstore in Thieves Alley, across the street from a honky-tonk glistening with flashing neon. The first time we met we talked, and you said, "Come," and you took me across the street by the hand, placed me in front of the bookshop owner, and bought me a copy bound in pale green silk of *Senryu*, translated by R. H. Blyth, a collection from the mid-1700s of darkly cynical and humorous verses similar to haiku. I mean, I was still a teen! What were you trying to lay on me? I still have the book, of course. Your fingerprint is on the title page, where you wrote, "To a nice boy from a wicked woman.—Yukiko, with love."

In fact, you mentioned that book in your second letter to me, which I received when I was at sea.

Dear Paul,

I receiving your letter this afternoon in the raining and was very, very glad to hear from you. And thank you for the haiku you found, but I don't know so much about that. Just I know this 5-7-5 syllabled verse, from the Senryu. I think you will be teaching me soon everything about Japan, so my plan to make you into a Japanese is working. Ha! Ha! Ha!

I think you received my first letter, and pictures of me also, but those pictures are only for a poet so handsome and charming.

Is there another beautiful girl, Mr. Great Cameraman-Writer? I hope no . . . not even a shadow of another girl!

The time is now 9:.00 in the evening, and I am sitting in my room, typing you this letter. I do not work for a few days. I am very lazy because there is not much business and sitting with customers who I am not interested to talk to. For me, this is just like sitting and listening to a very long Buddhist invocation since you left. Human beings can be so boring if they are not poets. Perhaps somebody has made me too lazy to work, someone who still possesses my heart so. As you said, many sailors come to Japan but they never really get to know we Japanese. I was delighted with that because this girl met such a so good person like you.

I know you like Marilyn Monroe. Oh oh! A caution signal: is a certain young man thinking somewhere of a sexy girl? Is he already drinking an aphrodisiac? Maybe you are on Okinawa which is so a hot and very strange place for we Japanese. Many witches live there, I think. They are not nice witches like me. They did not come out of the snow and ice like me. For many years I needed the warmth of fire. Then you gave me your friendship. Your friendship included

```
your helping hand. Is that the reason I
smile?
   Love,
   Yukiko
```

You wrote this letter after you slashed your wrists. But I know now that you attempted suicide not because of me. Even if other conversations are just fragments, I can remember word for word the story you told me when we were able to meet again at the Mozart café word for word, as if it had been written on a scroll you gave me to take care of for the rest of my life.

"A certain girl has to tell you a story," you said. "You see, this girl had a daughter . . . *I* had a daughter. She was ten years old. For a long time, my daughter was sick with tuberculosis. My mother died from TB. It was terrible, and unfortunately my daughter caught TB from my mother. Don't ask me about the father of my daughter. He is dead, so long ago . . . My daughter was my last relative alive. When I got the news from the hospital that she had died and I was not there because I had to work at the bar to earn money, I wanted to kill myself. She was the last of my family. Now I am alone. She was so bright and funny . . . not like me, her so serious mother. So I decided to die . . . I am so sorry to have to tell you this because you are a good boy and now my story is your story too. I am part of you and you are part of me.

"I need to tell you that I put on that white dress because in China it is the color of mourners and because I knew that somewhere I would meet my daughter again, and I wanted to be pure. Yes . . . pure. So pure, which I am not. I am not, Paul.

I am not a good woman . . . And then somehow, by fate—I think that is the right word—you came to my room at that hotel. You were like a star shining bright above me. I had to use my dictionary to look up those words.

"Yes, you are young. You are full of hope, and even though I am a very bad woman, because of you I glow with light because you care about me in the most beautiful way, like a man who is good of heart. Yes, like a man, even though you are not yet a man. And now I am here. I am still living. I will always be a little bird in the tree, singing, singing, always happily, I hope. Yes, I can hope. Please remember me and listen for my song."

Chapter 3

BLUE WOMAN

You girls who were seeking
the great love, the great and terrible love,
what has happened, girls?
Perhaps time, time?

> —Pablo Neruda,
>   from *"Las muchachas"* ("Girls"),
>   *Los versos del Capitán*
>   (*The Captain's Verses*)

It occurs to me that after you cut your wrists—and I became part of your story—you started writing much more poetry. First the blood flowed from your body. Then came a flood of verse. The ship sailed away on a three-week cruise to the Taiwan Strait and to Hong Kong. And then it returned to Yokosuka. As soon as I walked down the gangplank to the dock, after saluting the flag and taking the obligatory rubber in a wrapper from the officer of the deck, I went looking for you. You were not at the White Rose. They said you were probably still convalescing. I walked in the rain to the Mozart coffee shop, stepping into doorways and alleys to avoid running into navy shore patrols that might have detained me for attempting to

31

enter a forbidden area. The Mozart was forbidden. The brute force of that rule was beyond my comprehension, even then.

Your head was cocked to one side. There was an open book on the table in front of you. Your eyes were closed. There was that smile on your face that happened when you were in the presence of beauty. You were listening to the Ninth Symphony of Beethoven, my father's favorite, and the needle on the record was getting to the point where the sublime "Ode to Joy" chorus would begin. I could see you were anticipating it: *Joy, o wondrous spark divine.* There was the first rose tint of excitement on your face for the coming force of the chorale. Your long fingers were tapping the table. I stood looking at you for a while. You were truly lost in something I was not a part of. It was wonderful seeing you like that, so alive, entranced, vivid in your private world. You were like my father, who stood and conducted the Ninth, as the 78 rpm records he treasured spun on the blond-wood Ferguson record player, while I sat there uncomprehending. You pulled a notebook from your purse and began writing, first slowly, and then hurriedly as the chorus swept you up. I knew that you were writing poetry. You suddenly saw me, and you jumped up, spilling espresso out of the tiny cup. You ran and threw your arms round my neck and said, your voice triumphant, "I knew you would come back to me, my sweetheart."

You stood and looked at me. Your eyes explored my face: first my eyes, then my lips, each cheekbone, the close-cropped black hair, and last, my grin. "You missed me, I think," you said, after you had studied all my details. You called those details "credentials." You looked at me as if the short time we had known each other was altering the boy I was. Your fists were clenched at the sides of your hips. You were right in front of me, and you were not going to move. The chorus was soaring. I had to help you back to the table. You started laughing. The manager nodded politely. Public displays of affection were rare in Japan in those days, but you, with your books and your love of music and that look you had, were one of the manager's favorite customers. I am sure that he had never seen a mature Japanese woman throw herself into the arms of a young foreigner. But he nodded in my direction, quickly brought coffee to the table, and then said playfully to you in Japanese: "So, he is the one, this young man. Your Anthony Perkins!" Your face turned scarlet. I am laughing now when I think about that. I blushed too, as I did when I was a youngster. How much I wish that I were nineteen again, and a woman such as you with your red lips, stalked by tragedy, who devoured literature and wrote poetry and who wore an unknown perfume whose fragrance I can still recall, was waiting for me.

"I have to tell you something," you said. "It is another secret. A certain woman is in love with a certain man, but he does not know it. Do you know that woman?"

I nodded yes. Do you remember that nod?

"A certain man is in love with a certain woman, but he does not know it. Do you know that man?"

I nodded yes again.

"In my country," you said, "that is the perfect formula for a love affair that will have a beginning and an end. I have always wanted to be in love with a man who did not know I loved him. How bittersweet that love. How unforgettable. A love that I can take with me until I die. Do you understand?"

Well, of course, I did not understand. You were talking to someone who was not even twenty. Bittersweet? What did I know then about bittersweet! All I knew was sunshine. Laughter. Sunlight. Adventure. Your secret unleashed a score of unfamiliar feelings. I felt as if I were an infant taking his first step.

The manager of the Mozart was watching us discreetly. I saw him go to the shelf where the record player was located. He turned up the volume. You took my hand and pulled me closer, so that we sat side by side.

"You know Beethoven?" you asked. The chorus was at its zenith. "You have come back to me," you said, "at my favorite moment." You tightened your grip on my hand, leaned back in your chair. "I love life. I love something as simple as sitting with you like this . . . Do you understand, Paul-san?"

Dear Paul,

Did you get my second letter? I hope to hear from you soon. I need that thing that is called joy. By the way, I will go to the book store day after tomorrow. I told you before, the book of French language for you is a present, if they have it, I hope, and a dictionary too that they will send to the store soon. The store has asked Maruzen [a big Tokyo bookstore] for me and the store said not easy to get the original of a new book, but I try.

I want you to read poetry in the French language, and then I want you to recite it

to me so that I will lose my mind. I will
send you Verlaine and Rousseau.

Today I will make you bust of laughing,
when you reading this, if you be happy, please
reading with humming. If you be angry, say,
"Why so stupid a student! Look! Mistakes
all over the page!" But please do not make
a grimace, OK, Mr. Teacher?

Anyway I'll start. A little girl like me
has written a poem. She was thinking if it
was only possible that I was little again!
The girl was thinking about lost leaves in a
storm because she did not get a letter from
you. Yes, there was nothing that time. So
much she were waiting for your first letter,
you will never know. That is a new secret for
you. I don't like this word wait!! That is
why I will never use it again in my letters.
Never! I am stubborn. Remember that.

After you are reading this letter, are you
already correcting it for me? I know it is
trouble for you, but please do it for pity a
student to study, when you have time.

Please send this letter back to me with
many intelligent corrections. Please write
to me soon even if you do not have the
opportunity.

But even better than that, come back to
me before the new moon in the darkness of
night. Come back to me so that I can hear

```
your steps in the night and enjoy the feeling
of impossible happiness.
    Keep well. Study hard. Read books. Imagine!
    Remember me.
    Thank you for saving my life.
    Please always be a good boy.
    Love,
    Yukiko
```

That was not the end of the letter. You delighted in adding a P.S., or a P.P.S., and even a P.P.P.S. on occasion.

"If I P.S.," you said, "it is going to be something special. It is not what you call an 'afterthought.' I can't send you presents when you are at sea, but I can send you a P.S."

"But how do you say *P.S.* in Japanese?" I asked.

"We say it this way," you said, writing into my notebook the kanji 追伸.

"No. No. No!" you insisted, refusing to tell me how those kanji are pronounced. "First, you have to tell me is it P.P.S., post-postscriptum, or is it P.S.S., postscriptum scriptum?"

I was too young to know the definitive answer. To this day I still do not know how to pronounce 追伸. Here are the "gifts" you sent me in that letter. You preferred to call your P.S. "gifts."

```
    P.S.
    Well, open the curtain.
    Now, a Paulownia leaf has fallen.
    Fancy and actuality:
    Between them is the life of sad people.
```

P.P.S. A girl is writing something again. The girl is listening to the radio which is saying it will play Ravel and Copeland just for me today. I was thinking. And I thought. And I wished for Ravel and Copeland and yes, they are coming to me today. I will sit and talk with the composers after they climb my mountain. I hope it is raining when they bring their music and I hope they like hot Japanese green tea.

I just saw the postman, but, and yet, he did not stop at my house. Today is very windy. I do not want to go to work. I am looking at the bay for the Shangri-La. Your ship. Looking. Looking. This girl is always looking. I am looking from the mountain, from the front of my house, from the window. If you saw me through the window you would see the face of a Japanese girl with the black shining eyes of a very impatient woman.

> That leaden sky is so very low,
> The trees rage, and do not suppress the agony.
> Any more there, those green,
> That many, many colors would glisten,
> Those thickets so deep and dark,
> And all hope to suck.
> I don't know how to stop that heartless wind.

P.P.P.S. Bolero is now finishing in the highest intonation. That was the music we heard the last time we were together. Do you remember? Until that time I was happy, so happy. You were here, and then, and then you went away.

Until, after you are gone then,
I didn't know this sorrow,
I didn't know this, it was not part of me.
My dear dead daughter. And now I so much miss you,
So much were cared of.
I cannot write this way. No! I cannot.
He is gone . . .
Perhaps, any more, we may meet, I may send,
I may call for his ship to come to the mountain.

The radio say for tomorrow, GASHUIN . . . Oh. I mean Gershwin. Rhapsody in Blue. Gershwin wrote that for me because I am a blue woman. You are young, but I think you know that. Blue women live only for the next available rhapsody, young man. Please never forget that. I started writing this letter at 3:30 PM. My dictionary is burning because I use it so much. My heart is in flames. Do you remember me?
Yukiko

Your letter reached me on the *Shangri-La*. When it arrived, we were somewhere on the ocean, somewhere near the island of Guam. At sea you are always somewhere. Where I was ex-actly, I never knew. I would stare out at the sea all the way to the horizon. If my gaze went all the way to where the sky met the sea and then beyond . . . that is where reality began and I knew where I was, like I did when I was with you. There was a typhoon that tossed the ship around as if it were a toy. They made an announcement from the bridge telling everyone to stay below. But I knew a secret passageway and ladder up to the crow's nest at the very top of the vessel, and I took your letter up there to read it again and again. The envelope blew away. But I held on to the two pages of paper. And after I read and read your poems I realized there was nothing I could do to make the ship come back to you. It would all happen in its own sweet time, as they say. I would come back and look for you and I would find you and I would ask you to tell me more.

I am the sort of person who needs to know. I was reading yesterday that Japanese is the most imprecise language in the world because it is so poetic. There are so many ways of interpreting each kanji—those Chinese characters you use—and nothing is said with direct intent. Things are suggested. You told me once that there are a basic 1,246 kanji in daily use, but the actual number of kanji known to exist may be as many as five thousand, although some of them were used only once or twice in obscure and ancient imperial court poetry written mostly by noblewomen and concubines coping with the long absences of lovers who may or may not have been killed or wounded on distant battlegrounds. Important things are only hinted at. Your country is a floating world, a place of dreams and mists and mirrors, not to mention the frequent tears. Somehow you came out of Manchuria wearing death as a shroud and with no purpose to live—or at least no purpose after your daughter died. Do you see how horribly direct and analytical my way of thinking is because I am from the West?

You would never frame your thoughts this way. The big heart-shaped leaves would be falling from the beautiful paulownia with its masses of blue trumpets in front of your house, and you would watch them silently, thoughtfully, as if they were a highly appropriate part of your loneliness. *How am I ever going to be able to communicate with you? How am I going to be able to know you?* Those were my questions. Those were my thoughts when we came back to Yokosuka and I found you at the Mozart coffee shop. I saw your instant of ecstasy. I saw you raised up. I saw you yearning to be joyful, to be happy, to be free.

In 2011, when the sea invaded northern Japan and those images of certain death swirled around the world, the first thought that leaped in my mind was: *Are you safe? Where are you? Are you alive?*

What of the Japan that I knew fifty years ago? The tiny bars, with stools for no more than six people, where I spent so many hours writing down words and phrases spoken to me with such care by so many good people: working men with bruised hands, lawyers in white shirts with their briefcases, the single gorgeous woman behind the bar pouring sake and flirting with me entirely in Japanese. Do those places still exist, or is everything now befouled by Kentucky Fried Chicken and Starbucks? Do you know that by the time I finally left Tokyo in late 1962 my command of street Japanese was so good that I was able to date Japanese girls my own age who did not speak English? And that is all really because of you and the effort you put into making sure I was learning your language every day. You called *me* "Teacher" because I sent back corrected copies of your letters. Hah!

You said to me soon after we met, "We Japanese use three different written languages." There is kanji. Each character can be read with both a Japanese sound and a Chinese sound. For example, the Japanese word *atarashi*, which means "new," can also be read as *shin*, which is the Chinese sound. There are many hundreds of words like that; scholars call them pictographs because each kanji originated as a tiny picture of something. But then there are also two written languages using characters that are entirely phonetic and are not a picture of anything. Those are hiragana, which sometimes appear alongside complicated kanji to indicate their sound and meaning, and also katakana, which is usually used to approximate the sounds of foreign words in everyday use in Japan, such as *basu*, which means "bus," or *kissu*, which means "kiss."

When I first started learning Japanese, I was not sitting in a classroom. Your life was my classroom. You were not my student. I was your student and your sweetheart. I am so lucky to still have your letters. "Fancy and actuality"—it sounds so Japanese. Dreams and reality: you understood that both happen in a love affair.

Yes, I can hear your voice. I can hear you singing your favorite song, done as a duet by the torch singer Matsuo Kazuko and the male singer Wada Hiroshi: *"Dare yori mo, kimi wo aisu"* (More Than Anyone Else, I Love You). You are still a little bird singing in the tree. It is a slow song. It is moody and flirtatious, sung by a worldly man and a worldly woman slyly tempting each other.

From the time I loved, the suffering began
Since the time of being loved, I have waited for the
    separation.
Ahh-ah . . . Still, when life is over,
More than anyone, more than anyone else, I love you.

Every time I hear that song I want to write to you again.
More than anyone. More than anyone else, I still love you.

In conversations with close friends about those days I have
often struggled to explain why a mature woman would become
involved with a young man who was so shy and inexperienced.
My experiences with girls who were not yet women had been
so limited. But here was a woman who, with great tenderness,
accepted that shyness as if it were a strength, not a weakness.
It took a while to become a man. But I was being groomed.
"Oh," you said one day, flashing me a sudden glance over your
shoulder in a way that made you even more beautiful. "You
will make many women happy. I will teach you. But first you
must learn how to smile, like me."

Of course, in later years, I was equipped with a smile but I
was still too shy to dance. The girls I met were now women.
If I trace relationships I have had back to 1959, often there
is a common thread: a kind of quest for a Yukiko. This was
especially true of Japanese women I knew later on. They
were not my mentors in the arts. But those friendships were
evidence, at least, that I had become a man. I had experiences,
the details of which I could share with male friends as young
men do. But I never was awed as I was when I was close to you.

Chapter 4

A CERTAIN GIRL

Great Imperial Concubine was utterly indifferent to the charms of the young rakes who flocked about the Court and of the handsome noblemen who came her way. The physical attributes of men no longer meant anything to her. Her only concern was to find a man who could give her the strongest and deepest possible love. A woman with such aspirations is a truly terrifying creature.

—Mishima Yukio, from "The Priest
of Shiga Temple and His Love,"
in *Death in Midsummer and Other Stories*

"Dear Yukiko," I want to write. But how many "dears" do I dare put in front of your name? If you are dead, am I addressing a grave, or maybe your ashes? You had no living relatives, as far as I know, but perhaps you married after I was gone. I wonder if you found some happiness? If you were able to become a wife and have more children. Somehow, sadly, I don't think that was the case.

I think you were one of those people who startled those around her—like a gorgeous short-lived rose—and then dropped her petals. We could not have had a life together anyway. Sweetheart was a good role for me. It was what you needed. Despite my youth, I was capable of being that, at least. But I have a new secret: in old age, I would be that way too.

You once told me that after you fled Manchuria no one had ever loved you. You had not allowed it. You grew up loving books and art and music and the idea of romance without the drama of actually making love with someone. I may have been a child but now I think that I knew this about you. After you met me, you wanted a sweetheart, a kind of courtly lover.

I remember when we took the train south to Kamakura and we stood in front of the enormous Daibutsu, that thirty-foot-high bronze statue of the Buddha made in the year 1250. You were so merry on the train. I had the lyrics to "Who's That Knocking" by the Genies on my mind, and as the train rocked I was singing, "Who's that knocking . . . On my door . . . doo doo doo-wah, bang bang bang . . . all night long." The other passengers watched, with solemn, confused faces, as I came down the aisle toward you, snapping my fingers. You were astonished. "No, no, no," you said, with some force. "You are the poet." I think that was the moment when you realized that I was really just a young man who insisted that "Smoke Gets in Your Eyes" was poetry, "Stagger Lee" was revolutionary, and Frankie Avalon's "Venus" should have been dedicated to you.

Soon we were standing in front of the Daibutsu, side by side, our heads bowed. You prayed for your daughter and your lost family and the snow country in Manchuria where your childhood was obliterated by war.

"What did your father do there?" I asked, trying to visualize a place I would never see. You shook your head, reluctant at first. You said, "He played piano."

I said, "I mean, what about his work?"

I had a thousand questions I wanted to ask. Kamakura probably now has a McDonald's, and people undoubtedly use smartphones to communicate instead of gossiping in sake bars and greeting each other in the street with a quick bow and a stream of exquisite pleasantries. But I remember Kamakura in those days as a small town by the ocean, where muffled temple bells could be heard, not like pealing church bells, but booming slowly, majestically, as if they were heartbeats, as if every day had a funeral. We were walking to the Engaku-ji Zen Buddhist temple, and you were trying to explain to me the significance of the massive *sanmon* gate, which I now know represents the three gates to spiritual emancipation. You told me you often came to Engaku-ji because it was built to honor those who lost their lives in war. "It is said," you began, "that this gate frees one of various obsessions and brings about enlightenment . . . Pass through the gate with a pure mind, Paul. Come with me, and I will tell you another secret."

So, I stepped through the gate, puzzled. You looked at me intently and you said, "My father was an executioner. He was a policeman. I am afraid to say this because I know he would be sad to hear the truth, but he was not a good man. He killed many Chinese. Bang, bang, bang." I looked at you and I could tell that this was such a burden, still, even though a dozen years had passed since your family was forced to start walking south, through the ice, hundreds of miles to the Chinese port of Dairen.

"He was a really talented pianist. He played the piano

because his life was so brutal, so terrible. He was so strict. He hurt my mother. His favorite pieces were by Satie. Do you know his *Vexations*, his six *Gnossiennes*, his *Trois Gymnopédies*? I know them all, by heart. In a way, they are like bells ringing for those who are in mourning. When I dream, they are the rhythm of my heart. But when I wake up, my face is wet and I know I have been crying in my sleep. I remember that none of us was allowed to move—not even a little bit—while he played. He would not open his eyes. It was as if he was living in another land. This was his ecstasy."

You were sobbing into the sleeve of your gorgeous kimono, silk the color of slate, with its undergarments in three different shades of grey. In Japan, grey in all its shades—from charcoal to silver—is one of three colors that express sadness, especially in kimonos. White is the second color. Black is the third. A single tear mixed with mascara, so that it looked as if black lacquer cut a line down one side of your face to the corner of your lips. You pulled out a cigarette and lit it with a match, something you never did at the White Rose bar. You inhaled deeply, as if you were a very tough woman, a gangster's woman maybe.

"Look, Paul," you said, your voice brittle and harsh, "you probably hate me now." You looked up at me as if I was going to walk away, forever. But I was young enough during an age when empathy was still possible. I was no cynic. I had not yet lived and lost, loved and lost, as you had. I gulped and choked. "Yuki," I said, "you were just a little girl. And now . . ."

I could not finish the sentence. What were you now? I did not know. You poured drinks at a bar where the music was country and western, and then . . . ?

I reached out. It seemed as if I were reaching across time, and I pulled you so close to me that you gasped, and the crowd of sightseers and pilgrims stopped in its tracks and stared at us.

You said, "All my life I have been waiting for that embrace."

On the way back to Yokosuka, you sang and hummed those moody *enka* songs that Japanese loved to sing when they were drinking sake. Both of us loved the songs of the singer Misora Hibari. The "Little Lark," you called her. The following week we took the train north to Tokyo to hear Misora Hibari sing at the Nichigeki Theatre. You gripped my hand. People were whispering about us. I felt uncomfortable. I did not want you to be hurt; I didn't think you could take it. But I was wrong. As the looks grew more intense, you held my hand even tighter and pulled me toward you so our bodies were touching, and you told me—you whispered to me, and I remember your lips were wet against my ear—"You are my love, and I am your love. I don't care if they look."

We sat that way for the entire performance. I looked down at your wrists. The scars were there, white, like cords of cotton lain across your skin. And when Misora Hibari had finished singing "*Ringo oiwake*" (Apple Folk Song), and the crowd, which was almost entirely women, was on its feet shouting her name and pleading for autographs, do you remember how she came down from the stage and looked at you with an appreciative smile? Now that I think about it, it was as if she could sense the bond between us. She was already famous, already bruised by her affairs, already capable of singing about the sorrows of a woman in a way that moved you and millions of other women to joy and to tears.

I remember saying, "Yuki. Did you see that? She noticed."

And you said, "It was a blessing. Things are changing. I feel as if I am drunk with happiness." There was a tear running down your cheek and you brushed away an identical tear next to my nose with the back of your finger and said, "Thank you so much for allowing me to feel your love and friendship."

Your fourth letter came when I was in Manila. I can't remember what I did there. My sailor friends got drunk and paid for tattoos—that I know. I did not do any of that because I am me. I am not a member of the herd. You taught me that. You said, "Be yourself. Be strong, no matter what. There is no other way. In my country there is a saying: 'When a nail sticks up, it must be hammered down.' It means you must be part of a group. You must not be different. You must conform. I don't like that saying. Don't ever let it happen to you. Do not let them hammer you." You also said, "Remember this: in this life, all men reach and fall. It is not so true about women, Paul. When women fall it is not because they have reached. Why do you think that is, Paul? You should know. Or maybe you do not know, because you are so young. I will let you think about it. When you become older, you will know."

Dear Paul.

Are you still stay in Manila? If so I sympathize for you because the ink became red it got that much hot. But you so clever. You used the red color in your last letter to me so that I would think hot. How about next time you send me the nice smell of Chinese food from Hong Kong? This Yokosuka is not yet hot. It is almost the same when you were here.

I received your letter yesterday. Before I open the envelope, I ran around the room laughing. I was waving your letter. So happy. Thank you for a very nice letter and also my letter which you corrected and sent back to me. I got very much pleasure out of reading it. I don't like ever, ever, feeling that I can remember even few and fewer things about you. I HAVE TO know you. All of you. You are far, far away, Paul-san. First you steal my heart and now you steal my memories. You know some secrets. Do you remember me?

I wish I could be writing like you so that I could think many things. I must study harder to be a writer. You must go to college so that can I read your book. Maybe you will write something that make me cry so happy even when I am a very old woman, a very old and still a wicked woman. But for now, your letter I put under my pillow. I want to dream about my happiness. I don't want to dream about my life and wake up with a pillow soaked with tears.

Now I am look at the calendar. This month almost finish, but more many days, many weeks. The next month is raining season in Japan and to think that makes me gloomy. But I can spend time (Not WAIT!!! Remember! I do not like that word!) for to talk to you in my letters even though many miles away from you until then. I will wear my gray kimono. Do you remember? It was the kimono of my mother. We carried it on our backs all the way from Manchuria and why was that? It was because my mother wore that kimono on her first date with my father, and my father told her, simply, "You are beautiful when you wear gray." That is all he said. Just that. But she never forgot it because it was the first time in her life she was beautiful.

A certain girl has to tell you now, thank you so much for the embrace of a lifetime. That embrace made me beautiful. Maybe my mother says this too because I wear her kimono. Shakespeare would say she was a thing of beauty—not like me, so ugly. Take care of yourself. I wish from you now. I wish. I wish . . . that is my secret. No, no, no. I wish you were here with me on my mountain, forever. I wish I would hear the big noise of your ship coming around the corner into the harbor. I wish I was running down the mountain to meet you. I wish. I wish. I wish.

How nice for me to wish when I am awake, instead of wishing in my dreams. If you were a teardrop in my eyes, for fear of losing you, I would never cry. Please don't look too deeply into my eyes next time we meet. Please. Please. Please! I am afraid of emotion that I have not had before. But I am thankful that I can feel the fear, finally, of a young girl falling in love because I was a young girl so long ago.

   Lot of think of you, sailor boy
   Yukiko

   P.S. I'll go the book store now. Then I will run down the mountain, singing. Can you hear me singing and dancing in the rain?

   P.P.S. I went to the library. I looked for these lyrics: "Si, Mi Chiamano Mimi" [Yes, They Call Me Mimi], from La Boheme. I adore Puccini. That is strange for Japanese because when we are with someone we love, we so politely conceal our feelings. But here I am, confessing to you, and I have not even told you I love you. This aria by Mimi is like a long poem. It is shy and modest. But her emotions shimmer like sunlight on the surface of a lake, don't you think? These emotions are not under the surface. They are free to dance ON the water, so they can be appreciated. Rodolfo is in love. He wants to know more about her. So she sings.

   Yes, they call me Mimi,
   but my true name is Lucia.
   My story is short.

A canvas or a silk,
I do embroidery at home and abroad . . .
I am happy, happy and at peace
and my pastime
is to make lilies and roses.
I love all things
that have gentle sweet smells,
that speak of love, of spring,
of dreams and fanciful things,
those things that have poetic names.
Do you understand me?

Chapter 5

TIME OF THE TYPEWRITER

To gaze at a river made of time and water
and remember Time is another river.
To know we stray like a river
and our faces vanish like water.

—Jorge Luis Borges,
from "The Art of Poetry,"
a personal anthology

Hummingbirds are sipping sweet red nectar out of a feeder hanging in front of the window through which I can see my garden. It is the mature garden of a man who is seventy-five. The garden is his creation. I am he. Roses, figs, bamboo, ginger, banana, papaya, white grapes, red grapes, mango, guava, pomelo, red hibiscus, pink hibiscus, white hibiscus, lemons, lemongrass, limes, tangerines, calamansi, pink grape-fruit, white grapefruit, jujube, oranges. The cuts on my hand and the calluses are from digging, cutting, and pruning. It is dignified work. If you have a garden and a library, you have everything you need, Cicero said, and I think he meant men too old and too lacking in idealism to go to war again. It is also the garden, full of fecundity and delicate perfumes and dazzling colors, of a man without a woman.

Every year these hummingbirds come and then they go. They are easy to forget, but I never forget them. Every year they are the same: ruby-red throat, shimmering green back, tan underside. They have no fear of me. In fact, they zoom right up and stare me in the face, hovering there like little incandescent gifts from God. Sometimes I even think they are carrying messages from you. They are here in the summer. In the winter, they fly to Central America without so much as a good-bye. They know when to leave. They don't have to think about it. They just go. But in the spring they always remember to come back.

I look back on 1959 now, and I try to imagine myself. I am accustomed to old age. I feel comfortable with the impact of time on my mind and my body. I have no idea where I am going—except occasionally I do go to Costa Rica in Central America.

In San José, Costa Rica's small capital, I have a circle of male friends all roughly my age: a former Marine with a combat grip who taught economics; a retired physician who suffers from a rare optical disease but still rides mountain bikes on wilderness trails; an itinerant musician who plays keyboards and composes unadulterated lounge music; a tough guy from South Central Los Angeles who mentors even tougher teens; and a painter who is perpetually on the run from US tax authorities and exults in every day he is a free man. The fact is, they are all in search of the perfect love, except me. I am still the outsider, just as I was in 1959 when I glimpsed perfection.

At this point in my life, I am searching for Shangri-La. It

does not exist, I know. I am looking, but for the time being my house is a kind of paradise full of boxes packed tight with memories: newspaper clippings; airline tickets from years of travel; a Vietcong booby trap I stepped on but that did not explode; and receipts from old hotels in Phnom Penh, Manila, Buenos Aires, Havana, Hanoi, Mexico City, where deep shadows helped me doze in the afternoons. Books line the walls from floor to ceiling, and an array of antique paintings from Bali, showing maidens in sarongs, is clustered by the front door. There are a lot of photographs in my house too, including some never published that remain hidden because they show shattered bodies in painful detail; these photographs were taken in Cambodia in the final week of the war.

Soon death will be my visitor. I wait for the knock on the door, made of cedar from Peru, that guards the entrance to my small paradise. I live day by day, aware through the mixed blessing of the Internet that friends and relatives of friends are dying or becoming seriously ill every week. Sometimes I wish there would be a clock I could set for the end of my life. If I set it now and it gave me a reading of 2,124 days, 13 hours, 25 minutes, and 14 seconds to go before the end, I would not procrastinate anymore. If I was aware that every ticktock of this clock was winding my time down to zero, I might not relish those deep sixty-minute naps I am taking every afternoon, from which I awake completely disoriented. I would be painting my house. Repairing cracked caulk in the bathrooms. Attending social gatherings and musical soirees. I would be driving my Alfa Romeo Spider as fast as I could every day of the week. Would the Yukiko you were in 1959 recognize me now?

To help me recognize that 1959 version of myself, as I write I have assembled a dozen photos of me when we knew each other. They show a slim young man with a piercing look and neatly arranged dark features, who could be Latino, Arab, Roma, Italian, Persian, or maybe a mix of some of those, with a little Japanese thrown in. Well, of course, there is some Japanese in me, put there for all time by Kaji Yukiko. One of these photos shows me in a white T-shirt and dark blue dungarees, painting a metal ceiling in an office space on the *Shangri-La*, with a shipmate named R. E. "Red" Downs, a genial African-American guy who was from Mississippi. I have a kind of sneer on my face. There is some stubble around my chin and above my mouth. I am standing on a chair, so I look down on the photographer. Do you remember that you told me this was my "imperial" look?

"You would make a very nice young emperor, Paul," you said at the Mozart coffee shop, when I was standing by the table that was your favorite. "Such a look you have," you said. "I did not teach you that. Where did you learn to make a woman feel afraid?"

I did not understand what you were trying to say. I also remember what I said: "There is a lot I do not know. I am trying hard to catch up. Maybe I am looking like this at you because I can't believe . . ." I did not finish the sentence. I was not yet a man. I was speaking like a child, and you knew it, and you knew if I had completed the sentence I might have said too much and robbed you of the chance to put your own ending there.

Other photos show me with an impish grin, packed with energy and ignorance and insatiable curiosity. They show me standing alone and confused, or maybe even overwhelmed, in front of the Zen temple in Kamakura, with my hands on my hips, not looking at the camera or at you but at something else. I still stand like that, with a slight lean to the left, all six feet of me. Despite age, you might be relieved to know that I have actually not shrunk one bit. Time changes us and then it doesn't. Isn't that strange?

The really strange thing is I still do not understand where my knowledge about the world came from in 1958 and 1959. It did not come from the one year of American schooling I had at Freeport Senior High in Illinois, Home of the Pretzels—what an uninspiring name!

Even stranger is the fact that as I was writing this paragraph I noticed Ben, the mailman, arriving by bicycle at my mailbox, into which he inserted a letter postmarked Freeport, from Herb Jacobs, a fellow graduate of the class of 1958, inviting me to the fifty-fifth class reunion: "Informal get-together at Ron Prasse's Barn on Lily Creek Road," followed by golf at the Park Hills Golf Course and a social hour and "2-Meat Hot Buffet" at the Freeport Eagles Club. I phoned my sister Mary in Ohio. "What is an Eagles Club?" I asked.

"I don't know," she said, laughing. "There are a lot of strange things about Freeport. Someone told me it is now run by the Mafia."

Did I know that in 1958? Certainly not. What I did know about Freeport was that during the year I went to that high school I did the following. It caused an unpleasant buzz. First of all, I accepted an invitation to have coffee with five other students at the home of a quietly intellectual black female classmate who wanted to discuss racial discrimination. I was so incensed by the evidence all around me of racial prejudice that I jumped to my feet and angrily denounced the United States—my adopted country. I was not trying to be a hero. I was upset that the other white kids in the room showed no evidence of outrage and said nothing. Our hostess appeared to be stunned by my outburst. She looked at me oddly as if she thought that explosion of rage was not called for. But I could not help myself.

One evening a couple of weeks later, I was at a soda fountain reading and thoroughly enjoying a forbidden book, Henry Miller's *Plexus: The Rosy Crucifixion #2*, published by the Olympia Press, Paris, and sold to me wrapped tightly sealed in brown paper, like a half-kilo brick of heroin, from under the counter at a dismally lit cigar shop. Four non-black classmates with bad-boy greased hair sauntered in, took one look at me, and shouted, "Nigger lover!" several times before sitting down and looking proud of themselves. No one in the soda fountain looked astonished or alarmed, except me.

But evidently word had circulated about the English boy who abhorred racial prejudice because the week after that several black male classmates stopped me on Douglas Street and invited me to join a high-speed night run in a souped-up Mercury coupe on US Route 20 to the bigger town of Rockford. At a small club down on the river they introduced me as "the English boy, and he's all right!" That was some night. I did not know how to drink. I did not know how to dance, or even how to move to music. I didn't do any sweet-talking. But I did have fun—the first completely uninhibited fun I had had in America. We were all squeezed into an overstuffed red velvet booth shaped like a smile, together with some long-legged girls who asked me—close up—if I knew how to kiss. I remember they were playing "Do You Wanna Dance" by Bobby Freeman and "Whole Lotta Loving" by Fats Domino. I was not yet eighteen. I was drinking beer. I felt good.

> I got a whole lotta loving for you,
> True, true love for you,
> I got a whole lotta loving for you

What were the roots of my hot-blooded response to prejudice? You often asked me about that when you could not understand some of the poems I started typing out, poems that were, in effect, howls of rage about America circa 1959. Something primal was stirring in me. There was also something in the air just then, especially at that point in time when we met. This was the year when Fidel Castro, my big hero then, came down out of the mountains to liberate Havana and force Fulgencio Batista to flee to the United States, which greeted the repulsive dictator with flowers. I have the poems I mailed to you on my desk here. They are heavy with political content.

It was the time of the typewriter, and carbon copies, and the thrill of underlining key passages of verse in red with the flick of a lever if you used a red-and-black ribbon. Many nights out in the western Pacific I was up late listening to vinyl LPs of Tchaikovsky's *1812 Overture* and Gershwin's *Rhapsody in Blue*. I told you that I pounded on an office typewriter with a soft lead editing pencil clenched in my teeth, writing poetry with a passion so strong I could not sleep later. I mailed all of these poems to you. I wonder if you have them somewhere. It

was the end of the decade and its deadhead politics: Dwight
D. Eisenhower was still president. There was still the smell
of Joe McCarthyism in the air. John F. Kennedy had let it
be known he intended to run for president. Segregation had
been struck down by the Supreme Court in 1956, but it was
an undeniable fact of life, even in smug little Freeport. The
struggle over the integration of Central High School in Little
Rock, Arkansas, was going on, with segregationist youth spitting, with no shame, at students who were black. All across
the South brave people were struggling to make equality a
reality in schools, at diners, on buses, at the voting booth. "I
AM A MAN" some of their protest signs read. Yes, indeed.

I remember our conversations about those topics. You were
appalled. The Japanese had treated their Chinese neighbors in
Manchuria with similar contempt, you said, sadly. I remember
how amused I was when some of my shipmates called me a
Communist. They even suggested that Security investigate me
for the pro-Castro viewpoint that I never tired of expressing,
even at the White Rose when Johnny Cash records were spinning. Do you remember how a drunk Marine with a broken
beer bottle, who was looking for a fight with anyone, slashed
the palm of my right hand and how I marched out into the
street with that hand held high to slow the bleeding? Blood was
running down my arm and dripping onto my white uniform.
You exclaimed then, when you were waving that big brown
bottle of Kirin beer over your head: "Don't touch that nice
boy or you will be a dead man." It is a fond remembrance.

Last night I was reading some of the poetry I wrote aboard
ship. I know that you read this too. It was probably an early
reaction to the bar scene in Yokosuka, where you worked

pouring drinks, slow dancing, and making conversation in baby talk, which was what sailors expected from you. They were not in the White Rose to discuss Dylan Thomas, after all.

Down the gargoyle alley he set his reeling gaze.
Through the snarling neon signs and shadowed doorways
To the ostentatious, incandescent bars
Frothing like lace frilled leeches
In this Thieves Alley of monstrous reality.
Through the jungle conglomeration of babbling
Assorted humanity to a certain electric white rose
High flowering on a dimmed corner where
Impeccably Occidentalized penny-pimps in
Ivy League mackintoshes cajoled with smiling,
Laughing eyes the drifting five dollar lonely.
There was a mistral wind in his hammered ears
And foreign rain beating his exhausted face as his
One-by-one footsteps methodically created
Disintegrating gasoline dreg portraits in the
Merry gutter pools. Up the rice alley and vooooooom!
Past the chilled octopus clinging hands and
Women-women clogged doors by.
Bar Texas (an entity unto itself).
Bar shit kickin' Western.
Bar Playboy (jumpin' jack rabbit, man!)
And the extravagant rajah of extravagance, Bar X!
Yokosuka slice. Japan of Hiroshige cherry blossoms
And exploding Kabuki Noh plays and the dastardly
Day of Infamy which brought me to you, Japan,
Where happy children, like me, can play.

Were there roots of my discontent in youthful experiences as a teenager earlier, back in England, where, when I was dragged off my bicycle while pedaling through a quiet residential area by a group of thugs, they yelled "Paki" (Pakistani) and other curses I do not recall? One of them hit me in the jaw with a full-bore thrust of his fist, a punch with such impact that it caused my teeth to dig into my lower lip, cutting it severely. The scar is still visible. This happened when I was sixteen.

Was my discontent connected to the long chats I had with my uncle John Brinkley, a loyal member of the British Communist Party, who served with the propaganda division of a British Army unit during World War II and whose bookshelves included a cache of red-bound volumes on Marxist topics? Uncle John, who later taught graphic design at the Royal College of Art in London and who wrote *Design for Print: A Handbook of Design and Reproduction Processes*, was at first refused a visa by the USA to lecture at American colleges because of his Communist affiliations. Later, after some academic protests, he was permitted to lecture at Yale University. He was an extraordinarily good-looking man; dark, lean, like a panther emerging from a jungle of deep shadows.

Or perhaps my discontent and occasional eccentricity was passed down to me from both sides of my family. Partly from my father, Gilbert, who delighted in driving Rolls-Royces loaned to him by car dealers because he was quite convincing in passing himself off as wealthy. Maybe it came from his glee in embarrassing my sisters with rambunctious behavior in department stores? Did it come also from my mother, Phyllis, whose side of the family had alleged Romany underpinnings and included an aunt, nurse Nancy, who with her friend, the

Irish nurse Katy Plante, drove a doughty little Morris Oxford sedan from Paris to Moscow two years after the end of the war to take a look at what all the fuss had been about?

My mother's eccentricities were connected more to her occasional "nervous breakdowns," which removed her every now and then for weeks from our household. She had a lot to be unhappy about. She wrote unpublished poetry, quarreled frequently with my engineer father, became involved in psychic matters, and was convinced that I had had a personal visitation from the Virgin Mary in front of our house in Ashford, England, before we emigrated to the United States. She also did not do much to squelch the rumors that I, her son, might be the illegitimate child of her very real romance with an Indian prince in the mid-1930s, when she was photographed wearing a sari and bearing a Hindu red caste mark—the bindi—on her forehead. The prince was killed as the result of an accident that occurred when he was riding at a polo match, this family yarn went. My father, who hit the glass ceiling as a works manager at a giant electrical engineering firm in England because of his working-class roots, was very much in love, all his adult life, with his wife, whose family had upper-class pretentions although it probably had a healthy infusion of Romany blood, which made me, my mother, my uncle John, and my aunt Nancy all look weirdly—even wildly—Middle Eastern. Who knows where my mother's affections lay.

We had several lengthy conversations about this, Yukiko. I told you that I did not know much about "nervous breakdowns" at the time. Recently, I unearthed several letters written by me to my mother in those years when she was hospitalized. These letters are written in pencil in a constantly developing and maturing longhand. I am guessing that I wrote them between the ages of seven and twelve. On the back of each letter I always drew a highly detailed map of some remote part of the world: Aden, for example, or Bombay Island or Socotra or the bleak Isle of Rona, north of Scotland, where no human being lived. I remember how surprised you were soon after we met when I sketched a map of Japan from memory on a bar napkin. "I thought only strange Japanese boys did that," you said, intrigued. "It is very nice to know that there are strange English boys too."

Those maps were my escapes, I suppose, from a world in which I was not content. I thought that over the years I had obliterated these memories, Yukiko. But when I reached for them this week, there they were like noxious bubbles from the swamp of childhood.

You remember this little story, I am sure: my account of the horror I felt the first time my father took me to visit the hospital ward in which my mother was confined. I could hear shrieks and screams coming from dark places as we climbed the concrete stairs. I was gripping my father's hand as tightly as he gripped mine. Fear of dark places still haunts my dreams. My father, always frank when he was anxious, gave me a detailed description of what he called "The DTs"—the *delirium tremens* of alcoholics experiencing withdrawal. He spoke with contempt about drunkards. But he did not mean my mother. My mother was not an alcoholic. I am not sure what ailed her. I have read about depression from time to time. Maybe what she suffered from was depression. You asked me several times about my mother. You said I looked sad. I tried to explain but I did not know exactly what to say, and you had trouble understanding me. I believe that the first time you held my hand was during one of these discussions. You listened closely. You spoke softly. I could see tears welling in your eyes.

Here are a few lines from one of my letters read by me this month for the first time since I wrote them. I must have been about eleven because I had just passed the Eleven Plus exams.

```
Dear Mum,
     I hope you are feeling well in Ward 6
and that you will soon be out of hospital.
At school today we had Brussels sprouts for
Biology but we did not need them so in the
French lesson me, Derrick Reid, and George
Evenden and Neil Hiscox, started breaking up
the sprouts and throwing them at each other.
Suddenly George Evenden threw one and it went
a big bang on the window. The teacher turned
round and said I threw it, but I didn't and
I was sent outside. Then he let me back in
and I made up a new French song to the tune
of "Two Lovely Black Eyes, Two Lovely Black
Eyes." And everyone laughed and so did the
teacher who told me to eat up my sprouts. It
was a blinking fiddle. The thing is at school
that when somebody does something wrong I
always get blamed for it. I am going to the
Saturday morning pictures tomorrow after I
make fried eggs for everybody. We had fish
and chips yesterday at the ABC Staines and
it was smashing. I think I want to have a
```

microscope for passing the Scholarship. I
hope you are making lots of lovely friends
in hospital. People always ask how you are
doing. But I don't know what to say. Are you
getting better? Did you like my poem?

How strange it is now to hear me talking like a British kid.
A blinking fiddle: that sounds so quaint.

My sister Mary and I talk only infrequently about my
mother. We do so out of curiosity. It probably sounds cold,
but for all three of her children, including me, my mother is
a mystery woman. Mary is warmhearted and is capable of the
greatest empathy. She took care of my mother in her final years
when she had Alzheimer's disease and she knew her best. If I
sound remote when I talk about her, it is because she remains
an enigma. I know, for example, that in the United States she
worked with the poor, she joined a circle of psychics, her interest in the occult was mentioned in a couple of books, she
changed religions several times, and she struggled with the
marriage and a husband she did not truly love. All of this she
kept locked up inside. She was not like you, Yuki. You were
vulnerable but you did not conceal that fact from me. My
mother was vulnerable, but her children did not know that.
All we knew was that she was ill, that she was sad, that she was
in the hospital, or that she was at her brother's place or with
her mother. She was unavailable. That is my view. She was
a beautiful woman who was desperate, needy, disappointed.
It was all tragic.

I was estranged from her at a very early age. I remained that
way into my adult life, treading carefully around her because

I never knew what to say. She could be cutting sometimes. If her children were truthful with her about difficulties in their lives she would say something like, "Just get on with it!" Maybe she did that because of her lack of happiness. That was your interpretation, I clearly remember.

Sometimes when my mother attempted to hug me, I would pull away. I have a box of journals she kept but I have not had the nerve or the will to read them. Most people might find this difficult to understand. Other people would treasure notebooks like these. But not me. My younger sister's husband burned the journals that came her way when my mother died. He made the mistake of reading, I was told, and he did not like what he saw. I could not summon up the courage to go to my mother's burial. I did go to a memorial service, which several inner-city people attended. They gave thanks for her involvement in their lives. They described her as sensitive and caring. I was surprised, but I am sure it was true. My mother is long gone now. On quiet Sunday mornings in my red room full of paintings and hundreds of books, I sometimes attempt to talk to her. I need to say "sorry" because I am aware she was in pain. I need to feel something I may have denied myself.

"It is terrible for a mother to lose her children," you told me with such a troubled face, after I said I was not close to my mother. "It is terrible for the child also, Paul." It was one of the few occasions on which I saw you cry. "Please learn how to love everyone," you said. "I was born in *mutsuki*, the first month of the year according to the old Japanese calendar. We say that *mutsuki* is the month of affection, of harmony and warm feelings. You were born in the seventh month—*fumizuki*. That is the literary month, the month of letters and books.

Your July is the month when young people write poetry." You looked at me intently and in a sudden gesture gently closed my eyes with your hand. "Poor boy," you said sweetly. "Poor boy! Boys are really little men and men are really little boys who need their mother's love forever."

I have tried, Yukiko. I have tried to love everyone. It is not easy or simple. I am truly a *fumizuki* person. I have a house full of Buddhas but I am not religious. I spend hours inside books, inhabiting them as if they were dwellings. New topics thrill me. For me, my mother is a "topic." She is more of a topic for me now when I am old than she was when I was a young man or middle-aged. I was talking to Mary today and I asked her why we rejected Mother. She was in such need of affection, Mary said, that she crossed a kind of mother-child boundary of comfort in pursuit of love. My father loved her, but not in the way that would give her comfort. It was not a gentle love. He was not a romantic. He may have worshipped Beethoven but he was no intellectual. She complained about being "raped" her entire life.

In her teens and twenties she had been a kind of golden girl. People would stop and watch my mother and her brother John on the dance floor because they were so sleek and good-looking. My father did not dance. My mother read widely but my father thought that poetry was "sissy," my sister said. When I phoned home from university in 1966 to tell my parents that I had won the Academy of American Poets prize given to students, my father ridiculed the news. My father and I fought viciously with our fists in the months before I enlisted in the navy. Mary remembers him chasing me round the kitchen table with a knife because I questioned his authority. I have always said I joined the navy to escape my family. "I'm going to murder you" was an epithet he sometimes used when he wanted to intimidate. But did I distance myself from my father? No! Why? I can't give a coherent reason. But I do know that my skin crawled when my mother sang the lullaby "All the Pretty Little Horses." I was afraid that in her care I might never wake up.

> Hush-a-bye
> Don't you cry
> Go to sleep my little baby.
> When you wake, you shall have
> All the pretty little horses.

Thank you for listening to me then, and now, Yukiko. I write vignettes and short stories for fun. I showed you my early attempts. You told me to write more. I am still writing. My mother would have almost certainly approved of that, I know. But would she have been able to show such pleasure? I related to my mother best when I read a four-page account she wrote—something not from her journals—about how happy she was on Sundays as a child. "Being the youngest," she wrote, "I would be the first to climb the stairs to bed, and through the open door the fire would be glowing, and the lamps lit upon the table where the family would be talking earnestly. I can see them now, watching me, smiling at me, as I climbed the stairs with the music of Chopin still hanging in the air and my bed waiting for me in the frightening shadows above and my whole world there in the warm, rich circle below." One good thing my mother did was defend my refusal in my teens to study to be an engineer. She fought hard—feeding me a special diet of plaice and codfish and glucose tablets to "increase" my brain power—to make sure I made it to Ashford County Grammar School, experimental place for bright, university-bound boys and girls, where I did not really excel, as I was always a year or two younger than my classmates and I was socially inept. I did not have many adult mentors. No one prepared me to be a man in this world. I grew bored and depressed at school and created a scandal by jumping off the bus and becoming a truant. The bus I took to school always made a stop at Henry VIII's Hampton Court Palace. I would get off the bus there and spend the day strolling around the astonishing gardens, reading books in convenient alcoves, and talking to the elderly men who served as guides about King Henry and all the women he loved. Billie, one of the men, once quoted a passage from William Blake's "Auguries of Innocence." "Now, son," he said in a kindly manner, "live your life well, and enjoy remembering this when you grow old."

> To see a World in a Grain of Sand
> And a Heaven in a Wild Flower,
> Hold Infinity in the palm of your hand
> And Eternity in an hour.

When the school wrote a letter to my parents saying I had been missing for a couple of weeks, my mother went with me to meet the headmaster, Mr. D. N. Atkinson. He actually let me off without any penalty because her tale of how I passed my time at the palace was not what he was expecting. I remember he said to her, "There was no crime here. Your son is not a delinquent. I can't really disapprove of a young boy who likes art and history and does something about it." In fact, he wrote a strong letter of support for me when I was enrolling at Freeport High. God knows what the American school principal made of it. I still have a copy of that letter.

"Paul has a tendency to be independent and unconventional, but not in a harmful way," Mr. Atkinson wrote. "He could go far in life, given proper direction."

America. America! The United States was not my father's first choice. He was an admirer of Lieutenant Colonel Percy Fawcett, the single-minded British explorer who vanished in 1925 somewhere in the jungles of the Amazon, where he was searching for the supposed lost city of "Z," a Latin American Shangri-la. Dad's destiny, and hence mine, lay in Brazil, he decided in the mid-1950s. He was frustrated by the fact that his working-class background prohibited him from rising further in managerial positions at big British electrical engineering companies. At our house, suddenly there were books and pamphlets about Fawcett and Brazil. Eventually, however, the prospect of having to master Portuguese killed that ambition and my father tried his luck in Canada. I am not really sure what happened there. But soon we were making plans to emigrate to America. We sailed aboard the luxurious SS *United States*, where we were served astonishing things like iced water and chocolate milk shakes. As we were preparing to dock in Manhattan I became seasick within sight of the Statue of Liberty. Dad was soon able to land a first-class works manager job with the Minneapolis-Honeywell plant in Freeport. His destiny was now set.

But my destiny was not defined. I languished. I had no

identity. I was, in reality, an unwilling immigrant. I escaped by enlisting in the navy after a stint working illegally as a file clerk with Standard Oil in the gigantic city of Chicago. I could have ended up as a man of absolutely no consequence. But you were so sure of what I could become, Yukiko. You pointed the way.

Chapter 6

MAN LIKE A BEAR

Whoever succeeds in the great attempt
To be a friend of a friend,
Whoever has won a lovely woman,
Let him add his jubilation!
Yes, whoever calls even one soul
His own on the earth's globe!
And who never has, let him steal,
Weeping, away from us.

—Friedrich Schiller,
from "Ode to Joy," 1785;
adapted by Ludwig van Beethoven
for his Ninth Symphony, 1824

The *Shangri-La* left Yokosuka on May 14 and did not return
to the Yokosuka harbor until July 13, ten days before my
twentieth birthday. The ship had made port during that period in Okinawa, Manila, Hong Kong, Okinawa again, and
finally in Sasebo, a smaller navy town in southern Japan.
Yokosuka was hidden in a fog. I left the ship with a two-day
pass. I was a little older and wiser. During the cruise I had
volunteered to go out on a US Marine Corps night-training

mission in Okinawa that involved firing lots of live ammunition. I woke up at dawn dotted with scores of phenomenally itchy mosquito bites, which I manfully ignored. My fingers were blistered because I had been stupidly gripping the steel barrel of the M-1 rifle I was firing at the moon. I did not like the idea of firing at human silhouettes even if they were just printed on cardboard.

Do you remember when I came back from Hong Kong from a fight at the famous Suzie Wong bar with the drops of blood on the cover of my copy of *An Outline History of China*? It was printed by horrible enemy forces in Beijing—or Peking, as it was known in the West in those days. I was not yet twenty. I was trying hard to be older than that. You reminded me that I was still a boy but you listened intently almost as if (I realize this now) I was your son and you were the mother I never had. A sailor with muscles tried to grab the book. Red Downs, my good-natured shipmate, moved quickly to get in the way. The sailor's many friends surged toward the table where I sat with Red and James L. Fowler, a pale, thin kid from Kansas City who was often called "Little Russia" by embryonic Tea Party partisans infuriated by contrary thinking. I struggled with the sailor, who was consumed with bone-cracking rage. I ended up with a long scratch on the side of my face but I had been able to give him a slap and a fat lip. Members of the shore patrol burst into the bar, pushing aside girls wearing tight, slit, silk cheongsam dresses that buttoned to the neck, accentuated their bosoms, pinched them at the waist, and exposed their legs all the way to the top of their flanks if they chose. The shore patrol began hunting for miscreants. I promptly sat down on the *History of China* and avoided arrest by adopting a nonchalant pose, which allowed me to enjoy the sight of the shore patrol dragging the sailor who hated books out onto the street.

One thing I discovered was that certain women were strongly attracted to men skilled at artful and deceptive behavior. I was suddenly popular. The Suzie Wong bar, like the fictional version in the film, was a nest of Eurasian vamps who moved deliberately with the restraint of snakes and who were especially good at slow-smoking black Russian Sobranie cigarettes with gold filters. A pretty girl sitting in your lap, kissing the wound on your cheek and blowing smoke into your eyes when you are nineteen . . . Ahhhhhh. Sublime. You may recall that I used that word when I told you about the incident and you laughed with a strange kind of regret.

I almost forgot. I believe I showed you that history book when we met on that July day in Yokosuka. You saw a couple of blood spatters on the cover. You seized the book, looked sternly at me, and said: "Oh. Oh. Oh! What is this? I told a certain poet to be a good boy." I explained at great length what had happened. You looked proud of me. "Fighting in defense of literature," you said loudly, as if you were making an announcement. "A noble sport!"

I still have my copy of the Chinese history book. The final paragraph in the book reads,

> The victory of the revolution of the Chinese people and the establishment of the People's Republic of China is a victory of Marxism–Leninism in China. It is the most important event in the world after the Great October Socialist Revolution (in Russia). It is a source of inspiration

for the oppressed people of the East as well as other people in the rest of the world and affirms their confidence in the ultimate victory of their struggle for liberation.

I remember reading that passage and thinking a forbidden thought: "I suppose that includes me."

I've just remembered another book acquired on that same Hong Kong visit. I still have that, too. It is *The True Story of Ah-Q* (阿Q正传). You know my habit, which you started, of wandering into used bookshops not in search of any particular book but in search of the great unknown. "I always have a book with me," you said mischievously in the White Rose. "When the world becomes too much, I open the book and slip inside. Would you like to know how to do that? Watch! See! Look, here is the book. I open the book. I start reading. I am in a trance. Now look at me. See? I am invisible."

When I die I want to be buried with *The True Story of Ah-Q*, the *Outline History of China* with the blood spots from the battle over literature, the *Senryu* with your fingerprint inside, and the antique bronze vase with the green patina you bought me because I said that if I ever was a writer I would use it to store pens and pencils and rulers and ink brushes and a long thin paper knife I would use to slit open the envelopes containing your letters. You can still write to me, you know. I am here, waiting, waiting.

"You want to talk to interesting people as much as you can," you told me. "The best way to do that is to walk into a bookstore, pick up a book—any book—and ask the person next to you if he has read it. A stupid person will just shake his head. An intelligent person will say, 'No, but I would like to read it.'"

I did not buy the *Ah-Q* book, which was written by Lu Xun and had been published as a magazine series in 1921 and 1922. It is considered a masterpiece in China. The story traces the "adventures" of Ah-Q, a peasant with little education and no definite occupation. He is a bully to the less fortunate but fearful of those above him in rank or power. He persuades himself that he is spiritually "superior" to his oppressors, even as he is hauled off to be executed for a minor crime. Inside the book I wrote, "Paul Rogers, Victoria, Hong Kong, 6/17/59. Bought for me by Paul Feng."

Paul Feng happened to be standing alongside me in that Hong Kong bookstore. He looked surprised, and pleased, when I not only asked him if he had read the book but asked questions about it after he said *Ah-Q* was a classic. "This is wonderful," Paul Feng said. "A young American wants to read the most famous book in China. Please let me buy that book for you." We talked for a while. We sipped bitter tea from small cups. It was good to feel like the equal of an educated man, I recall telling you. It was good not to be the stereotypical young American but to be the object of friendly curiosity. Nonetheless, because I had tasted the fruit of seduction by book with the volume of Chinese history, I raced back to the Suzie Wong bar, sat down at the same table, pulled out *Ah-Q*, and attracted yet another swarm of Sobranie smokers. In the midst of these adventures, I received an extraordinary letter from you, dated June 5, 1959.

Dear Paul,

    I envy you because you can visit many new places. These places should be exciting for a creative mind with the desire to be the poet I want you to be. They are especially interesting for a journalist. You can be a journalist too, you know. It is not as wonderful as being a poet, but I will allow that. Journalism is a side pocket of culture. It is not appreciated very much. But it is thrilling. Thank you very much for the nice letter (May 27th) from my utopia, Shangri-La. I think just reading your letter is better than writing to you because me . . . I am having such good feelings when I read your letter.

When I am writing to you every time there become funny sentences every time, and mistakes all over and of course rotten grammar all the time. Are you not yet tired of my letter? I am sorry for my errors. But I simply just have to write to you because, first of all, I enjoy it, and secondly because I don't want you to forget me.

Since we become friend I feel from you every time something that remind me of an emotion that we almost be forgetting here at this kind of work I do. I appreciate it profoundly. You make me cry with joy. The girls at the bar worry about me crying. But I say "No. This is happy crying. Happy!!" Because they are good girls, they understand. They are so kind to me even though I am a bad woman.

After they see me enjoying your company and after you have gone, always they talk about you. This makes me jealous but I love it so. Yes, I do. I love watching you walk out the bar because no one walks the way you walk and at the last moment you always turn and give me such a shy smile that I have to hold my heart because I am almost fainting. But of course, I am Japanese, so I would not be fluttering and torn like a woman's precious scarf caught in the thorns of this thing foreigners call LOVE. No one has ever said I LOVE YOU to me, by the way.

Now I have to tell you, Paul, that sometimes I saw in your eyes a special glittering. I hope you can translate what I try to say here. I can't express this very good in English. So this is the secret I give to you today. TAKUSAN (much) NO SAINOO (ability) WO MOTTA (have) HITO (man) GA, SONO KANOOSEI (possibility) WO DEKIRU-DAKE (as much as) HAKI (exhibit) SHITOO TO (to do) KIBOO (hope) NI KAGAYAITE (glittering) IRU KOKORO (mind). There. Can you understand that? I know I am also your teacher, but I know your mind was made up—your good mind existed, sailor boy—even before you left the United States to come to Japan.

Dare I say it? I am WAITING your letter from now on. I HATE that word WAIT!! I am

WAITING. I am hating that word. No! No! An ugly woman like me should accept she will spend her whole life WAITING!! I wish I could write more but I'm tired of my bad English. Even sometimes when I don't write to you Paul, I am always thinking about you. Take care of yourself.

Love,

Yukiko

P.S. Please remember always and forever, for all the years you live, this simple thing: in my womb there will be a memory of who you were and everything you could be. Maybe some day, many years from now, some tiny thing will remind you of me. Maybe you will read this letter again. Maybe you will remember me: a certain woman from a such long time ago. Maybe you will hear the sound of my voice. Maybe you will remember how hard I fought to vanquish the demon of broken English.

Again Love,

Yukiko

You were laughing very hard on the train platform at Yokosuka station as I told you stories from the cruise. You clutched my arm and squeezed it tight. "My plan is working," you said. "You met me when you are a boy. Now you are becoming a man. I am responsible for that. I am so happy." If there is one image of your face that has persisted over the years it is the way you looked at that moment. The way you looked at me remains—the look a woman of the world gives a man in his youth that can never be repeated again.

We were waiting for the train to Hayama, a small resort town with a beach southeast of Kamakura. You had reserved rooms there.

"Yes, I am a wicked woman," you said, with a sly smile, when I looked embarrassed. "But don't worry. We will read books and write poetry all night because we cannot be lovers."

You were chuckling. I was even more embarrassed.

"Do you know that many hundreds of years ago at the court, there were always beautiful women reading books and keeping diaries and writing poetry? Love affairs often began when a gentleman saw beauty in a woman's calligraphy before he even saw her face. In the diary of the aristocratic woman Shikibu Izumi, there is a poem. I can remember this poem. Yes, here it is in my notebook. Please listen carefully.

> "Thinking of the world
> Sleeves wet with tears are my lovers
> Serenely dreaming sweet dreams:
> There is no night for that."

I remember many stories you linked to your recitation of verse, Yuki. Sometimes I wondered if you had been a schoolteacher at some point in your life. I would listen closely, very closely, because these tales often were magical and you delighted in my delight as I listened. You created a hush of silence by putting your fingertip on my lips. And then you told me that many of these women were locked away with nothing else to do but think and imagine a world outside those great court walls and castles. Lady Murasaki, for example, wrote the world's first novel, the first psychological novel, the first modern novel: *Genji monogatari* (*The Tale of Genji*), an esteemed classic about love and intrigue familiar to Westerners doing Japanese studies. Also, you said that a noblewoman, Sei Shōnagon, wrote *Makura no sōshi* (*The Pillow Book of Sei Shōnagon*), a journal packed with poetry, gossip, observations about court life, and lists of things to do. Both books were first published almost exactly one thousand years ago. Here is the brief passage from the *Pillow Book* that has always made me laugh, even as it did the first time we discussed it, Yukiko, when you behaved, in a fit of giggles and tickles, as if you had written it yourself:

It is important that a lover should know how to make his departure. To begin with, he ought not to be too ready to get up, but should require a little coaxing: "Come, it is past daybreak. You don't want to be found here . . ." and so on. One likes him, too, to behave in such a way that one is sure he is unhappy at going and would stay longer if he possibly could. He should not pull on his trousers the moment he is up, but should first of all come close to one's ear and in a whisper finish off whatever was left half-said in the course of the night . . . Then he should raise the shutters, and both lovers should go out together at the double-doors, while he tells her how much he dreads the day that is before him and longs for the approach of night. Then, after he has slipped away, she can stand gazing after him, with charming recollections of those last moments.

"I take books like those when I travel by train so I can also be transported back to those lovely times as well as to my destination," you said, slipping that big fat notebook full of pillow-style notations into your purse. "Those great women were strong. Sei Shōnagon was a court official. Many of these women writers carried swords. They knew how to use them . . . like me. That is one new secret about me, Paul-san. I have a sharp sword. I can fight. I have fought. I am a fighter . . . Do you like my use of tenses?"

I was listening to you like a tall, thin fool. I think you sensed that I felt deeply inadequate. I felt as if I were a tight-rope walker trying to get from one side of a cultural chasm to the other. So to help steady me—maybe even to make me laugh—you said, "But what else do you think these women from ancient times were doing? They were WAITING. They were waiting for their lord to call them to his chamber. So patient are Japanese women. Always WAITING! Waiting women wrote so many great poems and books because they were thinking and thinking while they were waiting and the men were fighting. Silly men!" Yes, it was the women who were the writers, you said, but they were also the concubines and mistresses and playthings of the highest caliber for those men.

You shivered. You had apparently just remembered something.

"I . . . am . . . a . . . ghost," you said, very carefully and slowly, making me wobble over the chasm again. "At one time in my life I . . ." But you did not complete the thought.

It was just after nine in the morning. You told me this was the beginning, according to the Chinese zodiac, of the hour of the serpent, so named because it is when the sun warms the earth and snakes slither forth. My British brain was declining to comprehend, even though my spirit was willing. How could I accept "hours" that were two hours long and were named after animals? I was born in the late-afternoon hour of the monkey and therefore I would always be irreverent and mischievous, you told me. "Take a look at yourself, sailor boy," you said. "Maybe then you will understand that there are truths even in ancient things."

We were waiting. We were talking. We were laughing. The train, which had come down from Tokyo, rattled and whirred to a halt. A loudspeaker was announcing the identity of the station. This happens every day, all across Japan. If I close my eyes I can remember, "*Yoh-kooo-skah! Yoh-kooo-skah! Yoh-kooo-skah!*"

Sleepy people rubbing their eyes tumbled out of the train into the daylight. Some of them were drunk or looked drunk or looked as if they had hangovers. I felt your hand grip me even tighter.

One of the passengers getting off the train was a heavyset man in his early forties with very short hair. He was wearing an undershirt with sleeves, a kind of heavy tan woolen belly warmer round his middle, and grey slacks cut tight round the ankles. On his bare feet were stiff zori sandals. He stood in front of us, his legs apart and rooted to the ground. There was no expression on his face at first. He looked at you. He looked at me. He looked at you again. And then he reached out and seized hold of your shoulder with a grip so powerful that he pulled you off balance. This was so unexpected I was frozen in place. He began dragging you to one of the exits. You looked at me with an expression I had not seen on your face before. It was an expression of complete hopelessness and submission. Passengers began running. I started to move toward him, and he growled at me like a bear, swung his other arm out toward me, and began saying something to me in the crude language of the streets—the language, in fact, of the yakuza, the violent gangsters whose code of honor governed murder, drug trafficking, black marketeering, gambling, smuggling, running nightclubs and massage parlors, pornography, and prostitution, in addition to making lavish "donations" to corrupt politicians.

I know about the yakuza now. But I did not know about them in 1959. To me, this snarling character, who had grabbed you as if you were a runaway, was an unknown force of evil. I followed for a while. He never took his eyes off me. I had no idea what was happening.

"Yuki! Yuki!" I shouted. I had a bad case of the jitters. I could barely speak.

"No," you cried. "*No!* Go away! Go away!"

But even then I did not believe you wanted me to go away. I made another move. He growled again, louder. Even the uniformed station workers were scattering. He let out another stream of threats, or obscenities, or maybe even something worse. You screamed. You screamed again. Your shoes fell off.

I actually tripped over myself, sprawled on the concrete surface of the station platform, and skinned both knees.

Out of nowhere, just as suddenly as the gangster had appeared, came the same police detective who two months earlier had investigated your suicide attempt and who had told me, like a father talking to his son, to leave and go back to the ship. He was wearing the same trench coat and black beret he wore when he came into that shabby hotel room where you were stretched out on the floor, blood everywhere. He skidded across the platform and wrenched the man's hand from your shoulder. They spun round and round in circles—his hands round the man's neck and the man's hands round his neck—until both men stood panting and shaking and cursing, facing each other. You leaned against the wall, crying and sobbing. Some station hands came up to help the cop. Out came a pair of handcuffs. The growls continued. I was convinced the man was telling me he would kill me if he ever saw me again.

"You!" the cop said loudly to me. "You!"

You were too badly bruised and shaken to go to the beach. My confidence and sense of well-being were totally upended. This time I had not come to the rescue. I was no hero. I had a glimpse of the consequences of yet another of your secrets. I got a taxi and took you to the foot of the hill where you lived. I felt that the friendship with you was suddenly over. You waved me away as you started climbing the hill. You did not even look back at me.

But then, halfway up the steps to your house, you stopped, and in a small voice said, "Come back tomorrow. I will explain. I told you I was a very bad woman, but you were too young to know I was telling you the truth."

Chapter 7

SPIDER WOMAN

I remain in a state of surprise, and this leads to heightened interest and hence perception. Like a child with a puzzle, I am forever putting pieces together and saying: Of course!

—Donald Richie,
from *The Japan Journals,*
1947–2004

Young men are likely to be attracted to the ripe beauty of women older than themselves.

—Tanizaki Junichirō,
from "Portrait of Shunkin,"
in *Seven Japanese Tales*

I could hear your voice above me on the hill. You did not sound like a little bird in a tree. You were rehearsing something.

"Dayne-jerrr-oooos! No, no, no! *Abunai!*

"*Dayne-jerrr-oooos! Nooooooo. Abunai! . . . Yes! . . . Abunai!*

"Day-uhhhhn-jerrr-oooos!

"I hate English," you said angrily, after you became aware that I was there. "I hate it. It is a stupid language. By the time you shout 'dayne-jerrr-oooos' you are dead. *Abunai* is a

87

wonderful Japanese word. *Abunai*. It is quick. Like danger. It is like ripping a page from a book when you shout, *ABUNAI!*"

It was the morning of the day after the incident at the train station. It was the day after the danger. You were outside your room, sitting on a ledge in the bright sun. Your black eyes looked deep violet. You looked devious. You looked different. You looked like a showgirl. Your hair was tied up behind your head in a ponytail. You were wearing a brand-new pale-blue cotton dress with a flared skirt over pale-blue high heels. You leaned back and put your feet up on a rock. Your lipstick was thick and scarlet. You wore red plastic earrings shaped like hearts and a red plastic necklace. You looked almost like a teenager, and I, after climbing the hill, was wheezing like an old man.

"Look," you said, without even a hello. "See. This is me, wicked woman." You kicked off your high heels and wiggled your toes. "Come here, Mr. Poet. Come here! I am dayne-jerrrr-oooos." You laughed not very convincingly.

"This is a joke," you said. "This is very funny." You pouted. "I am a Hollywood girl. You supposed to bust out laughing. But no. So serious. So serious you are, young man. Why you no laughing at me?"

And then you stopped the teasing, or the make-believe, or the deception—if that is what you were doing. There must have been something in the way I reacted. I was as startled and fearful as a chicken about to have its neck broken. I think I probably looked annoyed. I had expected a serious Yukiko. I had expected a big mug of hot green tea, and then a solemn, unfolding, engulfing, and maybe even bewitching story. I had expected an explanation so that I could understand the violent actions of the man who became a bear.

"Well, I will tell you almost everything," you said nervously. "I can't tell you everything. If I told you everything, some of it would be lies. Some of it I have had to paint on a canvas so that when I look at that self-portrait I can see what I want to see. I can live comfortably, like a nice woman, like Doris Day. Happy, happy, like a big bath of bubbles, with a nice husband, Mr. Rock Hudson, so . . . so . . . so very handsome. So you will get the almost-truth, and then you will have to use your imagination. Imagine you were reading my life as if it was written by Franz Kafka. He is my favorite writer. Do you think it is strange that a bar girl would read Kafka? If you had to deal with what I deal with at the White Rose, Kafka is like a medicine. What he writes is surreal. Do you understand? But in his surreal creations is a reality . . . the truth . . . my reality in which there is no Doris Day. If you had lived my life from Manchuria and Japan and Hiroshima and then Tokyo, all bombed and life lived in chaos, you could understand. Do you know that when we were finally repatriated and we landed in Japan, there was a sign greeting us, which said, 'Thank you very much for your hardship'?

"But you can never understand. You are too much of a nice boy. You are a golden boy. You are like the four seasons, but the longest of your four seasons is spring. The sun always rises on your world. The moon is always there. The stars keep you company. Your sunsets are always painted for you by Heaven . . . But me . . . I already lived my life. I have lived all of it, to the end. And now, there is Hell. Dancing devils are chasing me, courting me, tempting me. If I have to fight, I will use my *tanto*—my sword.

"Oh no! Oh no! I forgot," you said urgently and abruptly,

derailing your presentation. You looked as if someone had slapped you. "First . . . First . . . What happened after you left me at the bottom of the hill? Where did you go? What did you do? . . . Oh yes. Oh yes! Tell me, Paul. Tell me! You will not be cruel if you tell me the truth. Do you hate me now? Do you belong to me?"

You started crying as if life consisted of nothing more than endless "battles without honor and humanity" (to quote the postwar Japanese novelist and filmmaker Fukasaku Kinji), battles "without meaning," battles for the sake of battles, battles without mercy, without a soul, without a thought, quickly dismissed with a shrug, forgotten after convenient funerals with everyone in formal dress, stone-faced, betraying no conscience and no purpose except to go on living.

I sat down beside you. We looked out at the bay. The flight deck of the *Shangri-La* was glistening with aircraft that had their wings folded. The ship was pointed out to sea, as if ready to make a quick getaway. In a few days we would be gone again, and then you would be waiting. I felt as if *I* had committed an unpardonable wrong. I was desperate to put things right.

But why? You should have been the desperate one. But then, of course, I was merely flustered and you *were* the desperate one.

Is that why you played Miss Hollywood? I started talking in my stupid English—my stupid English that I spoke with an English accent. At least I could spell, you told me once. That is how I ended up on the ship's newspaper. I could spell "seaman apprentice," which was my rank, a rank comparable to that of a worker ant or, better yet, a termite hidden from the light. Eighty percent of newcomers to the ship could not spell *apprentice*, the personnel clerk told me when I first came aboard. I could spell *apprentice*, and they did not know at first what to do with me. So they put me to work cleaning the brass-and-chrome toilets and showers used by sixty men who lived in the same vault-like "compartment" as me, until someone said, "Hey. That weird British kid who can spell *apprentice*. The ship's newspaper needs a writer. Where the hell is he?"

In fact, I told you the work I had done on the *Shangri-La*'s monthly *News Horizon* had impressed the ship's brand-new number two, the executive officer—Commander Davy Crockett—born and raised in Dallas, Texas. He was a former fighter pilot with an exceedingly square jaw and eyes the color of ball bearings.

After I left you at the foot of the hill on the day of the danger, I retreated to the ship. I was obviously upset. I was also angry. I also understood absolutely nothing at all. Red and Jim asked me what had happened. I told them as much as I knew. The next thing that occurred was that the meek little ensign who was in charge of us three seamen apprentices found out about it and informed a more senior officer, who in turn informed Commander Crockett.

I was told to report to Crockett's office IMMEDIATELY!

I walked in, expecting a red-hot blast of uncomprehending rage from Crockett. He was well known for being the human equivalent of a battleship. But, strangely, he greeted me calmly, with a boyish grin. He put down his copy of *Playboy* magazine with a wink. He looked up at me from his chair and said, "Son. What you are doing is dangerous. Dangerous!"

I gulped.

"It is dangerous out there in those alleys of goddamn Yo-kosuka. There are whores and thieves and bandits and murderers, not to mention goddamn Soviet spies! Goddamn it! You are just a goddamn kid. Are you even fuckin' shaving yet, seaman? . . . Oh, jeez. Oh, jeez. Mother of God, have mercy! The goddamn thing that saves yer ass is that you have talent. But you know what? If Satan himself came around the corner in the light of day, you would not recognize him." He leaned back in his chair again to study the effect of his broadside on my pimpled face.

"Now look, son," he said, "I am just trying to scare you. This is not a disciplinary hearing. I am going to give you some advice. Japanese women. God love them! You gotta love them. They are loyal. They have honor. They will never, never, never divorce you, even if you are a hard-drinking, panty-chasing son of a bitch! They are as sweet as sugar candy and every man aboard this ship should take one back home to introduce to his mother! But Japanese women . . . they see a young American, and they spin a silken spider's web. They sit there like a spider, waiting to catch gnats and flies. You are a gnat, Rogers! A gnat. But you are a smart gnat. So if I tell you that all of those girls working in the bars have a history that would scare you to death if you knew just ten percent of it, what would you say?"

"Uh . . . Um . . . Well, sir," I said, "I am not actually a 'young American.' I am actually a young Englishman. There is an important difference."

"I know that, goddamn it," Davy Crockett exploded. "I *know* that you are a goddamn foreigner. But you are in the goddamn United States Navy, God love it! You are a goddamn

Englishman, and we can't give you a security clearance even if we wanted to because you are an alien—an alien!—and that means we can't trust you, and that means if you end up in the arms of a Japanese floozy and she is a Russian agent then you have no loyalties to the United States. Nothing! *Nada*, goddamn it! . . . Oh, jeez. Jeez Louise! I need a moment. I need to catch my breath . . . I mean, what I am trying to say is that you can write and you can spell and you can go far if you are not eaten up by one of those goddamn Japanese spiders. In other words, we goddamn need you, you bastard!" He paused for a breath. His face was red. His khaki shirt had been dry and starched when I entered his cabin. Now there were dark circles of sweat under his armpits. "Look," he said. His voice dropped several octaves, and there was a tone to it that sounded unexpectedly kind. "What are you trying to do, kid? There is a girl involved. I know. There has to be a girl! A goddamn bar girl, and you have lost your mind because she has sweet-talked you like no other woman can. Not even your mother can do that, goddamn it!"

I shook my head, respectfully. "Sir . . . There *is* a girl. She is a *woman*. She works in a bar. But she knows a lot about literature and classical music and history. I have not had sex with her. She is a very nice person."

"Sex! Sex!" the commander roared. His voice sounded like a saw biting into a very dry log. "Good God Almighty, Rogers! That is the worst kind of woman. A real devil! A man-eater! Goddamn! A true spider, I am sure. And you . . . and you . . ." He looked me up and down, paternally and with pity. "You don't have any idea. Any clue. And she has you wrapped around her little finger, and all of her fingers have very long red fingernails. She's got ya. Ohhhhh, jeez. Oh, Jesus! Oh, my God! Goddamn! God in Heaven!"

I gulped. I quaked. But I remembered at that moment the tall-masted schooner *The Torment* maneuvering, escaping a great thundering hunk of steel.

"Now, look," Davy Crockett said, after taking yet another deep breath. "You wrote a real nice story. No one else could have written a story like that." He was referring to a long piece set to appear in the October edition of the ship's newspaper, after we sailed away from Japan forever in late September to return to the United States. I knew the senior officers on the ship had read the piece carefully. It was not the typical dull military story full of boring technical terms. No. This story glowed with emotion. The headline had already been written: "*Shang* Bids Sayonara to Japan." The layout for the page included a drawing of a Japanese woman in a kimono holding a parasol over her right shoulder and looking out at the ocean from the side of a hill. I had found a magazine illustration of a geisha looking out to sea and had told the seaman who was the ship's artist to adapt it for the article. He depicted the mighty *Shangri-La* as nothing but a tiny silhouette disappearing over the horizon. The ship was no larger than a flea. The woman was a hundred times its size, and she had an intelligent profile and a sensual twist to her body as she watched the Shitty Shang sail away.

Our leader, the ensign, was terrified about how all this would be received by his superiors. "I just don't think this is appropriate," he whimpered. "It creates the wrong impression. We should have an illustration of an American wife waving from the shoreline of the United States, or at least from a beach in Hawaii. And your story: it makes all the men on this ship feel as if they had a love affair in Japan. We print this story, and every man sailing back home is going to feel guilty."

Guilt? Maybe. Love affairs? Unlikely.

Nonetheless, I had been told that Commander Crockett liked that drawing, and the story, and that he had also approved another piece I had written for the same issue about the marriage in Japan of Lieutenant Junior Grade Pat Bauschka to a beautiful graduate of Hiroshima University, Niishi Mieko. I told you that I treated this story in exactly the same way I would have written it if he had married a girl from Texas. Bauschka, a radar controller on AD-5W Skyraider aircraft, was a tall young officer from rural Wisconsin, completely without guile, who fell in love with Miss Niishi on a previous *Shangri-La* cruise to the western Pacific. There was a lot of grumbling on the ship about this union. Chaplain Peeples strongly opposed the marriage on the grounds that Niishi Mieko was not American and not Christian and also not worthy of being a wife and mother loved by an American commissioned officer.

I interviewed Bauschka for the story, and I could tell his heart was in it. He was truly in love. He became one of my heroes, in fact. During the brief weeks I knew him, he urged me many times to go to college. He also urged me not to reenlist in the navy. "You are not quite the right fit," he told me. Bauschka went on in life to command several ships. He has passed away. But Mieko, his wife, still lives.

Recently I exchanged emails with the Bauschkas' son, Chris, who is an electrical engineer. When I asked Chris whether he thought I could interview Mieko about her life with Pat, he replied:

Paul. Wow, this is most interesting. I can almost guarantee that my mom would not be willing to talk. But I have forwarded your message to a couple of my sisters in the hopes [they will try] to help me convince her . . . my reasoning being that since my father passed away when I was quite young (and he was not home much of my life growing up), I have not been able to talk with her about anything related to Pat. Basically, I know very little about my dad. I have small snippets of stories, and some small memories, but that is it. Please don't feel like a nuisance by continuing to check back with me if you haven't heard from me in a while.

You would probably recognize, Yukiko, the regret in this email—the regret of a child of a military man who did his duty for the naval service but who was, as a result, seldom home. Regret over a mystery that can never be put right, or understood, at least until old age makes acceptance and comprehension possible. Then there will be peace. At death, this father and son will be reunited. I am sure you would agree.

But what of Commander Crockett? His talk with me ended, and he waved me away, but not before he attempted to plant horror in my soul. I saluted.

"Don't salute me, son," he said. "You will do well. But keep your nose clean. Stay sharp. Don't drink too much. Don't smoke. Don't kiss strange women. Do kiss your wife if you ever marry. Of course, kiss your mother. Make goddamn sure you always use a rubber. When you get all hot and bothered, remember the training films about your health that we showed you back in boot camp! Be truly scared of *non-specific urethritis*.

You don't want someone shoving a glass rod up your dick! And be especially scared of *chancroids*. You don't want your balls turning black with rot! No more fighting, son. No more contact with the police."

"Police?" I asked, trembling. "Police?"

"Yes," he said. "The goddamn cops. I had a few words today with a smart-ass detective, who told our liaison that a kid sailor had been involved in two incidents ashore, including one in which a woman almost died."

Almost died. Yes, you almost died. I could not hold back the tears.

"Now, now, son," Crockett said. "Be a man. I know you tried to help her. I know that. You did the right thing. But can you imagine if that got into the local newspapers? I would have the God Almighty US ambassador in a three-piece suit on my neck. The mayor of Yokosuka. The foreign minister of Japan. Maybe even the emperor of Japan. God help us if the captain, and the goddamn admiral, and the chief of naval operations heard about this. God help you, son! God help me if you get into trouble again. Stay away from Japanese women, if you can. Love them and leave them. That's the navy way."

"So," you said, Yukiko. "Everything is all right, then?"

"What?" I exclaimed. "What? No! . . . Everything is *abunai*! *Abunai!* You understand *abunai*?"

"Oh," you said. "I am sorry . . . so sorry, Paul. I did not know how much trouble I caused." You reached out and took my hand, and you would not let go when I pulled away a little, not sure if you were a spider or the woman I hardly knew.

"Please, let me say 'I love this hand,'" you said. "Just this hand. You will let me love just your hand. I can't say 'I

97

love you,' because that is impossible. It is impossible for one hundred reasons, most of which you do not know. It is better if you do not know. You are going to leave me. You will go down the hill and back to the ship and you will never come to the White Rose again."

You started weeping.

Like a man, I did not know what to say.

"I am only going to go when the ship sails away in September," I said. "It is still only July. I am going to have a birthday soon. There is lots of time."

You shook your head slowly. You looked up at me. "There are just a few days left," you said. "There is not enough time to make everything perfect. There is not enough time for you to know me so that you will never ever forget me." The tears came again.

I blurted out, "They did not order me to stay away from you. They just told me you are like a spider."

"What?" you said, jumping up. "How dare they! How dare they! What an insult that is to a poor Japanese woman. How unkind! How ignorant! How rude! How *American*! What do they know about anything? What do they know about me? They know nothing!

"No. No," you said, releasing my hand, your face clouded, furious, dangerous. "No. No. Take your stupid English and go back down the hill and find some stupid girl you can talk to like a stupid boy. That is what you should do. You don't want to be with an ugly woman like me, so old, so evil . . . A spider!"

It took me some moments to realize I still knew almost nothing about your past.

Chapter 8

NICE SIMPLE BOY

Yamaguchi Momoe, raised in Yokosuka by a single mother, had a wildly popular singing career that capitalized on her dark, damaged image. But she retired in 1980 at the age of twenty-one to marry and has not made public appearances since. It was strictly her choice to end her career, she said. Her biggest hit was *"Hitonatsu no keiken"* (Experiences of Summer Youth), which included the lines, "I'll give you the most precious thing a girl has," and, "We all experience sweet seduction at least once." This prompted salacious questions such as, "What is a girl's most precious thing?" She replied, *"Magokoro!"* This translates as "a true heart" or "devotion."

I did not retreat down the hill. I stood on the topmost of the 101 steps that led to your house. The city, the ship, and the train station were all laid out neatly below me in the haze as if they were toys. One lesson I had learned that summer, even in the face of countless sights and sounds I did not understand, was to stand my ground. I did that in Vietnam and in Cambodia, in Buenos Aires and Caracas—any place there were barricades and rocks, tear gas and bullets. Defiance became my style after we met. You taught me well, Yukiko. I gripped my left wrist with my right hand, leaned slightly to the left, and stood right in front of you—and waited calmly and resolutely for your rage to subside. It was a way of looking and asking a question without words.

I had climbed the hill thinking that I would tell you that during 1945 when the *Shangri-La* was brand-new, its aircraft bombed Yokosuka and other places, deep in the heart of Japan, seven days a week, until the atom bombs were dropped on Hiroshima and Nagasaki in August of that year. Japanese air defenses were so shattered at that point that there was nothing people could do except watch their neighborhoods go up in flames. The ship became known as the "Tokyo Express" for its regular deliveries of destruction and death. I was going to tell you that I had noticed that major military powers often delight in sugarcoating their instruments of war, as if this would enable their citizens to sleep at night instead of picturing in their mind's eye—as I did aboard ship—that moment when the bombs detonated in the sky, killing 225,000 of the 590,000 people in the two cities. I wondered whether Heaven had the capacity to receive all those souls at once, or if those shrieking spirits still flew around, unable to respond to the grand chorus of loved ones in Heaven awaiting them. And now that I mention Heaven, I give thanks to whoever it was who restrained me from telling you about the *Shangri-La*'s role in the ruination of Japan.

We looked at each other uneasily for two or three minutes. The expression on your face was slowly changing. I could sense that you had accepted the fact that I was not leaving. There was a flicker of approval in your eyes, as if I had passed a test. I had the feeling that you had never come to this point in your life before—the moment of revelation. Your history was hidden. It was left behind. It was forgotten, locked up, buried, not even real anymore. I was not sure what I should do if you started talking. Should I just listen? If there were tears, should I cry? Would you need comforting? Should I put my arm round you? There was a part of me that knew the answers to those questions. There was a part of me that still did not understand what it was to love unconditionally, even when there was no hope of a happy outcome.

You took a deep breath. "Please wait here," you said in a very small voice. You turned and went inside your room. I could hear the rustle of the blue dress you were shedding, and the sound of satisfaction you made when you pulled the obi sash tight round the waist of your *yukata*—the long, simple cotton kimono the Japanese wear at home in the sultry summer months. You were humming a lighthearted melody popular in the shambles of postwar Japan, "*Ginza kankan musume*" (Ginza Street Girl).

> The rain falls on the kankan girl
> Standing there without an umbrella.
> She pulls off her sandals, saying, "Ha! So what!"
> The Ginza is her jungle. She is not afraid
> Of tigers or wolves. She's the Ginza street girl.

It was you, I suppose, who hung the small bells in the bushes and in the lower branches of the paulownia, together with little jagged, folded strips of pure white paper on which, you told me, you wrote your prayers. A breeze came up from the sea with the smell of brine and the coolness of the ocean, and your prayers and bells waltzed in the bright light. Many years later, when I was listening to the pianist Cristina Ariagno's performances of Erik Satie's mathematically precise pieces, I was reminded of that scene. I also remembered that when you came out onto the porch again, the *yukata* was draped loosely around your shoulders so the nape of your neck was exposed to the top of your spine. Your hair was piled up and held in place with four long metal-and-tortoiseshell *kanzashi*, which stuck out like chopsticks at odd angles. Long strands of wet hair hung down over your cheeks. Your eyes were moist, and so were your lips. Your face was flushed, as if with excitement. When you moved you took such short steps, confined as you were inside the *yukata*. You held the upper part of your body above the narrow sash cinched tightly round your waist extraordinarily erect. You glided toward me, luminous, as the bells tinkled. This was all so new to me. For the first time I realized how profoundly different we were: you, the older woman from a culture I knew almost nothing about, and I, the young man so keenly aware that he was totally out of place, defenseless, dependent, enchanted. I tried to remember Commander Crockett's dramatic warnings, but they were entombed in that great mass of steel called the *Shangri-La* and they did not resonate up here on the hill, which was, I was sure at that moment, much closer to paradise.

"Are you all right?" you asked. I sat down to mask the fact that I was trembling. How funny, I thought, that in front of Crockett I was petrified but I understood why. Here, however, in front of this woman with that exposed neck and beads of glistening sweat moving slowly down her skin toward her bare shoulder, I was truly awed, and frightened, but I did not understand why. We were no more than two feet apart.

"Do you like my *yukata*?" you asked, a little amused. I nodded. "Are you sure you are OK?" you asked again. You lit a dark green stick of temple incense. The trail of fragrant sandalwood smoke curled round and round, turning into near nothingness as it gathered around you. I shook my head slowly in response to your question and I tried to smile. But I did not have enough experience in this world to tell you what was on my mind. In fact I did not know what I was thinking. I still do not know, although if I look out into my garden and see the dense, deep red blossoms on the Rouge Royale French rose, I get a hint.

"In Japan," you said, "this is not supposed to happen. You are really a child, you know. An older person does not confide in a younger person. It is supposed to be the other way around. But I do owe you some kind of explanation. It is the polite and correct thing to do. You are very young, but in the last few weeks you have become wiser . . . Not cynical, like me, but wiser, maybe like a cat." You laughed. "Yes, like a *kuroneko*, like a black cat, cautious but curious and ready to pounce." You laughed again as the bells clinked in the breeze and your prayers fluttered, attracting the attention of celestial beings, I suppose. "My friends ask me about you, and I tell them, he is really my pet. But be careful of his sharp teeth and his very sharp claws.

"I am going to tell you something," you said. "I am going to start talking. I am going to use my broken English to tell you about three parts of my life. This may take a while, and also I have to use your so stupid language. You will struggle to understand. Maybe I will give you a severe headache. Don't worry, though. I have aspirins, and if you are in pain, I will so good massage your head and your shoulders.

"My life has been full of pain and I believe that you have been sent to me to share that burden. You are still like the sheet of writing paper that you were on the first day we met. You don't know about we Japanese. You don't know that according to our religion, life is supposed to be happy. If your life is not happy, and the place where you are is not happy, and there is no harmony, we clap our hands and we pray and we are purified. Yes, Mr. Paul, you will share with me and you will be instantly unhappy. But in the end, maybe many hours or even days from now, we will say a prayer together and we will be happy. So happy. Do you remember when I did not die on that day—when I decided to die so that I would be happy? That was a mistake. You . . . a nice simple boy . . . you gave me one more chance at happiness so brief that I will almost die from that happiness. But first you have to suffer." You laughed yet again. You reached out and touched my hand. "Don't be scared," you said. "I will show you the way."

Yes. You would show me the way—a pathway, maybe—as you talked about your past. But I knew enough about your ways to realize that I would have to be patient. I remember that one day you were reading a magazine, and you pointed to a full-color reproduction of Monet's famous painting of water lilies. "There is too much beauty in this painting," you said, suddenly. "It is too overwhelming, too bold. Beauty is best presented when it is concealed. And secrets? Secrets are like beauty. You will never know the reasons for beauty. They are so secret, no one knows."

If you were going to show me a pathway it would lead to someplace unknown. Would it lead to happiness? Again, I realized I was in such an unfamiliar place. The *Shangri-La*, with its hoard of nuclear weapons, was close at hand but so far away. Neither prospect was comforting. So I stood my ground.

"I have been thinking about this for several days," you began, sitting down beside me, so close I could feel heat from your body. "Please forgive me." I could smell just a hint of that perfume you used whose name I did not know and will never know. "I have been planning what to tell you, in my own way, so that you will understand who I am. I hope so. Please try. You will remember all of this, one day, long, long after you sail away and I am a memory.

"Once upon a time a small girl was born in Harbin. This was a beautiful city in north China, in the land of the Manchus. This was my home. This is where I came from. I am 'Japanese,' but also I am not Japanese. I am like you: you are 'American,' but you are not American. First, Harbin belonged to China. Then it belonged to Russia, and then it belonged to Japan when it created Manchuria. Those were very confusing times. My father was a policeman—a military policeman. We call them *kempei*. You call them . . . ?" You looked at me closely for a response. I gave none. You adjusted the temple incense. You clapped your hands to attract the attention of your deities, which I am sure were now attentive. "I am going to pray now," you said. "For a few minutes I will be pure. This will permit me to tell the unpleasant truth."

What did I know then about *kempei*? Absolutely nothing.

You plunged into the truth with such determination. I still could not take my eyes off the back of your neck. I could tell that you had done some rehearsing, as you had rehearsed the English word you detested so much, *dangerous*. I could sense that you were laying out history as if opening a window and allowing light to fall on your statement in Kamakura that your father had been an "executioner." Further down the pathway would be new light, spilling on the evil man at the train station and who knew what else.

"My parents were Japanese, of course. We were from Ōtake, a small town near Hiroshima. My mother married below her class. Her father—my grandfather—was a doctor who had studied in Germany. Like my father, he loved Beethoven, especially the piano concertos played by the great Artur Schnabel."

That was a shock. "Really!" I exclaimed. My father also loved Beethoven, and when he was a young man he held a short conversation with Artur Schnabel outside the Royal Albert Hall in London and told him how much he admired his technique. "And do you know—" I began, before I thought better of it and silenced myself. Maybe I can end that sentence for you now. It would have been, "And do you know that Schnabel's mother was deported from Austria to the Jewish ghetto of Theresienstadt in 1942, where she quickly perished, which was one of the reasons Schnabel never returned to your grandfather's beloved Germany or to Austria after the war." How can it be, I asked myself, that two human beings from countries so distant from each other could share the fact that their forebears admired the genius of Artur Schnabel?

By the time my thought was stifled, you were already explaining why your mother married your father. "You see," you said, "one evening my grandfather heard a young student pianist play at a concert in Hiroshima, and he admired his determination to finish the piece even though he made many mistakes. His mistakes were 'brilliant,' my grandfather said. After the concert, my grandfather invited the student, my father, to play piano at his home." You said your mother, who was only sixteen at the time, shared that admiration, because in those days your father always played piano with a lot of mistakes, as did Schnabel. He did that until the marriage was arranged with your mother. Your father could not find work as a pianist, so he did the next best thing—he joined the military police intelligence service, where he used his mathematical skills to become an expert at breaking codes, and then he started playing Erik Satie and seldom made mistakes again.

I nodded. This I could understand. "You know," I said, "there is no emotion at all in playing Satie. Satie never called himself a musician. He called himself . . . what is that word? A *phonometrician*—a person who measures sound, a technician, a person working with formulaic precision . . . almost as if he had contempt for those who listened to his music."

You slowly began explaining that Harbin was at the far end of the railroad connecting it and other big Manchurian cities with the port of Dairen, where there was a large Japanese garrison. Dairen linked the industrial riches of Manchuria with resource-poor Japan. In 1932, the Imperial Japanese Army caused consternation back in Tokyo by striking northeast-ward from Dairen—without authorization—and seizing all the manufacturing centers of Manchuria, one after the other, including Harbin. The Japanese went to great lengths to es-tablish and legitimize the idea of a Manchurian state, which they called Manchukuo.

I have not forgotten all of this, Yuki. But there were often gaps in my understanding until I began writing to you again, like this. Recent research I did showed that, in 1940, there were 42 million people living in Manchuria, of whom more than 1.7 million were Japanese settlers. According to Japanese government planners, the Japanese population was to have grown to 5 million by 1950. At 380,000 square miles, Manchuria was bigger than Texas by a third. It had its own emperor, P'u-i, of the Manchu dynasty, appointed by Japan to preside over the puppet state. Various Manchu warlords swore allegiance to Japan. Some Chinese patriots joined guerrilla groups to contest control, but the Japanese military was highly trained and well equipped, and its "punitive expeditions" ensured that Japan kept control of urban centers.

You said the army also opened up large areas of forest and farmland for colonists from Japan who, starting in the late 1920s at the dawn of the Great Depression, responded to government-sponsored exhortations to leave Japan and occupy this new frontier as "pioneers." You spent some time laying out all of this. It was as if you were delivering a lecture about a subject dear to your heart that no one cared about anymore.

Harbin was a relatively remote railroad hub with an unusual history. You told me it was home in the 1930s to more than twenty thousand Russian Jews who had been living in exile in Siberia. It was also home to a good number of Europeans, including quite a few Polish Catholics, seven thousand of whom had been sent to Manchuria in the early 1900s by the Russian czar to build railroads. The city's international mix also incorporated a host of adventurers, including many anti-Jewish White Russian fascists who fled Russia in the years after the 1918 revolution. Japan built steel mills and established other heavy industry in Harbin, knowing that it was secure from long-range bombing sorties if war ever came.

The Jewish community had its own schools, hospitals, and civic centers, you said. Harbin became known to the outside world as "The Paris of the Orient," and also as the "City of Music." The intellectual life was rich and varied. Many Japanese children, such as you, had Jewish friends. Jewish social gatherings were multilingual.

No wonder, I understand now, your English was so much better than that of the average Japanese. No wonder you could make the big leap to forge an intense bond with a young foreigner drifting around the fringes of Asia. No wonder you read Western philosophy and poetry and were so familiar with the great composers, and no wonder you needed to listen to classical music on the radio and to talk about poetry even with an unschooled primitive youth like me. Harbin was an ideal place for your father to continue his piano studies. His rigidly severe Satie recitals at home gave him an opportunity to escape the rigors of the work he was assigned, and to ensure that his control over his household was total.

Because it was out of sight of most forms of scrutiny, Harbin was also an ideal site for the Imperial Japanese Army to establish Unit 731, part of the military's so-called Epidemic Prevention and Water Purification Department. You were reluctant to talk about this in detail at first. But it was quickly apparent that your father's role as a *kempei*, terrorizing civilians—although not the Jews—was as shameful for you as your father's desire to subjugate his wife and his children. You mentioned briefly again that your father often beat your mother and his sons, but that he never touched you, a fact that caused you to be truly terrified because you were so certain that he would lash out at you sooner or later. Your brothers were fearful, but having experienced his wrath, they were able to live with their terror. You, however, spent a lot of time, even when you were a very young girl, at the homes of Jewish neighbors, where you were given the love and affection missing at your home.

"I did not hate my father," you said hesitantly, as if you had never uttered that phrase before. "My mother was devoted to him despite everything. But she became so worried, and she became ill. People said she caught tuberculosis because the beatings made her weak. When my mother was living, I always knew her as a sick woman, as a suffering woman. She neglected her health. Maybe she wanted to die. It was only after I became a teenager and I had heard rumors about the kind of work my father did, that my mother took me aside one night and warned me never to mention Unit 731 to anyone. My mother said, "Your father is doing his duty. I have to accept that. I have no choice. He does what he is doing as a service to the country."

You stared at me with what looked like stark fear. I knew then that you had never been able to escape those memories. If they were not part of your daily thoughts, they were part of your conscience. They were also probably part of your worst dreams. You told me once that even then, when I knew you, sometimes you were afraid to sleep. I knew that because you sometimes told me you were so envious that I had funny dreams I could share with you.

I could see how uncertain you were about continuing. You held my hand again, and leaned your weight against me. It was the first time in my life a woman had been that intimately physical with me. "Please give me a moment," you said, "before I continue. Let's pretend we are happy, happy. Happy! Happy! Oh yes, until this moment with you, sailor boy, I had lost my happiness. My happiness should have been a butterfly, visiting flower after flower, just looking for a taste of sweetness. But instead my happiness became one of those big crows, cawing at me with his cruel voice from the trees behind my house. Do you know they have feathers so dark you cannot see even the blackness of their eyes? But now, I have my happiness again. It has come back to me."

You smiled such a thin smile. Oh, that smile!

"Let's listen to the bells," you said. "Let's watch the wind carrying my prayers to Heaven."

Chapter 9

THERE IS NO FORGIVENESS

I'll give you my life. I wander around and I get to Tokyo.
There, in the neon garden of Shinjuku at night,
a flower finally blooms.
[. . .]
I'll give you my life. I'll even lie so that I can survive.
I'll get drunk on sake if it means I can survive.
I don't want to be cynical but
if you like a woman like me . . . I'll give you my life.

> —*Enka* blues sung by a woman
> gangster in the film *Zubekō Banchō*
> (Delinquent Girl Boss)

For several minutes, we watched small birds attacking a big
hawk soaring as if it was a malevolent kite on a very long string.

"Look, Paul. Look at those brave birds," you said. "They
are mothers protecting little baby birds in their nests. My
mother tried her best to look after her children. On those nights
that my father came back drunk from his job, she gathered us
in a dark room of the house. She hugged us tightly until we fell
asleep because there was nowhere to go and my father had a
gun and a sword. She hugged me like this," you said brightly.

You suddenly shifted your position so you had your arms tight round me. "I am going to tell you more, but please do not be frightened. Please think about beautiful poetry when this certain girl is talking. She would appreciate it if you would give her that poem after she finishes her Manchuria history. If there is no poem, I will be very worried. Maybe you will hate my country. Maybe you will hate my family. You might hate me.

"I have to put my arms round you when I am telling you this because you were once a child in England and your mother hid you under the stairs when the bombs came. Were you afraid? In 1945 you were already six years old. Yes, I know you had that experience. That is why you listen so patiently to me. Thank you for that.

"But you did not have a father like me," you said, your voice hardening. You released me from that very long embrace and pushed me back. It was another of those instances when everything froze in place and you studied me from head to toe, slowly and carefully. You stared especially closely into my eyes, as if you could somehow use them to gain entrance to my mind. You stared, and then you slowly shook your head. In your eyes I could see tiny crystals of ice and blood. I looked deeper and I was afraid of what I saw there: your history and a life I would never be able to comprehend.

"You are without guilt," you said suddenly, with a strange smile of resignation. "You are a very nice boy . . . I share a guilt. As long as I live, it will always be that way. I share that guilt with my father. But for the time being, please remember I only want happiness. So far, you are perfect . . . You are a handsome young man who is respectful. You think like a poet. You look at me and you feel fear because you see the truth—evidence of the truth—and that I cannot hide from you. You are a friend. You are a pleasure and a joy. *Are wa taihen okashii, da wa! Hen, da wa! Hen na gaijin, daiyo!* [That is very strange indeed! Very peculiar! You are indeed a very strange foreigner!]

"You see," you said, with the saddest of smiles, "I am ready to tell you now something I did not know myself until very recently when I came to Yokosuka to work. My father—like you, once a sweet man—worked at a place that was truly the entrance to Hell."

"Hell is here?" I asked. "Here on Earth?"

"Yes," you said. Now your mouth was twisted, as if someone had just struck you, or as if someone had pushed needles under your fingernails. "A Japanese Hell is not only a bright light that blinds you. It is also darkness. In that secret Hell, you are trapped no matter what you do. All you know is the pain, but you are alive. You are not burning. You are living your life . . . laughing and suffering . . . To me it is all the same, unless . . . unless . . . someone, a nice young man, is brave enough to love me."

You said you found it so strange that the average human being who puts on a uniform or swears an oath or who marches to the sound of trumpets cannot resist becoming inhuman when the order comes to kill. You said you did not mean the ordinary soldier who fires his weapon in battle in order to attack, defend, and survive. What you meant is the man who does not flinch and who does not resist when he accepts that it is his duty to torture.

"That is very, very bad," you said. "There is no forgiveness." But the truth is, you said, that those men murder with a strange fascination and satisfaction. "I did not know this myself," you said, "until I met someone who knew what my father did at Unit 731."

"Who is that person?" I asked. "The man at the train station?"

"Oh no," you said. "Not that very bad man."

"Another very bad man?"

"No. A man who is not good or bad. A policeman."

Commander Crockett's words about a conversation with a detective were ringing in my ears. I nodded. Nodding is what dolts do, I thought to myself, when they see the flood coming and know they are going to drown.

"But this unit . . ." I blurted.

"Yes," you said patiently.

"This unit . . . what did it do, and what did your father do there?"

"How can I explain this?" you said. "I will try."

Harbin was a city of culture, you began. It was also a city of infernal intrigue. On the one hand Harbin had a direct link by rail and mail—from Eastern Europe all the way across Russia and through Siberia to Manchuria—with the Japanese vice-consul in far-off Lithuania.

When I was reading your letters, I remembered how you struggled with this explanation. Research on my part recently enabled me to determine that this consul, Sugihara Chiune, decided to issue transit visas good for resettlement in Japanese-controlled territories in the Far East to more than six thousand Jewish men, women, and children, mostly from Poland, fleeing the Nazi campaign of murder in occupied Europe. Sugihara did this not only for humanitarian reasons but because the

Japanese government adopted a policy in the early 1930s that favored encouraging Jews to settle in Manchuria and also in China proper, including the international settlement in Shanghai, which eventually came under Japanese control. The reason Japan decided on this policy was because the Japanese looked upon Jews as people with strong business skills and the spirit of enterprise, who would help facilitate commercial and industrial growth in areas where Tokyo planned to settle millions of Japanese colonists. However, the Japanese Ministry of Foreign Affairs never gave direct approval for Sugihara's actions. For twenty-nine days, he and Yukiko, his wife, handwrote more than three hundred visas per day, until the Soviet government closed the consulate. Sugihara was raised in the strict Japanese code of ethics of a turn-of-the-century samurai family. According to the 1995 book *Visas for Life* by Sugihara Yukiko, "The cardinal virtues of this society were *oya koko* (love of the family), *kodomo no tameni* (for the sake of the children), having *giri* and *on* (duty and responsibility, or obligation to repay a debt), *gaman* (withholding of emotions on the surface), *gambatte* (internal strength and resourcefulness), and *haji wo kakete* (don't bring shame on the family)."

The Imperial Japanese Army was told to keep the Jews in Manchuria under constant surveillance, you said. That was one of your father's duties as an officer in the fearsome *kempei*. But your father studied music in the thriving Jewish community in Harbin. You had Jewish friends. I wish I had known about Sugihara when I knew you. The diplomat had been stationed in Harbin by Japan's Ministry of Foreign Affairs while you lived there. Sugihara converted to Russian Orthodoxy in Harbin. He had a brief marriage to a White Russian woman. You were too young to have known him, but it is possible your father may have met him. Who knows whether they would have been anything more than acquaintances. Sugihara resigned his Harbin post to protest the brutal treatment of Chinese citizens by the *kempei*. His Russian-language tutor was a Jew, and he had friends in Harbin's large Jewish community. Some Japanese, you said, were convinced that the Jews and the Japanese had much in common in terms of culture and religion and also in terms of being a "special or chosen people." In fact, you told me, when a new Shinto shrine was dedicated in your neighborhood in Harbin, Japan sent a Shinto priest to the city, whose job was to invite rabbis and other Jewish community leaders to this sacred event.

"They thought that our Shinto religion and the Jewish religion were linked."

I am not Jewish. Part of my extended family has probable Romany—Gypsy—roots, and I knew about the history of suffering at the hands of the Nazis, who killed more than 220,000 Roma across Europe, in addition to the millions of Jews, in the Holocaust.*

---

* In the early 1970s, when I was working as a *Newsweek* correspondent in the magazine's Tokyo bureau, I remember several conversations I had with my boss there, Bernard Krisher, who often said that many of his close friendships with the elite of Japan came about because he was Jewish. Bernie, who married a Japanese woman, was always bemused by comments made by people in Tokyo about his religion—it was almost as if they were in awe. But as for the supposed filial linkage between Judaism and Shinto, that topic never came up with Krisher. By the time I worked for *Newsweek*, I had already received an undergraduate degree in Japanese history and I would have rejected any notion that Shinto—a nativist religion centered on the belief that the members of the imperial family are direct descendants of a sun goddess—had anything in common with the Jewish religion.

"So you see," you said, at a moment when I clearly did not understand what you were telling me, "that was one thing my father did."

"That is what the policeman told you?" I said.

"Yes. Very recently."

"But why would he suddenly tell you this?"

"Because he suddenly met me."

"Oh," I said. It was the first time in my life I felt jealous.

You could see the jealousy, I know. So you suddenly veered off subject. The Japanese did not kill Jews. But the Germans did kill Jews. This made no sense to me at all because were the Japanese and the Germans not allies? For me, things had to be either black or white, hot or cold, virtuous or evil, ugly or beautiful, and I was too young to know otherwise. How could the world be that complicated, I remember asking you.

"Oh," you said. "Oh . . ." But beyond that, you did not answer.

Instead, you went inside to make *ocha*, the green tea Japanese people drink for all sorts of reasons, but especially when they are being thoughtful, or they wish to retreat a little from disagreement or controversy or anything else that upsets their need for that all-important harmony, which for Westerners does not really exist.

Large thunderhead clouds were gathering overhead. From the ocean came a rumbling, like distant cannon fire. During all this time when you had been talking, a Tokyo radio station you favored was having its weekly opera recital. "Who is that woman?" you exclaimed. "She has such an extraordinary voice." The singer was finishing an aria. The male announcer was explaining something.

"The singer was someone called Carras," you said.

Carras? Who is "Carras"? I wondered. My knowledge of opera was fragmentary at best. But then I remembered reading something about Maria Callas and I realized you were having problems pronouncing the letter *l*, a problem common to almost all Japanese.

The children of another tenant down the hallway were laughing and banging on a galvanized steel washtub with sticks. You leaped up in a fury, as if someone had stolen something precious from you.

"Urusai!" you shouted. *"Urusai!"* That was one of the first Japanese words I learned. It means "Be quiet," and if spoken loudly and rudely it means "Shut up!"

"I will not have this noise," you announced to me, before you made the even louder announcement in Japanese. The children had scattered. They were truly terrified.

Again, I could not understand your rage.

The radio announcer was continuing with his analysis of the opera and its star. "How wonderful," you said, your voice suddenly gentle again. "I have always wanted to sing like that. But . . ." Your voice faltered. The fury was returning again. I so much wanted to understand you. Language was not the issue. Something else was the issue.

It is only in recent months that I have come to understand that you had been listening to a rebroadcast of a 1955 performance of Puccini's *Madama Butterfly*, conducted by Herbert von Karajan and recorded at La Scala in Milan. This was the legendary one and only appearance at La Scala by Callas as Cio-Cio-san (*cho-cho* is Japanese for butterfly). The announcer was continuing with his commentary.

"Oh no! Oh no!" you said suddenly. You reached out to hold my hand. Your fingernails dug into my palm, and I winced.

"Oh no! Oh no!" you said again. "That aria. That beautiful song. She sings in Italian, but I can understand just from the sound of her voice how lonely she was and how she never gave up hope. How sad! That poor Japanese girl. How sad! So much sadness. But she was no *cho-cho*," you said, explaining that *cho-cho* is a Japanese word also used to describe someone who is unfaithful or a flirt, a butterfly flitting from one lover to another.

"She had a true heart," you said, "like me. We Japanese call it *magokoro*! Puccini should have named her Yuki."

"OK," I thought. "Now I know *urusai*. And I know *magokoro*." I pulled out the small green notebook I was rapidly filling up with penciled Japanese words because you told me, Yuki, that I was *erai*—smart—and I needed to show you the notebook, every day, to show you what I had learned. I still have that notebook, and to this day it reminds me of my diligence when I was nineteen and I was enthralled about everything without exception.

You gave me a cup of tea. It was hot enough to burn my hand. "That is something else you need to learn," you said. "How to drink Japanese tea correctly." Sooner or later, you said, I would probably have to get into an *ofuro*, the Japanese bath where you do not use soap but you soak and turn bright red like a boiled lobster. "The *ofuro* is hot! This tea is not hot!" you exclaimed, like a schoolteacher.

"Now," you said, as if you were announcing an event. "I am going to tell you one other thing about Harbin."

I sat firmly and squarely on the top step to your house, and steadied myself.

"Yes, yes, yes," you said. "The tea is burning your hand. But now I have to tell you that although my father had a good relationship with the Jews, part of his work as a *kempei* was to torture and kill many people—but not Jews."

I put the cup of tea beside me on the step. I got a good grip on the surface of the stone. You sat down beside me. I could feel the heat of your hip, a heat more intense, it seemed, than the scalding tea.

"Do you mean the work he did at that unit?" My voice was hoarse. Hot green tea does that to my throat sometimes, even today.

"Yes. The unit," you said.

You explained quickly. It operated in the suburbs of southern Harbin. Surgeons and doctors were assigned there, together with *kempei*. Your father, you said, told his family he was working at some kind of clinic where the Japanese government was studying diseases and the effect of severe cold on the body. Your father made it sound as if this was humanitarian work of some kind. But you said that the man you met recently told you that actually Unit 731 performed hideous experiments on unwilling human guinea pigs—most of them Chinese guerrillas or political enemies rounded up in suppression raids by the Imperial Japanese Army—to determine the effects of germ or chemical warfare. The unit also did experiments on some American and other Allied prisoners transported to distant Harbin from far-flung theaters of war. In addition, you said, these prisoners were subjected to exposure to the astonishingly severe winter temperatures that immobilize much of Manchuria, so that the effects of endurance and frostbite could be monitored.

"This is one reason why I have been saying that I am a guilty person," you said, suddenly tearful. "This is a reason why I said I am a wicked woman. It is because I am my father's daughter . . ." Your voice fell away into a strange silence. You put your arm round me with a tenderness I had never felt before.

At that moment a heavy rain began to come down. "I guess I owe you that poem," I said.

"Please," you said quietly.

"All right," I said. We were still sitting there in the rain.

This poem came out of nowhere. Maybe out of the sky. Maybe out of that moment. Maybe out of my inability to accept what I had been told. You still had your arm round me tightly. Your heat was still intense, even in that cold rain.

> Around a couple of mountains,
> And down the deserted shore, he flew,
> Killing time, I thought.
> But hardly had he touched the earth
> When his loved one asked him,
> Do you love me?

Chapter 10

FIVE SIMPLE RULES

Her's [*sic*] is an extremely well-drawn character, beautifully played [by Nakakita Chieko]. From the very first we know that she is good—in the way that Japanese girls so very often are. She is truly generous, truly unselfish. She likes to pretend that things are better than they are—the model house, the imaginary coffee shop, the imaginary concert—and this helps make them so. At the same time she knows her own failings. Her very compassion is apt to catch her.

—Donald Richie, writing about
Kurosawa Akira's *Subarashiki Nichiyōbi*
(*One Wonderful Sunday*, 1947),
in *The Films of Akira Kurosawa*

The next day, late in the afternoon, I went to the White Rose, took a quiet corner booth, and waited for you to arrive. It was raining again. I had ducked into a "locker club" where I kept some civilian clothes, including a plaid long-sleeved shirt with button-down collar, two pairs of corduroy trousers, and a brown suede jacket. Navy regulations did not permit swapping one's uniform for civvies, but if I didn't, how would I ever be able to visit you at your home? In my uniform in off-limits Yokosuka neighborhoods I would be a moving target for the military police; Commander Crockett would be alerted and he might not be so forgiving next time. Maybe I would even be locked up in the brig, deprived of sunlight, raindrops, books, and the company of an extraordinary woman whose life was better than a book. I was artful and conniving and determined. I was standing my ground. I was taking a calculated risk. I was a youngster, so I could be cleverly foolish. At twenty, I might be mature and boring. At twenty-one, I might be dead, or married. Also, I had a British passport, and my fallback plan was always to whip that out if I was ever challenged for wearing civilian clothes and committing the crime of loitering at the Mozart coffee shop.

The White Rose was crowded with sailors in their white uniforms, sitting together in groups, noisy but sheepish, not knowing what to do except hope that pretty hostesses would pour their beer and tease them mercilessly for an hour or two.

Reiko came to me with a pout, slid across the vinyl with a squeak, and nestled against me as if I were her big brother. "Excuse me, please. Do you know any gentlemen?" she asked in her excellent high-school English. She had just had her hair permed into a series of waves, one of which hung over her right eye, in an imitation, maybe, of the style made popular by American film actress Veronica Lake.

"What kind of gentleman, Rei-chan?" I asked. I addressed her with the affectionate diminutive version of her name.

"Well . . . a handsome gentleman," she began, "suitable for a Japanese girl."

"Oh," I said. "Let me see . . ."

I was curious to know what was appropriate, and what was not. I was curious, but not because I intended to have a Japanese "girlfriend." Yuki and I had never used the term *koibito*—which means both boyfriend and girlfriend—to refer to each other. She always introduced me to people as either "my dear friend" or as "the English boy," to distinguish me, I suppose, from American sailors who, lumped together, were "barbarians," according to Kaji Yukiko.

I could not think of anyone at that moment, except for a couple of navy pilots who sometimes dropped by the office on the *Shangri-La* where the ship's newspaper was published. These pilots liked to bombard me with politely voiced questions such as, "Have you met any girls you like a lot?" and, "Where can we meet college girls?" as if I, who was still a virgin at the time, had a secret life when I went ashore in Yokosuka. Little did they know! You would think that virile navy pilots would already know the answers to those questions, but the truth was that command policy, constantly enunciated by Chaplain Peeples as if it were an addendum to the Ten Commandments, dictated that virtually everything ashore was off-limits to commissioned officers. I knew I could not recommend to Reiko that she meet these pilots because if they were seen escorting a Japanese woman around Yokosuka they would be severely reprimanded by their superiors, and that reprimand would be entered in their service record and possibly result in a denied promotion. Navy fliers could get falling-down drunk in bars in Honolulu, for example, and they could chase American girls there without any chaplain's disapproval. But Japanese girls were *verboten*. Lowly seaman apprentices such as myself were not restricted, as long as they remained in the Honcho district's three narrow streets jammed with neon-lit nightclubs and bars, immediately opposite the main entrance to the navy base. Also, of course, fliers were discouraged by their chaplains and also by American embassy or consular personnel if they had the temerity to get married in Japan and then attempted to bring their brides to the United States.

So, I asked Reiko, what kind of male qualities were acceptable to a Japanese woman? She giggled. "I am really too young to tell you that," she said coyly. "I am only twenty-two. I am a girl from the countryside. My father is just a farmer. What do I know?"

I looked at her closely. Why did some of the girls at the bar call her "Pumpkin," I wondered? She was no beauty, but she had already shown me that week you slashed your wrists that she was loyal, affectionate, and sturdy both in frame and in temperament. Reiko was a "sweet apple," you said. "It hurts me when I see sailors touching her because she is such a good girl. Do you know that almost all the money she earns here at the bar goes back to her family in Aomori?"

"Please, Reiko," I said. "Tell me. What kind of man do you like?"

"Well . . ." she began, followed by a big tumble of carefully phrased words. "I long for the special man appear in my life. I hope we could accompany with each other to walk together for the rest of the life, no matter if it is storm or wind. We will always join together to experience the sour, sweet, bitter, and hot in the life.

"I am saving my love in four parts. One part I will give to my family, because they give life to me. One part I will give to my future husband, because he will be the one who will accompany with me for the rest of the life. The third part I will give to my husband's family, because if it was not for his mother and father I would not have him. The fourth part I give to myself, because if a woman does not love herself, how she could love another?

"Also, I believe that you can't make someone love you. All you can do is be someone who can be loved. The rest is up to the man who recognizes your worth. That is what my grandmother told my mother, and that is what my mother told all her daughters including me. All my aunts agree too. Every woman in the village agrees. Every woman in Japan agrees too, probably."

"How many sisters and brothers do you have?" I asked.

"I am the youngest," she said. "I have five sisters and four brothers. At one time we all lived in my parents' very big farmhouse. Maybe you have not seen a traditional Japanese farmhouse? In the far north where I was born and it is very cold in winter, we are all sharing warmth under the thick thatched roof. My brothers and sisters. My parents. My grandparents. Three cousins who lost their parents. Two aunts who lost their husbands in the war—killed by Americans. The family altar where we honor our dead ancestors because those ancestors are living with us . . . Oh yes, also a horse. Many chickens. Several big lazy dogs. Several fierce small dogs. Cats with no tails that get fat in the winter. Big bags of rice and seeds and sweet potatoes. Big boxes of tea. Onions too. Many barrels of sake . . . Let's see. Have I forgotten something?"

I laughed politely. I was trying to imagine living that way. In my family it was myself, my mother and father, two sisters, a highly devious Siamese cat named Chang, and that was it.

"Is there anything else?" I asked her. She looked up at me. I think she sensed at that moment the vast differences in culture and habit. Also, maybe she was thinking that living on a housing estate in the suburbs with 2.5 kids and a Buick station wagon might not be a wise choice for someone raised in the Japanese countryside who suckled her mother's breast—as was the custom in her family—until she was eight years old. (Reiko always enjoyed telling sailors that.)

"Yes, there is more," she said. "I am very definite. This is the way I want to live my life. All the women in my family say that the measure of love is when you love without measure. Do you understand?"

I nodded in the affirmative. In the back of my mind was the friendship I had with you, Yukiko.

"In life there are very rare chances that you'll meet the person you love and that he will love you in return," Reiko said. "So, once you have it, don't ever let go because the chance might never come your way again.

"It's better to lose your pride to the one you love than to lose the one you love because of pride. All the women in my family believe that too. We spend too much time looking for the right person to love, or finding fault with those we already love. Instead we should be perfecting the love we give. That is a woman's duty in Japan. That is what we Japanese believe with all our heart.

"So can I tell you the five simple rules in my family? You are not Japanese, but maybe you can remember these rules that will make you happy. I tell your friend Yuki-chan this, many, many times. But sometimes she forgets because she has so much on her mind.

"One: free your heart from hate. Two: free your mind from worries. Three: live simply. Four: give more. Five: expect less.

"I follow these rules," she said, "because even though I am from the countryside, I know that the world is so big. I know there must be the *one* man who would love me and care for me. I would like to be his sweet wife only. I seriously want a simple love that a man could share with his woman.

"Happiness is my destination," she said.

She poked me in the side to make sure I was listening.

I could see that you had just entered the White Rose, Yuki. You were shaking the raindrops off your big black umbrella. The collar of your tan trench coat was fastened high around your neck. You wore a black French beret. I could see the glitter of your cocktail dress—standard attire for the hostesses at the White Rose—as you hung up your coat and scanned the crowd for faces you might recognize.

"Quick," Reiko said. "This I say to Yuki-chan a lot. She is my *onesan* [honorary big sister], and it is not my place to giving her advice. But she is the kind of woman who has to be guided because she has never accepted that people can be unkind. I tell her, so many person chase love and happiness here. I am a kind girl. I have a warm heart. I am serious about love. I am lovely, sweet, honest, and I can always be nice to my family and friends. I love life. I always have a smile in my heart. Like Yuki-chan, I want to share my life with someone special. But who? Please, can you help me find someone who knows how to cherish the beauty in life, and cherish a little happiness? Especially, please be honest with Yukiko and please be understanding and please remember my rules and remember that lies have short legs."

Before I could say anything, Reiko slid across the vinyl to the dance floor and ran with a little skip to your side. She had a smile on her face that I was sure every woman in her extended family had under the huge thatched roof of the farmhouse. She whispered in your ear and then she scampered to a table where there were many sailors and started making them laugh. I have wondered many times what happened to Reiko and whether she found a happy man.

You waved at me. I felt the full flush of happiness spread across my face. Could you see it, I wondered, through the shadows and the darkness inside the bar? What did that flush of happiness mean? It was so unexpected. I think that even now, after all these years, that feeling I had on the cusp of adulthood has never gone away, never faded. I have to tell you that fifty-five years after the long summer of your letters that same happiness still emerges when I think about you. You are more than just memory. You are alive.

Your next letter, by the way, arrived on ship after it docked at Yokosuka. I had read it just that morning, before I went ashore. Why it took so long to reach me I do not know.

Dear Paul,

    It is a very nice day. That is because the air mail came. Yes, I got your letter but it took several weeks to get here and that is very strange, very rare. But maybe it is because it is the rainy season in Japan on my calendar. There has been flooding and terrible weather.

    I am so glad you had so nice time there

in Hong Kong. Or was it Manila? You have made some good friends by talking and meeting people, I am sure. I am sure you spent a healthy time there, not like the bar in Yokosuka. Not like with me on days when life is cruel and you are fighting demons so that you can understand.

You are growing up! I am very glad for you because of the way you live your life. Your character makes me imagine that one day you will go to Tokyo to be a student so that you can learn about my country. Maybe you can help me learn about Japan too. I came back to Japan only 10 years ago and still I am in big trouble. Still I do not understand. When I feel confused, it helps me put my imagination upon you—like this—so that you are discussing the arts and music with friends, and sometimes with a hard-looking face you are speaking of life and philosophy and politics. This always makes me feel relieved from any bad feelings—any sad feelings—when we part again.

I imagine the day when you will be a civilian. You will meet many, many wonderful people. You will write a book yourself and you will be a big success. I will be here in Japan with such a warm feeling in my womb. It will be such a cold winter day, but I will feel warm. I will feel like you are my son. I shall read in the newspaper of your activities. I will see your picture. There will be an article that explains to me your life history and I will keep that article forever and never let you go. How wonderful your future!!! I say that with happy tears, because I know it to be true. I have nothing critical to say about your character. You are a brave and handsome man and I know that sooner or later I will have to let you go. When that happens, I promise that you will not see my tears. You will see me with a happy face. I want to let you know that, so that you will always remember me . . . this certain girl . . . Yuki.

Please remember my name even if you cannot remember my face. I am Yukiko Kaji from Yokosuka. I am Kaji Yukiko from Harbin. I am "Japanese" and I am not Japanese. Please hide me somewhere in your big man's heart. I want you also to know how happy I am today, and because I am happy I can laugh at danger. I feel that you are with me even when you are far away. Now I must hurry down the steps to the mail, so I will close now. Nothing will stop me from getting to the post office. Take care of yourself until we meet again.

Love,

Yukiko

Chapter 11

THE POLICE KNOW EVERYTHING

Thus the ideal man is the leader type, the "manly" man, one who has suffered, a man of courage and endurance, strong-willed, quick, decisive and forceful in situations where lesser men would hesitate out of scrupulous regard for detail, frank in the expression of his opinions without excessive regard for etiquette or convention, disdainful of underhand scheming, direct in his expression of emotions, a good loser, generously lacking in petty resentments, but ready to avenge insult whenever it is proffered, capable of deep passions but able to conquer them if necessary, a loyal friend, ready to act on the promptings of the heart, and as a leader of men ready to give his life for his subordinates and chivalrous in his protection of the weak.

—R. P. Dore, from a 1958 survey of Japanese housewives, in *City Life in Japan: A Study of a Tokyo Ward*

I walked into the Mozart coffee shop the next day to wait for you. You had made a plan to take me to see a black-and-white film from a Japanese director at a new theater, where we could hold hands in the dark without getting disapproving looks and comments from those who thought it was unacceptable behavior.

It was Franz Schubert day at the Mozart. The café was celebrating the composer's *Impromptus Opus 90*, to be exact, with its fantastic introductory chapter building upon itself until the complete landscape of Schubert's vision was made clear. I remember my father saying the world was fortunate that Schubert wrote all of that just two years before he died, otherwise it would have been lost instead of remembered for eternity.

I looked at the Schubert announcement chalked on a small blackboard posted at the entrance in Japanese script and in English. There were always engaging errors in the manager's English: "Today so wonderful concert. Please enjoy your happiness." These errors caused me just the hint of a smile. I did not want to embarrass the manager, Mr. Ito. He was one of the few Japanese in those days who appeared to accept our friendship as a harmless fact of life. He also seemed to be in awe of you and your style and your looks.

I opened the door. The manager greeted me with his usual, "Mr. Anthony Perkins, *konnichiwa* [good afternoon]! So nice to see you!" which always made me blush deeply. Groups of uniformed high-school girls reading Jean-Paul Sartre and Simone de Beauvoir and *Gigi* by Colette—in French, of course—suddenly snapped their books closed and looked up with worshipful eyes above rosy cheeks. Their uniforms were dark blue sailor suits with pleated skirts, white ankle socks, and black leather shoes, and the girls wore no lipstick, no mascara, no jewelry, and no other embellishments of any kind.

Mr. Ito motioned me to my usual seat by the record turntable. There was always a humming noise coming from the amplifier in this shadowed corner, and the sound provided a good cover for discreet conversation. I slouched down, doing my best imitation of Jean-Paul Belmondo sans smoking cigarette.

But then, a real horror, more horrible, maybe, than having to deal with Commander Crockett, or you when you were frightening children with shouts of *"Urusai!"* Seated at the window, about a dozen feet away, was that detective, the one who yelled, "You! You!" at me at the train station after he had subdued the man who growled like a bear. He was staring right at me, with no trace of recognition on his face—a seasoned skill that froze me in place and prevented me from adopting my usual cunning or calculating countermove. Then a scowl of some kind darkened his face. It reminded me of the scowl on the face of my family's cat when it anticipated a live morsel. He lit a cigarette, got up, and thudded across the floor to where I sat. He bent over slightly and produced a business card, holding it out to me with the thumb and forefinger of each hand gripping either end of the card, as if he were a waiter delivering a tray. I could smell liquor of some kind on his breath, and his raincoat reeked of tobacco. I knew nothing, of course, at that time of my life, about the elaborate etiquette involved in exchanging *meishi* (business cards). But I suppose that did not matter, as seaman apprentices, whose job it was to follow orders without question, did not have business cards. I am sure they do not have them now.

I was about to slip his *meishi* into my wallet, when he stopped me with a command in English: "Read!"

"Yes, sir," I said, my face bleached with fear, I am sure.

The printing on one side of the card was in Japanese. I turned the card over. On the other side, in Latin letters, was:

KANAGAWA PREFECTURAL POLICE DEPARTMENT
YOKOSUKA POLICE STATION DETECTIVE
GORO NAZAKA

"There is no telephone number," Detective Nazaka said. "The important thing for you to remember is that the police know everything. Just ask for me, anywhere. Everybody knows who I am. If you want me, I am just minutes away, all the time, every day. Do not make the serious error of forgetting that in Japan the police know everything."

Thank God, I thought, Commander Crockett was not there to see that, because if he were there they would have had to call an ambulance to take him away. The other thought that flashed like a streak of lightning was the description of a Yokosuka jail cell given to me by my pal Red Downs after one of his friends spent a night there, for "insulting a policeman and offending the public," whatever that meant. "They put you in a cage," Red said, "and you have to sit there with your legs crossed, not moving, for many hours, while they threaten you with castration . . . although that is probably just your imagination because the interrogation is done in Japanese until they acknowledge you don't speak it and they have to hand you over to the US Navy shore patrol. So, in other words, your life, as you know it, is over."

Nazaka sat down at my table with a sigh, as if he was devastated by weariness.

After telling me with some satisfaction that Japanese business cards are "vastly superior" because they are a standard 91 by 55 mm—"much larger" than Chinese business cards, which measure, he said, exactly 90 by 54 mm, and "many times larger" than American business cards, a mere 88.9 by 50.8 mm—the conversation went like this:

"You have not ordered your coffee," he said. "Please order!"

"Yes, sir. *Kohi kudasai* [coffee, please]," I told the manager, who was looking at me with amusement.

"Oh," Nazaka said. "You speak Japanese. Very impressive."

"Oh no, sir. That is just something that Yukiko taught me."

"Yes, Miss Kaji Yukiko. You are both troublemakers. But you are interesting troublemakers. That is why you caught my attention. I don't like trouble. But I do like to have my intelligence challenged. My imagination is important too. Thank you for stealing my patience."

"I am so sorry. I did not mean to do that."

"Well . . . I see. There is evidence that you are not an American. You apologize rather well."

"Oh! Thank you. Good detective work! I am British."

"British! British . . . A noble island people with a long history, like we Japanese. Of course, you were savages until the Romans came to conquer you. Your warriors were decorated with blue dye. So your cultural history is not as long as ours. We have never been conquered!"

"That is true, I suppose," I said.

I forgot on purpose that Japan had very recently been conquered—or maybe it was just defeated—by the United States of America. Because I was not sure who had conquered and who had been seduced and ravished after the end of the fighting, I decided not to raise this as an issue.

But I did remember the heroics of Boadicea, queen of the Iceni, who was, in effect, the last queen of the Britons in those ancient times. After her daughters had been raped and she had been flogged, she fought the Roman legions in her chariot. Roman historian Cassius Dio wrote that she was "possessed of greater intelligence than often belongs to women," I recalled from my English schoolboy days.

"We had Boadicea," I said, trying to sound proud.

"Oh yes," the detective said. "She was tall and had red hair to her waist. Boadicea also had a piercing glare, like your friend Miss Kaji." There was a sudden smile, which just as quickly vanished.

"That is an interesting thought," I said, wondering what you would look like, Yuki-chan, wielding a spear in defense of your house on the hill. I also wondered again whether I should remind Detective Nazaka that although it was true that Britain had been conquered by the Romans, Japan had been conquered by the Americans. But I did not, fortunately.

"Boadicea was an excellent national hero for the British," Nazaka said. "She was defeated. Of course, we Japanese had Amaterasu, the sun goddess, the founder of our imperial dynasty. Yes. You had a queen. But we had a deity! Deities cannot be defeated!"

I wondered where our chat was going. I was piling hope upon hope that you, Yukiko, would not enter the Mozart.

So I summoned up courage and said, "Thank you for your help at the train station the other day."

"Yes," he said slowly. "Yes. You are a lucky boy."

"Thank you also for your help at the suicide scene."

Again, he said slowly, "Yes . . . Yes. She is lucky you were there."

"Can you tell me about the man at the station?"

"You are lucky he did not have his sword," the detective said.

"Sword!" I exclaimed in a high octave, not believing what I had just been told.

"Yes. That man was a minor gangster. Gangsters often carry a sword. If they carry a briefcase, they have a short sword—a *tanto*—inside. It is a matter of honor, as well as a good means of defense. If it *is* a matter of honor, they can use it to kill."

"Really!" I was stumbling to express myself. *"Really?"*

"Yes. I will explain. English is not a problem for me, by the way. I was educated in Manchuria. Like your friend Miss Kaji, I was repatriated at the end of the war. It is not a problem for me to speak with foreigners. I rather enjoy it, in fact . . . I even enjoy talking with foreigners who are trouble."

My face turned red again. The palms of my hands started sweating.

Detective Nazaka was in total control. I had no power, no cards to play, other than the odd fact that I was a British kid in the American Navy, which must have caused the worldly Nazaka to take a small amount of interest in me and my fate.

"You should remember that man's name," the detective said. "It is Shinoda Yusuke. Do not go near him. I don't know if your friend Miss Kaji told you this, but Shinoda is her boy-friend."

"Her boyfriend?" I said loudly. My hand holding the tiny coffee cup was trembling.

"Her boyfriend," the detective said again. "We Japanese call that kind of man a yakuza. He is a gangster. He is an *aniki* ['big brother' or leader of a small squad of gangsters]. We know all about him. The police know everything."

"I don't understand. She never mentioned him." I looked alarmed, maybe even annoyed or jealous.

"Well, you see, Miss Kaji left Mr. Shinoda. He had beaten her with his fists. She ran away. When she arrived in Japan from Manchuria she settled in Hiroshima. Most of the city was destroyed by the *genshibakudan* [the atomic bomb]. There was a lot of open space there. Lots of refugees built shacks or put up tents. There were many guns in Hiroshima because the Japanese military had many warehouses and depots around the edges of the city. Many bad men got hold of those guns. That is where the yakuza criminal culture of my country began. With those guns they controlled all the thousands of black markets set up in Japan after the war."

I was saying, "Yes . . . Yes," over and over again. I was struggling hard to accept this information. My understanding of things Japanese was limited to the occasional glimpses of the small magic kingdom of fantastic emotions ruled by you, Yukiko, who had trapped me there for reasons known only unto yourself. Like a spider, I thought in a moment of terrifying inspiration, like the spider feared even by an authentic American hero, Commander Crockett.

The detective gave me a minute to absorb the shock. After I blinked, and rubbed my eyes, he began again, but carefully, as if he were torturing me.

"I have given you warnings," he said. "I am interested in you. I am interested in the history of Miss Kaji because as

Japanese born in Manchuria we are both strangers in Japan. We were both educated in Manchuria too. I don't know much yet about Miss Kaji's history in Japan, but she is clearly an educated woman. I am still trying to understand why she took such an interest in you."

"Yes," I said, remembering her letters. "I think she just needed someone to talk to."

"Maybe," he said. "Maybe it was for reasons only known to a woman. I am no expert. I have never been married. I am a man who likes to drink . . . excuse me: I am a man who has to drink. The only women I know, I know from the bars. They are good, strong women . . . survivors, I suppose. Strength of character too! Admirable, in fact."

Suddenly, I was able to see Nazaka not as a policeman but as a man. He was looking at me closely too. I think at that moment he saw me not as a puny military juvenile but as a very young man.

"You should know," he said, "that from our police records we know that Mr. Shinoda violently assaulted Miss Kaji when she was a young person in Hiroshima. In this country it happens sometimes that when a young woman is attacked she will demand that her attacker should marry her. No one will want her, you see, because her honor has been taken. In this case, Shinoda's big boss did not order him to marry her. So she lived with him. She was his woman. He treated her very badly. I am sorry I have to tell you all about this, but for several weeks I have been feeling that you should know."

I tried to say thank you. But the words would not come. I stayed silent. It was as if I had been hit by a bomb blast.

"Also," the detective said, "we had to let Mr. Shinoda go.

He did not have his sword or any other weapon. He came to Yokosuka to look for Miss Kaji and take her back to Hiroshima. He found her by accident. You were there. Mr. Shinoda did not know what to do, because you were there. But he is still in the city, we believe. Please be careful. I have already told Miss Kaji to be careful too, but she said she has the means to protect herself."

"What kind of means?" I asked.

The detective's face became grim. Before it became grim he had looked a little like a schoolmaster counseling a schoolboy. But now he tugged at the collar of his rumpled white shirt. He pulled at the knot of his ultra-narrow brown-and-gold tie. He brushed the tobacco ashes from his raincoat. His teeth were bad. His eyes were bloodshot. He pulled a floppy hat of the kind usually worn by children out of his pocket and planted it firmly on his head. He looked at me closely again, as if he were sizing me up, as if he were measuring how much backbone existed, to the exact millimeter, in a British kid's spine. He sucked in his breath and said, "*Saaaaaaaaa*." This is the expression, I came to know later, that Japanese often use when they don't know, or don't want to know, or don't want to explain. "*Saaaaaaaa*," he said again. And then he was silent.

The manager came over to ask if I wanted more coffee. I looked at my watch. You would be arriving soon.

The detective got to his feet. "I am not going to say anything to the US Navy liaison officer about this conversation," he said finally. "This conversation is not official. In fact, it never happened."

With a nod first to me, and then to the manager, who bowed deeply, the detective headed to the door and quickly vanished, leaving me in a state of confusion, the like of which has never been equaled. If you had not shown up that day to continue my "education," as you put it, I probably would have accepted that as the best thing, under the circumstances.

But suddenly there you were, with a smile on your face that caused me to gulp several times. It was as if the sun itself was smiling on the first day of spring. Maybe it wasn't the smile. Maybe it was my reaction to a combination of this new glimpse of your past and the realization that you were so happy to see me, and that life would go on and on, no matter what. You studied the look on my face, and I could see from your lips that you liked what you saw when I was so happy to see you again.

I thought at that moment of a fragment of verse by the impossibly handsome British poet Rupert Brooke, who my mother once told me she wished had been her lover. He died at the age of twenty-eight during the First World War, killed of all things by an infected mosquito bite.

> The way that lovers use is this;
> They bow, catch hands, with never a word.
> And their lips meet, and they do kiss,
> —So I have heard.

"Come on!" you said with an impatient delight. "Come on! Come with me!"

You tucked your hand under my arm, got a firm grip, and marched me to the door.

The manager beamed, and even discreetly clapped his hands, so I could get just a hint of applause.

The uniformed schoolgirls dropped their French studies again and twittered like so many busy finches. I could hear their voices, their wonderment, at the sight of Anthony Perkins leaving the Mozart in the company of a mysterious woman.

"Who was she?" I am sure they were asking each other. "Are they lovers? Are they friends?"

Chapter 12

YUKIKO'S LIST

For truth or illusory appearance does not reside in the object in so far as it is intuited, but in the judgment upon the object, in so far as it is thought. It is, therefore, quite correct to say that the senses do not err, not because they always judge correctly, but because they do not judge at all. Hence truth and error, consequently also, illusory appearance as the cause of error, are only to be found in a judgment, that is, in the relation of an object to our understanding. In a cognition which completely harmonizes with the laws of the understanding, no error can exist. In a representation of the senses—as not containing any judgment—there is also no error. But no power of nature can of itself deviate from its own laws.

—Immanuel Kant, from *Critique of Pure Reason*

You were taking me to see *Rashomon*. This was the first film you and I saw together. It was screened in a small, damp theater, the odor of which replicated the smell of a dark English forest, but with added Japanese touches of burned tobacco, dried fish, and *umeboshi*, the sour pickled plums you nibbled with teenage abandon.

"*Umeboshi*. Very good!" you said with extraordinary enthusiasm. "*Umeboshi* keeps you young. *Umeboshi* keeps you strong. Do you know that long ago samurai ate *umeboshi* to stay strong in battle? You are a military man. You should know that! *Umeboshi* are good to eat when you need to fight. Also, many famous poets and writers eat *umeboshi* too, because the sour taste stimulates the imagination . . . Yes! Yes! You must eat *umeboshi* too. You must eat right now!"

"But I am already young. I am already strong," I protested. "Also, I am not really a 'military man' at all."

"Yes. Yes. I know that. But you will need to fight. It is natural, you know, for young men. It is not good to spend all your time in thought. Sometimes there has to be action. You have to act. Sometimes you have to act and fail. But you will probably mostly succeed. I believe that with all my heart . . . Please have an *umeboshi*. They are *suppai* [sour]. You will suffer, but that is a natural part of being man too. Women know those kind of things, by the way. Please respect that. Women raise their sons to suffer, and to die. It is very, very sad, but you must accept that truth. If you accept truth, then you can be happy, happy! Also, women raise their daughters to give life. Yes, give life. But *not* to suffer."

I understood immediately when I bit into one of those salted plums that you needed to be very brave indeed to be able to love them as much as you did. Maybe it was you who was anticipating a fight. Maybe you were thinking about the future. For the moment, I had decided not to tell you about my encounter with Detective Nazaka. I wanted to see whether you would tell me more about the man who growled like a bear, and whether you would specify how you would defend yourself if he attacked again.

"What is this film—*Rashomon*—about?" I asked, unaware that asking the question would prompt you to launch into fifteen minutes of feverish explanations marked by hand waving, finger pointing, exaggerated facial expressions, much biting into *umeboshi* to stimulate the imagination, frantic questions ("Are you sure you understand me?"), and such statements as, "Please open your mind and try not to be stupid . . . Oh, I am sorry, I forgot. There are no subtitles."

We saw at least nine films that summer. Sometimes we saw two and even three films in one day. I know now—thanks to the availability of vintage films on DVD—that I had a front-row seat to what has become known as the golden age of Japanese cinema. I also know now that you bought tickets for both of us, resolutely pushing my hand away if I offered to pay, because you were determined that I should know something about cinematic art. You were also trying to show me the totality of postwar Japan—including the often desperate plight of its women—by insisting that I watch films with a strong social or political context, especially those that dealt with devastation caused by war.

Rashomon was the first of these films. You said in reply to my question about the meaning of the film, "No one knows what this film is about . . . Some say it is about truth, or the relative lack of truth."

I stared at you, not understanding. The only films I had seen to date were at the so-called Saturday Morning Pictures for children at the Odeon Theatre on the banks of the River Thames in Staines, England, and B movies at drive-in theaters in Freeport, Illinois. In England: *The Cisco Kid*, *Hopalong Cassidy*, Gene Autry flicks. In the United States: *Attack of the 50 Foot Woman*, *Teenage Monster*, *Teenage Cave Man*.

Also, I was in the navy, where everything had to have meaning. There were manuals and diagrams and charts and rules for everything, all outlined in excruciating gibberish. There were, of course, those training films on venereal diseases illustrating in great detail the meaning of voluminous amounts of pus, hideous sores, spots, rashes, itches, and painful swelling of the testicles. Everything was labeled on the *Shangri-La*:

> Urinal
> Men's
> Aim (not on deck)
> Flush
> Button*

"But, how can that be?" I said of the plot of *Rashomon*. "How can there be any doubt about truth? Man bites dog. Dog bites man. That's a story, right?"

"Oh no," you said. "In this story—*Rashomon*—I have read that no one knows who did what to whom. A man is killed. A woman is raped. There are four witnesses. They all tell a different story. But you never really know who did what to whom. Do you understand?"

You so delighted in saying the word *whom*. "No American

---

* There were no zippers back then in sailor pants, the reason being that the metal crocodile teeth in early zippers could severely injure private parts, a danger that persisted until the Japanese company YKK (Yoshida Kōgyō Kabushikikaisha) perfected mass production of toothless nylon zippers.

ever says that word," you exclaimed. "That is why I love to say it. I say it at the White Rose too, you know—'To whom should I bring this beer?'" You giggled. "Sailor boys always treat me with respect after that, you know! I can wear a very sexy dress but no sailor is going to pinch the bottom of a woman who says 'whom.'"

My face turned scarlet.

Number one, I could not imagine anyone ever pinching your "bottom." That was the truth, believe me.

Number two, I did not even know you had a "bottom." You had a face and eyes and lips, a long neck, and small narrow hands with enameled fingernails. You wore lipstick the color of flames. Your perfume was still a mystery; "Ancient China," you once called it. I was vaguely aware of your legs and your back. That was it. After all, I was still a virgin.

"So to whom should I ascribe this film?" I asked. You giggled again.

"Oh . . . The director is a great man. Great in Japan. But not great in America, I am soooo sure. Kurosawa Akira. A very great man. Japanese, of course!"

"I see," I said, not knowing that *Rashomon*, released in 1950, won first prize at the Venice Film Festival for the "unknown" Kurosawa, or that the film afterward received international acclaim (though maybe not so much in the United States, where it may have flickered briefly at a few art houses and college campuses). So I sat back, listened to mice foraging for tidbits, squirmed in the seat a little after one mouse bumped my shoe, and waited to see a film that no one could understand. The understanding factor, of course, was made even more Byzantine in my case because there would be no subtitles—

just you occasionally whispering guidance in my ear while my brain was short-circuiting as it might if this theater had been on Venus and this film made by aliens.

Rashomon burst onto the screen in naked black and white with shimmering silver shadows and one thousand shades of grey. There was constant motion in the leaves and branches of the forest where the murder and the rape occur. The sun's rays stabbed at the unfolding scene and blinded the protagonists. Drums were beating. I could smell the mildewed interior of the theater. I could also smell the rotting ferns and leaves on the screen, the sweat of the rapist and his victim, the stale scent of tears, and even the odors of despair, exultation, and fear. But who was telling the truth? Who had really murdered whom? Which of the four witnesses to the crime were giving accurate descriptions? Were they describing reality as they saw it, or did they have ulterior motives? And how could the murdered man—the husband of the woman raped by the bandit—speak at a court hearing if he was dead?

I staggered out into a fast-fading sunset, intoxicated. I could smell rain advancing from the sea. "You were right, Yuki. You were right!" I said.

"Of course," you said, poking my chest with your finger. "Do you feel that?" you asked, as if you had stabbed me with a knife. "That was a *tanto* with a very sharp point. I have returned you to reality!"

We made our way to the Mozart coffee shop through the late-afternoon sidewalk crowd of people going back home after work. There were a lot of haggard faces. Those were hard days. But everyone, good and bad and those who were a mixture of both but did not know it, had a purpose in life. The men in their white shirts and suits had endured yet another day at an office and they longed to swap that straitjacket for a *yukata*. The women in straight skirts below their knees, simple blouses, and flat-heeled shoes were coming home to their babies and husbands, exhausted from the office too. The workmen in hard hats and oil- and rust-stained tough cotton pants and work shirts were walking in groups, headed to their favorite sake bars, where the *mamasan* could soothe their pain with sweet talk and professionally perfected flirtation. There were bar girls in heavy makeup, too, headed in the opposite direction, toward the garish lights of the Honcho entertainment district, to which sailors were just arriving. It was a living.

Bar owners were putting out signs such as "Ugly Girls. Lousy Beer. Rotten Music" and "Special Stinko Express Night Train." One carefully painted sign on a folding easel read, "The following practices will not be condoned by this establishment . . . picking nose at table, scratching nuts with swizzle stick, indiscreet petting, indiscriminate goosing, failure to button pants, hunting female navels, taking off pants, loud farting, biting hostess tit, wiping ass on curtain, screwing hostess out of turn . . . Failure to comply will result in a fine of 500 yen ($1.40) to be presented to the manager." You detested these signs and disapproved of me copying them into my notebook. "Gangsters write those signs," you exclaimed. Bar owners were also posting in their windows the bow numbers of the destroyers, cruisers, oilers, supply ships, and the occasional aircraft carrier, as if the bar were reserved exclusively for those crews.

Shangri-La's number was CVA 38. What did CVA 38 mean? In military-ese: Carrier, Attack, hull number 38. I never knew what the letter *V* stood for. They never told us. *V* for valor? *V* for victory? *V* for vicious? It was as much a mystery to me as the name of the ship itself, *Shangri-La*, which came from a 1934 British novel, James Hilton's *Lost Horizon*, and not from an American battle or a president or some famous warship from the Yankee past. Shangri-La was the novel's mythological, permanently happy land of virtually immortal sages lost in time, somewhere in Tibet. This ship was an enigma to me, but not to you, Yuki. "Oh yes," you said. "Yes! *Shang-ri-ra. Shang-ri-ra!* Oh yes. Sound like a Korean name, or a Chinese name. But never mind. *Shang-ri-ra* is a very nice name. So nice for a big ugly ship with too many bombs."

Many years later I discovered that President Franklin Delano Roosevelt had claimed that the famous Doolittle Raid on Tokyo, launched in the tightest secrecy in April 1942 from the deck of the aircraft carrier *Hornet*, had originated from "Shangri-La." The audacity of the raid—it was the first time American bombs were dropped on the Japanese homeland and was just months after the attack on Pearl Harbor—stunned Tokyo and boosted American morale. Roosevelt later named his retreat in Maryland Shangri-La (now Camp David). Today, hucksters have seized upon the name: for example, Zhōngdiàn, a remote mountain region in southwestern China, has been renamed Xiang-ge-li-la, in hope of luring gullible tourist dollars.

We pushed open the door to the Mozart just before the heavy rain came down. But we were still wet. I was in my illegal civvies. I shook myself, spraying water as if I were a dog. You wore your trench coat, buttoned up to just below your chin. The manager stepped up to help you remove the coat. You were telling him we had just seen *Rashomon*. He was nodding in excitement to everything you said.

"See," you said proudly. "He too knows nothing. He doesn't know the meaning of that film. Do you know why? I will tell you. It is art—like a modern sculpture, or a modern painting. People are always saying 'What does that mean?' It means what the artist—the creator—meant it to mean, and it is up to us to enjoy the pleasure of discussing that. For every single mystery of art there are ten thousand opinions, most of them worth hearing. Isn't that wonderful?"

You outlined the film to me and gave me your thoughts. It wasn't easy for you. But I understood what you were saying. Your English was sometimes limited, but you spoke with such enthusiasm and force that my mind lapped up everything you said as if I had a terrible thirst. "There," you said suddenly. "Now I have given you a complete picture. Your job is to think about it. Please remember that there is no truth in our lives. Many things happen. You may never know why. You may be in love, but you don't know why. There is no answer. No truth. Nothing! For example, there is me. There is you. Your eyes show you things that I will never know. There will be things you will not be able to define, like love. For me, love is a kind of surrender. It is like the interior of a nunnery at night. Think about what I said . . . When I see you again, I expect you to be enlightened."

Enlightened, I thought? Where did you get that word?

But then I remembered that at your house you showed me a small stone figure of the Buddhist deity Jizo, which you said nourishes the souls of dead children while simultaneously comforting their mourning parents. Your Manshu

Jizo (Manchurian Jizo), you said, represented the dead child of a parent born in Manchuria, as well as the sorrow of that child's parent.

"This is my Manshu Jizo," you said. "This is for my daughter. She died but her spirit lives with me." You pointed to the black night sky and to the myriad of stars. "With this Jizo we will always be connected." I didn't know whether you were talking about your daughter or me. "How do you call that when you suddenly understand something?" you asked.

"Enlightenment," I said. "Yes, enlightenment."

"Oh . . . thank you. Thank you! Enlightenment is so beautiful. Enlightenment! Light! Shining a light so that you can see. Enlightenment is such a pleasure. I try to have enlightenment every day. How about you, Paul-san? Do you like that kind of pleasure too?"

It is a tragedy, I think, that most Westerners and probably most Japanese have not seen the films you took me to that summer. In the past three months I have bought more than thirty DVDs, thinking I would be able to identify the films we saw. Some of my purchases were *chanbara*—films about samurai with slashing swords. I realized quickly that those were not on your list. But every now and then, I would pop a disk into the player, watch for ten or fifteen minutes, and then with a flush of excitement say, "Yes. I know I have seen that before." Every time that happened, I was swept up in a flood of nostalgia. The scenes would fade and dissolve, fade and dissolve, but as that happened my memory would come alive with your comments, your explanations, your unyielding efforts to have me understand these classic films with no subtitles. Of course, the DVDs I have been ordering do have

English subtitles. So I have two layers of understanding: the Kaji Yukiko version, which enables me to remember your voice and how pretty you looked when you were perplexed, and the official translated version, which, although fine and useful, does not have quite the same charm and insight.

I am sure that modern Japanese think of these films—if they think of them at all—as hopelessly outdated. We exist in a time of cheap thrills after all. Every year in Japan there are scores of vapid *pinku eiga* (pink films), which depict women tied up, gang-raped, sodomized, slapped. Those films are now, apparently, a norm. The yearly crop of yakuza films becomes increasingly violent and bloody as audiences demand more gangster gore. It is just as bad in the United States. Almost every Hollywood film features high-speed pursuits, crashes, explosions, vampires, zombies, and romance so saccharine, so stupid, and so unappealingly sexual that I sometimes wonder whether the kind of romance of two minds we had is even possible anymore.

THE KAJI YUKI LIST, 1959

Rashomon, 1950, Kurosawa Akira

Nihon no higeki (*A Japanese Tragedy*), 1953, Kinoshita Keisuke

Bangiku (*Late Chrysanthemums*), 1954, Naruse Mikio

Ukigumo (*Floating Clouds*), 1955, Naruse Mikio

Akasen chitai (*Street of Shame*), 1956, Mizoguchi Kenji

Yoru no onnatachi (*Women of the Night*), 1948, Mizoguchi Kenji

Kurutta kajitsu (*Crazed Fruit*), 1956, Nakahira Kō

Himeyuri no Tō (Tower of Lilies), 1953, Imai Tadashi
Ningen no jōken I (The Human Condition I: No Greater Love,
the first film of three), 1959, Kobayashi Masaki*

We said a quick good-bye outside the Mozart. This was not the time to discuss your boyfriend, or the detective, or how you would deal with a threat. It was my impression that you were resigned to handling that problem alone. You had not shown any new alarm. You had not laid out a plan of action. Instead, in a sudden change of mood, you appeared to be focused on the fact that I would soon be gone again. Early the next morning, the *Shangri-La* would steam slowly out of the harbor, round the headland, and head south by southwest again for two weeks, to the Taiwan Strait and to Hong Kong once more. We sailors would line up on the deck in our pure white uniforms and gaze back through the cold morning mist at Yokosuka. Many of us were convinced we were watched by hundreds of pairs of womanly eyes. The idea of romance dies hard on a ship made for war.

The rain had stopped.

---

* After I wrote to my friend and classmate Ogawa Wakako, in Tokyo, about these films, she expressed a strong interest in your history. At the end of the war, she said, women could either stay in traditional marriages, if their husbands had survived, or for the first time in Japanese history they could choose "to go out" into the workplace and make something of themselves, without marriage. The workplace in those years included the vast *mizu shobai* (literally, the "water trade") nighttime entertainment scene, where jobs ranged from geisha, which is a true art form, to cabaret or bar hostess to massage-parlor girl. Today that industry, geared to pleasing men, is more complex and brutal than in any other country in the world. Yukiko believed she was one of the emancipated—emancipated, at least, in her own mind.

You hid in the shadows of the alley and would not let go of my hand.

It was cold. There was a wind. I tried to hug you one last time, but you pulled back and shook your head. You seemed to be smaller. It was as if you had shrunk by a foot. It was as if your verve for life were spilling out onto the ground.

You pulled the belt of the trench coat very tight round your waist. I could not see your face. "Go now," you said. "Do not forget."

Chapter 13

THE MOST BEAUTIFUL

I found that I was fitted for nothing so well as for the
study of Truth; as having a mind nimble and versatile
enough to catch the resemblances of things (which is
the chief point), and at the same time steady enough
to fix and distinguish their subtler differences; as being
gifted by nature with desire to seek, patience to doubt,
fondness to meditate, slowness to assert, readiness to
consider, carefulness to dispose and set in order; and as
being a man that neither affects what is new nor admits
what is old, and that hates every kind of imposture. So
I thought my nature had a kind of familiarity and relationship with Truth.

—Francis Bacon,
from *On the Interpretation of Nature*,
1603–4

It was July 24, the day after my twentieth birthday and the
day after the *Shangri-La* left Yokosuka and headed into an
approaching typhoon. I could see the storm advancing across
a violent sea of bottle green. With every hour the gale in-
tensified. The wind sounded as if it were a chorus of scalded

devils. Black clouds swarmed above us, and the rain slashed down through the air in ice-cold squalls.

I went belowdecks to get shelter. I took the seat in front of my desk in the cramped *News Horizon* office. Warnings came over the intercom to tie down aircraft and machinery, and I wanted to make sure the large typewriter there was firmly secured. The ship was groaning and grinding, and every now and then there would be a huge thud and then a shudder as a giant wave crashed over the bow.

Red Downs and Jim Fowler were quizzing me about my friendship with you, Yuki. I was trying to maintain a low profile, because so many things had been happening to me that were confusing and threatening. I had not announced I was having a birthday. I did not even tell you on which day it would occur because it did not seem to me to have any significance at all in a summer during which typhoons of another kind pushed me to the limits of understanding.

Jim, who had a gorgeous black-eyed girlfriend named Connie back in Kansas, whose eight-by-ten-inch photo stood watch over him on his desk, did not probe too hard. He liked you. He liked women. Sometimes I would catch him whispering things to Connie's photograph. He often sat in the White Rose to watch you talking, a smile on his pale midwestern face.

One day, he told me after looking at you that he was "entranced." "What do you mean?" I asked.

He shook his head in disbelief. "You, of all people, should know what I mean. If you don't know, maybe it is because you haven't slept with a girl before . . . have you?"

Red could not believe that you and I had not even kissed. He could not understand why, if you and I were close, there was no sex and no one was attempting seduction. If I had tried to tell him about the effect on me of a single bead of sweat running down your neck, he would have laughed in my face. "You ever been with a girl before?" he asked aggressively in his deep Mississippi drawl. "What are you doing when you go ashore? Why are you even in the navy? You got that fine woman back in Yokosuka writing you that she loves you. How did you get a woman to do that, if you haven't slept with her? I just don't get it. You want me to show you how to chat up a woman—you know, kissing, squeezing, hugging—until she gives it up?"

"Gives it up? What do you mean?"

Red rolled his eyes and laughed. "Man," he said. "In Mississippi that girl would be having my babies!"

I was too embarrassed to engage in this kind of conversation. I certainly would never have dared to tell you what Red said. If I gave even a hint of what was going on between us— the drama, the poetry, history lessons, the cops, the boyfriend, the executioner, Commander Crockett—I knew it would circulate like a jet-fuel fire through the ranks of Division X, which included me, Red, and Jim, and the guys who worked in the print shop, in photography, and in the administrative ranks. If they knew I was still a virgin, and that I was actually not on a mission to cease being a virgin, they would be merciless. They would drag me to the nearest Wan Chai bordello in our next port of call, Hong Kong, to experience an important moment of truth; they would probably bribe a Suzie Wong girl who really knew how to wriggle to do whatever women do in the cribs in the darkened rooms above the bar.

Red continued to probe. He was enjoying it. I stood my ground. There was no way I was going to answer his constant question—"Are you in love with her?"—because it was a secret and, to be truthful, I did not know.

Then we heard a sailor running down the all-steel corridor linking the various offices. Soon other crew members were running. They were banging on the metal. There were some rebel yells. What was this, I wondered? Red stuck his head out through the opening left by the watertight door and asked what was going on. Was it a fire drill? One of the planes had crashed on the deck? There was a fight? A mutiny? What?

"Sweet Jesus and glory be to God," Red said. He lifted his hands up to a sky we could not see, in a gesture of salutation.

"A Japanese girl has just won Miss Universe!"

His brown eyes were somehow bigger. He had a grin that went from ear to ear.

I grabbed Jim's arm. Red grabbed me. We jumped up and down, without really knowing why. You would have liked seeing us enjoying our happiness, Yuki-chan.

Then the squawk box on the captain's bridge came to life. "Now hear this! Now hear this!" someone announced. Then a high-pitched boatswain's whistle blew, which was usual when there was an important announcement such as "COMNAVFORJAPAN departing" (the admiral commanding US naval forces in Japan leaving the ship).

"Attention! Attention!" an official voice barked. To me, it was a familiar bark. "We have just been advised that a young woman from Tokyo, Akiko Kojima, was selected over four other finalists, including Miss USA and Miss Brazil and Miss England and Miss Norway, for the Miss Universe title in Long Beach, California."

There was a pause, and a cough.

The voice resumed. "According to press reports, when asked what she wanted to do with her life, Miss Kojima said, 'I want to be a lovely wife.'" There was another pause and another cough. "So, if we can get this cruise to Hong Kong out of the way and keep everything shipshape and keep our noses clean, maybe . . . maybe . . . one of you goddamn swab jockeys [vernacular for 'sailor'] can get lucky when we return to Japan and make Miss Kojima your blushing bride." Silence. *Cough. Cough.*

We three friends shot glances at each other. I mouthed the name "Crockett."

Cheering erupted up and down the corridor. It occurred to me that all this joy indicated that many members of the crew were in love. Their hearts had been stolen, somewhere, by someone, some sweetheart, back in Yokosuka. I had a sweetheart too, and what a sweetheart! No one was as special as Yuki. I wanted to jump up and down as well, but I was cautious. Were you my girlfriend? Well, not exactly. Had you stolen my heart? How wild and dramatic that sounded. But there was no doubt that the selection of Kojima Akiko was vindication to those among the crew who had an "only" (a girlfriend ashore); it meant they had made a good choice, and maybe even their mothers would approve now if they brought a Japanese bride back home. I knew, however, that my mother, who cherished her complete set of cruel and dark novels by Charles Dickens bound in green and gilt gold, would never approve. I had written to tell her, happily, that I had made an "important" woman friend in Yokosuka, and she had written me back quickly, and curtly, to tell me that I was being an "idiot." Yes, an idiot. At least she did not call me a gnat!

The jubilation was continuing aboard ship. Some men began comparing love letters. Those lucky enough to get a red lipstick kiss on the paper flashed that around in triumph. We were all about eighteen to twenty years old. Evidently, we had all been severely bitten by spiders.

I wondered if there was equal excitement in Yokosuka. I imagined a scene in Honcho with hundreds of bar hostesses in their cocktail gowns running out onto the streets in a near riot. And you, you . . . you would be reading a book, no doubt. Maybe you were reading the *Selected Poems of Rainer Maria Rilke*, which I had purchased across the street from the White Rose in Japanese translation, spending an entire week's salary, because you had told me that elements of your most intimate dreams could be found in Rilke's verse. For example:

THE COURTESAN

The sun of Venice will prepare
with gracious alchemy gold in my hair:
a final triumph. And my slender brows
resemble bridges—can you not see how

they span the silent danger of my eyes
which cannily with the canals arrange
a secret commerce so the sea may rise
in them and ebb and change?

Who sees me once is envious of my hound,
on which betimes in a distrait caress
my hand (which never charred to any passion),

invulnerable and richly jeweled, rests.
and noble youths, the hopes of ancient houses,
are ruined on my mouth, as if by poison.

Yes, you would be reading, I thought. If there was a celebration you would be shaking your head dismissively and telling Reiko-chan that she would be foolish to believe that Japanese girls were only now being looked at as the most desirable women on earth. "Of course we are," I knew you would be saying. "I already knew that! Japanese women are the best. But we should be appreciated for our minds and our loyalty and dedication, Reiko, and not for our bodies and our teeth, as if we were horses."

The typhoon was mostly gone when I woke up, groggy, in my bunk, from an intermittently sleepless night. I showered and got into my dungarees and had a breakfast of stale scrambled eggs, cold French toast, and maple syrup that had the consistency of carpenter's glue. This came with obligatory slabs of Dole pineapple that were a startlingly bright yellow. I also had two cups of scalding-hot coffee that did nothing at all to wake me up, unlike those tiny shots of super-sweet espresso served with such gusto by Mr. Ito at the Mozart café.

I headed straight for the office. I wanted to see if anyone had been able to beg, borrow, or steal a photograph of Kojima Akiko.

Chaplain Peeples was sitting on my chair with his feet up on my desk, scanning the several copies of *China Reconstructs*—the monthly picture magazine published in Peking by America's "Red Chinese enemies"—I had acquired the last time we were in Hong Kong.

He put his left hand up in the air, with his index finger pointed straight up. His gesture stopped me in my tracks.

"To tell you the truth, Rogers," he said, "I am not convinced that you are an appropriate person to be working for the *News Horizon*. I found this photograph of Akiko Kojima on your desk this morning. I hope you are not planning to use it in the next issue of the newspaper." He continued, clearly alarmed, "I am going to have to report that you are reading Communist publications. We don't do that in the United States. SEAMAN ROGERS!" he shouted, his voice suddenly loud. "I know you are English—or is it British? But that is not an excuse."

"An excuse?" I asked politely but insincerely.

"Yes, England—Britain—is full of Communists. Marxists. Socialists. Freethinkers. Radicals. Freemasons. Spiritualists. Gypsies. Fortune-tellers. Homosexuals. Fakirs. Feminists. Fu Manchu. Eccentrics too, I suppose. They are all really bad, unfortunate people who want to destroy our way of life. Do you want to destroy the American way of life, Rogers?"

I have often wondered how Chaplain Peeples got that way. I never really made an attempt to probe further during that summer because he was a senior officer and I was nothing, although he did take a peevish interest in me. Whenever he and I talked, he was angry at me, or upset, or anxious, or offended, and he always laced his words with a strange kind of venom. I could never decide whether this was the way he really was, and he really believed what he was declaring, or whether he was doing this for effect. If it was all playacting, it did not make me falter. Commander Crockett was different. He too had taken an interest in me. The only time he addressed me was when he was upset also. I was not accustomed then to barrages of four-letter words. But he gave me glimpses of a Texas-size humanity that always caused me to look at him as a hero and a guardian. But Peeples was a living myth, a caricature created by himself and not created, I have always thought, by a merciful God.

"You have been to England?" I asked the chaplain, trying hard not to say that with a sneer or smirk.

"Of course not!" he said loudly. "I am a Baptist!"

"Oh," I said, not knowing what a Baptist was. "I see."

"Why is this photograph of Miss Japan on your desk?" Chaplain Peeples demanded.

"Umm, she is now Miss Universe," I said.

"Are you trying to correct me?" There was a hint of outrage there. I could sense he was trying to lay a trap. Maybe he would accuse me of insubordination or something devilish like that.

"Oh no, sir," I said respectfully. "It is obvious that you know she has been selected by the judges as the most beautiful woman in the world."

There was a silence as cold as a severe frost clamping down on the earth, the kind of frost that froze the surface of the goldfish pond in my Auntie Nancy's garden back in England every year, leaving the fish under the ice motionless, as their life-support systems closed down to almost zero.

The chaplain picked up the photo of Kojima Akiko. I got a quick glimpse of her—such elegance. He inserted the photo into one of my copies of *China Reconstructs*—the one with a pretty girl on the cover wearing an olive-drab cap with a red star on it and a dazzling smile on her face designed to corrupt young male Americans, no doubt. He rolled up the magazine and tucked it under his arm. He looked back at me with some hostility.

"Come with me, Rogers," he said, as if he had divine power that could move heaven and earth. "There is something sinister about you, young man."

I followed him into the officers' quarters, where there was a lot more mahogany paneling than there was grim grey metal. Two funny fliers I knew passed by. They gave me a thumbs-up. "It must be time for prayers," one of the fliers remarked. Chaplain Peeples unlocked the door to his office. It was full of toys and boxes of playthings he had been collecting in Hawaii and California to hand out to poor Chinese and Filipino children on behalf of the US Navy under what he called Operation Handclasp. We often ran photos of the tall, severe Peeples shaking hands with various small Asian gentlemen in suits, who looked both embarrassed and intimidated by the sheer size of *Shangri-La* generosity, backed up by nuclear weapons.

He told me to sit down on one of several swivel chairs. He went out to the wardroom to order coffee and cookies. I glanced at the objects on the chaplain's desk. There was an assortment of obviously heavily read pulp novels, each one showing white American women—blondes mostly—partially unclothed, sometimes with a leering man in the background. I knew instinctively that these novels were not written by Marxists, but I decided to save that thought for future discussion. Titles included *Hard to Get*, *Red Bone Woman*, *The Night and the Naked*, *The Chiselers*, *Strip for Violence*, and *A Matter of Morals*. Standing vertically between bronze bookends cast in the image of Abraham Lincoln were smut magazines: *Confidential*, *Rave*, *Stare*, *Foto-Rama*, *Hit Annual*, *Whisper*, *Adam*, and *Eyeful*, whose lead story on the cover, which featured a voluptuous brunette some men might call a broad, was "Are You Broad Minded?"

There were, in addition, two copies of *Lady Chatterley's Lover* by the British author D. H. Lawrence. That was a novel I had not read. In 1959, in the United States of America, it was a brown-wrapper book, sold from under the counter in shops that specialized in men's magazines, horse and greyhound racing journals, and stinking cigars rolled in Tampa by Cuban women whose signature finishing touch in the rolling process was rubbing Robustos and Lusitanias against the skin of their inner thighs—or so a tobacconist once told me. Up until July 21, 1959, two days before my birthday, it had been illegal to even send this book, deemed "lustful, lewd, lascivious and prurient," through the US mail. In other words, the book was obscene, and not "art," until the US Supreme Court ruled that even "ideas hateful to the prevailing climate of opinion" were protected by the First Amendment. Mr. Ito had told me about that at the Mozart coffee shop. I have to confess I sorely wanted to slip one of those copies of *Lady Chatterley* into the pocket of my dungarees, but I figured I was in enough trouble already and that if I was reading something prurient as well as something "Communist," I would be flogged or made a castaway on one of the many small Pacific Ocean islands US Navy vessels used for target practice.

After taking a quick look at the reading material, I sat there, trying to look innocent. I was innocent. I was innocent of, and about, everything. But chaplains, I remembered, do not deal with the innocent. They deal with sinners, the depraved, and the guilty.

Chaplain Peeples reentered his cabin, whistling merrily. He had a shiny metal hotel tray in his hands upon which sat two pure white mugs of coffee with "USN" stenciled on the side, a dainty pitcher of milk, a small ceramic bowl of sugar cubes, and two dozen buttery cookies encrusted with sugar particles. I thanked him for the coffee and started sipping. It was not up to Mr. Ito's standards, Yukiko!

"Well," Chaplain Peeples said. He made a motion toward the lurid publications on his desk. "Here, you see, is reading material confiscated from frustrated young men who do not understand that this is pornography. Your soul, Rogers, is like a piece of cheese. Obscene publications are like worms that eat holes in that cheese. Masturbation follows. You can imagine what comes next."

"No," I said, truly shocked. "What comes next?"

"Consorting with loose women . . . prostitutes . . . Japanese girls . . . bar girls."

"Oh, I see," I said. It was another one of those moments when an older person—a superior officer—was addressing me as if he thought I understood what he was talking about. But I did not understand at all. So I said, "Oh, I see," and waited for clues.

"Yes. We will forget for the moment your relationship with a woman in the White Rose bar. I have heard that it is not a proper relationship. That woman also apparently speaks Russian, and she may have an understanding of Hebraic grammar. Where there are Jews there are Marxists. Are you aware of that? Also, you are clearly violating the rules against entering off-limits areas, although I can't prove it yet."

Here we go again, I thought. I was close to panic. I did the

Zen thing and let an inner voice inside me say "*saaaaaaa*." I found repose. I stayed silent.

"You are reading Communist material," he continued. "You have opened up to brainwash. Clearly, someone has gotten to you . . . upset your balance of mind, and your judgment. That is not good if you are working on the ship's newspaper. Also, this matter of the photograph of Akiko Kojima. This is not good. We can't have a photo of a Japanese woman in our newspaper, Rogers. That newspaper is read by our wives and girlfriends back home, not to mention our mothers and all the other wonderful women in the United States."

"Yes, sir," I said. "I understand."

But there was no way I was going to allow Chaplain Peeples to prevail.

Chapter 14

THE TOWER OF LILIES

The manners of the Japanese possess in a very high degree the requisites of true politeness; they are never presuming, officious, nor arrogant; and if they are sometimes bored or impatient in their social intercourse, they possess strong powers of concealment, as no feelings of the kind are ever permitted to become visible . . . And it would certainly appear, that with all our intellectual supremacy, and spiritual enlightenment, we might learn from the unchristianized Japanese the secret of inward happiness and contentment.

> —Lt. James D. Johnston, from the chapter
> "Manners and the Japanese," in
> *China and Japan: Being a Narrative
> of the Cruise of the U.S. Steam-Frigate*
> Powhatan *in the Years 1857, '58, '59, and '60*

Mr. Ito had urged me in the past, when I looked as if I were on the verge of being overwhelmed by events, to adopt a certain aspect of Taoist thought called *wu wei*. He guessed, I suppose, that *wu wei* might suit my temperament, even though I was young enough, according to Mr. Ito, that I "still had the memory of a mother's love." He said I needed to toughen up and wise up.

Mr. Ito's English was fragmentary. But he said to me soon after my chance meeting with Detective Nazaka, "Something good to remember, Mr. Anthony Perkins. If you are pushed, do not push back. Action can also be inaction. Sometimes you win by doing nothing."

This theory from ancient China, he said, maintains that human beings who live in harmony with all surrounding forces should behave naturally, without artifice. If there is a challenge, such a person will instinctively know when to act. He will not make a conscious decision. He will just do it, and sometimes doing nothing—inaction—is action. Action without effort can also, in effect, be a martial art. Remember the samurai who moves his sword down and steps back, relaxed, right at the moment when his opponent decides to raise his sword and attack with a "mighty roar," Mr. Ito advised. "Who wins? If you know who wins, and why, you understand *wu wei*."

I had mentally typed up this suggestion from Mr. Ito and secreted it away in a cabinet of my brain that was never locked. It was filed in the drawer labeled "New and Intriguing Ideas" and placed under the heading "Theories to Be Tested in Emergencies."

The discussion with Chaplain Peeples, which now was irritating me as he struck a supercilious pose, was fast becoming an emergency. After trying to determine whether he had knocked me off balance, he reached into a desk drawer and pulled out a copy of *The Torch of Life: A Key to Sex Harmony*, by Dr. Frederick M. Rossiter, BS, MD, Licentiate of the Royal

College of Physicians of London, published in the year of my birth, 1939. The dust jacket was midnight blue.

"There is one thing about Communism and premarital sex," Chaplain Peeples said, with a blink and a wink. "Good instruction in what it takes to be in love defeats Marxist dogma and running after whores, every time."

"Yes, sir," I said, in a state of complete relaxation and inaction. "Yes, sir. Thank you."

He smiled. "This is a British publication," he said, "so it is probably to your liking. I don't normally give young men this book because it is not American. As you can see, the book starts with poetry, and poetry, even from the Holy Bible, is not something that will grab our attention." He had opened it to a passage that went on for seven pages in the front of the book, "An Ancient Love Song: The Song of Solomon." "This typeface is much too small for me to read, son," he said. It was indeed small. Even I had to squint hard to be able to read:

THE BRIDE: Let him kiss me with the kisses of his lips;
Surely more delicious than wine are thy love favours—
    your caresses!
Thy renown, like the fragrance of thy own exquisite per-
    fumes, is
Wafted like scent.
Therefore do the maidens love thee.

Because I was furtively employing *wu wei* strategy I did not question the appropriateness of this gift. I left his office walking backward, and I gave him a small bow as I nudged the door open, just to be polite, like a Japanese. I was also able to grab one of the pulp novels from a second heap of confiscated books by his door while his back was turned: *Morning, Winter, and Night: An Absolutely Frank Novel About the Exquisite Torment of Adolescent Passion* (by John Nairne Michaelson), a subject I knew nothing about. The book cover showed a young white male kissing the neck of an Asian woman whose head leaned back in ecstasy.

Red Downs was on the phone in the *News Horizon* office, desperately trying to convince someone in communications to give us a second photo of Kojima Akiko. Photos in those days were transmitted by radio-telephone and received, slowly and primitively, by a kind of fax machine. Red asked me where I had been. I told him I had had a "session" with the chaplain, which caused him to state, "You are in trouble again."

It would not help the situation, I thought, to try to explain the skewed world of Lieutenant Commander Peeples and his gift of *The Torch of Life*, so I said, "Did you know he has a big collection of confiscated books and magazines?"

"No kidding," Red said. "He took them?"

"I don't know. He has them. Maybe he put the word out. Something like, 'Bring me sex books. They are bad for morale.'"

Red laughed. "Bad? I got a few of them myself. Do you want to see?"

"Oh no. No. Thank you, and all that. But I have enough problems already. He also gave me this book on 'sexual harmony' and I think he wants me to read all of it so I can block my interest in Marxism and Yukiko."

I showed Red the book. Out popped a small postcard marked "Place 1¢ Stamp Here" and self-addressed to the Eugenics Publishing Company at 317 East 34th Street, New York, NY.

On the reverse side of the card, under the wording, "I am interested in unusual books dealing with sociology, sex and related subjects and would like to be kept on your mailing list to receive announcements of new publications which you intend bringing out from time to time," the chaplain had used a pencil to fill out his name and a street address in the civilian world in a New England state.

"He must have forgotten to mail it," Red said. "I'll put a stamp on it and send it off and alert the guys in the mail room to expect sex books for the chaplain. You know what that means, don't you? Gossip."

Then Red said, "You have another letter from Yukiko." He slid it across his desk. It had been written one month previously. Where it had been all that time was a mystery. I cut the envelope open with a penknife and read.

Dear Paul,

It is a very nice day. As you know, this is the beginning of the rainy season, but I have never seen such a day like this since I came to Yokosuka. Actually, all my recent days have been good ones. I hear crows cawing in the morning and at sunset. Sometimes I see the crows in the trees but I realize I cannot be a friend to them because they make me feel something unlucky might happen. You know what I mean, I think. For me it is so strange to have such soft and maiden feelings for a man. I sigh. That never happen for me for such a long long time. I can sit in my chair in front of the window and enjoy those feelings of friendship and joy and suddenly I am a young girl again. My imagination is full of dreams again. I know they are impossible dreams, but I get a feeling like the opera—like Maria Callas—when I feel such emotion so long denied to me. I want to sing an aria. Oh yes. BUT, unfortunately, there have been signs of danger that have nothing to do with you, Paul-san. The danger is my history. I have to live my life as if I am in a tall castle . . . I quote here from a poem by Fu Hsuan. He wrote this in China in the year 210.

Woman

Bitter indeed it is to be born a woman!
It is difficult to imagine anything so
    low.
Nothing on earth is held so cheap.
Boys stand leaning at the door
Like little gods fallen out of Heaven.
Their hearts brave the Four Oceans,
The winds and dust from thousands of
    miles.
No one weeps when you, a girl, are married
    off.
Your husband's love is as distant as the
    Milky Way.

Yet she must follow him like a sunflower
   follows the sun.
Their hearts are as far apart as fire
   and water.
She is blamed for all and everything that
   goes wrong.

I am sorry to put the burden of this poem
on your broad shoulders, Paul-san. I have
tried, but it is so difficult to explain my
life. I feel that here in Yokosuka I have
come to the end of the road. I can't go
back to the beginning of the road because
it is so far away. I would get lost trying
to find myself. I would never find the way
I was before I arrived in Japan. And then,
after I arrived, everything was bad too. I
made some terrible friends. I was trying to
survive. You are a nice boy. This is strange
for you. But please be patient. We are lovers
of literature and music, but we will never be
lovers. I know that already. It is impossible.
I am an old woman. I am a bad woman. You have
your whole life to live. I have depended on
you for comfort. You were generous with your
time and affection for me. How precious to
me is your loyalty, and your respect! Thank
you for that. Thank you also for your blue
letter to me. That was such beautiful paper.
Your letter I put in my pillow. Please be

careful when you go to Hong Kong. There are robbers, you know. I had that experience when I lived in Manchuria. My father killed. My brothers killed. I saw that. That was not a dream. The terror. Such terror on that day.

I am sorry if this bad letter is making you tired. That poem might rob you of happiness, but it is true. Please study my letter and that poem as if I was a student who submitted an examination paper. I am sorry that I do not have the sensibility to be a poet.

My heart is sensitive.
My mind is hard.
My body is a shield.
My spirit is armor.
When I cry, I cry inside.
In this world, I am a woman.

Of course, you already know that the English poet, Stephen Spender, says that a poem does not talk truth. You feel something that is truth when you read the poem and then you examine the feelings in your heart. I read that in the newspaper about two years ago when I had to be a refugee again. I ran from Hiroshima. You know that, I believe. Please excuse my poor letters and my typing and also my sentence construction. Thank you for being so kind to me. Sometime I imagine you as a strong young samurai in an ancient book of poetry written by a woman of the court. That certain woman is lonely, longing for the lover who CAN NOT be her love. Do you understand? Will you promise to always remember me? I send you love wrapped in silk, like the kiss of the first morning breeze after lovemaking.

Yukiko

P.S. Do you like the melody, Love Somebody in Blue, by George Gashuin? Oh yes, it is Gershwin. You told me that already. So sorry. Is the title Love Somebody in Blue? Or is it Rhapsody in Blue? It is the same thing, right? Love is blue. Love is not kind. How could Mr. Gershwin say love is rhapsody?

Yukiko: you signed your name in kanji—Chinese characters—for the first time. The characters were firm, assured, artistic, as if a poet had written them, I thought. Kanji: that was something new.

I folded the letter and slipped it back into the envelope. I was dealing with such a surge of emotions. I felt as if I had been talking face-to-face with you, our bodies close, in a hot room. It was like the first time I met you. My whole body was flushed. My shirt was damp with perspiration. That kind of reaction usually happens to me only when I am talking to a beautiful woman, and I am trying hard to sound coherent while at the same time my eyes are studying her face and her eyes for evidence of life lived. You might remember, Yuki-chan, how closely I studied you, as if you were white marble at the Louvre.

If there had been a safe in the office, I would have locked the letter and all your other letters inside. I had the uncomfortable feeling that if they were not locked away someone would be reading them. It was just a thought.

About that same moment, a senior Marine Corps sergeant, assigned to the USMC detachment aboard ship that guarded the nuclear warheads, dropped by to say he was retiring and to ask if we would like to write about his experiences on Iwo Jima. Red took notes. I listened. I knew a lot about Iwo Jima and the titanic struggle there in February and March of 1945 between the Marine invaders and the Japanese defenders, who were well dug in and ready to sacrifice their lives to help protect their homeland six hundred miles to the north. A total of 6,821 Marines were killed, and more than twenty thousand were wounded. More than twenty thousand Japanese troops died; only 1,083 were taken prisoner. It was hand-to-hand combat of the heroic kind, the cream of manhood from two aggressive nations.

I listened to the sergeant talk about the fact that two hours after the landing, only twelve of the 220 men in his Marine Corps company were still fighting. I did not say anything. A few weeks earlier I had sat in a Yokosuka movie theater with you, Yuki, and watched a double feature. I know it was part of my education, but it was an ordeal unlike any other. First on the screen was the American film *Sands of Iwo Jima* from 1949, starring John Wayne as the flawed and fearless Sergeant John Stryker. The Marines used flamethrowers, bayonets, rifle fire, machine guns, artillery, mortars, tanks, and bare muscle to slowly kill the Japanese one by one. Every seat was occupied in the theater, and many people were standing in the aisles. In an odd way, it was as if they had all come to church. As far as I know, I was the only foreigner in the crowd. Except for the noise of war on the sound track, there was absolute silence in the theater. These were ordinary Japanese people watching American Marines and crack Japanese troops in a fight to the death, which is the way the war in the Pacific had to be fought as the Japanese Empire began crumbling.

There was a short break. You would not look at me. I was the enemy and you were my Japanese friend.

Paired with *Sands of Iwo Jima* was the 1953 film by director Imai Tadashi *Himeyuri no Tô* (*Tower of Lilies*), which was never shown in the United States in those days because it was perceived by the Japanese studio to be anti-American. It was, however, a spectacular hit in Japan. Of course, there were no subtitles. I imagined the dialogue. You did some interpreting. The audience reaction was completely different this time. The theater was mostly full of women. They had come for the Imai film, not for the *Sands of Iwo Jima*. The women were crying, gasping, sobbing, almost from the start. You were rocking back and forth in your seat, clutching my arm sometimes, putting your hands in front of your eyes at other times to hide from the bloodshed on the screen. I cried too.

Later, Yuki, I found this description of the film that I would have loved to have shared with you. It is from the American author Donald Richie's pioneering book from 1959, *The Japanese Film: Art and Industry*. I could attempt to describe the film myself, but every time I try to visualize it my hands start shaking and I start choking up. Those emotional reactions did not happen to me during the *Sands of Iwo Jima*: it was about sacrifice, but it was also about flag-waving and thus not quite real. *Tower of Lilies* was also about sacrifice—but the Japanese killed during the invasion of the island of Okinawa were schoolgirls. It is a true story. There is a monument—the Tower of Lilies—on Okinawa to the memory of the more than two hundred teenage girls and their eighteen teachers who were shot or were killed by flamethrowers or committed suicide rather than surrender during the ninety-day battle. These girls and young women had been hastily conscripted by the Japanese military as nurses. They had been given a few hours of training. They had believed there would be a quick battle, the Americans would be destroyed, and then they could return to school to resume their studies and play basketball and softball, which they were good at. It was their duty to tend to the Japanese wounded, not in a hospital, but in caves, in the trenches, on the front lines. They were not warriors, they were children, and this film, for me, was far more real than the one made by Hollywood, Yuki.

Tower of Lilies, Richie said, acquired the reputation overseas as

> the most scurrilous of anti-American projects. If it is "anti" anything, the film is anti-war. It is the story of the girls of the Okinawa Prefectural First Girls High School, often called the Lily School, who just before the pending American invasion are mobilized as special combat nurses. Their unit was named The Lily Corps. Under the American attack they are all killed . . . In the film Imai had almost nothing to say

about the enemy, and the terrific pounding given the area
by the American forces is not implied to have been one of
terror against the civilian populace; rather, it is presented
as a straight battle between opposing military forces.

More than two hundred thousand human beings died in the
battle—soldiers from both sides, civilians, and the members
of the Lily Corps, in their medic uniforms of white headbands,
school satchels, straw sandals, black shirts, and black skirts
and pants. They were teenage innocents, you said, more innocent even than me. The US Marines won a titanic victory.
There have been countless stories through the years about
their valor. To their credit, the Marines often tried to convince
Japanese soldiers to surrender. But they would not. There was
no valor in surrendering. It was not honorable, the Japanese
military code declared. Often the Marines watched in horror
as Okinawan civilians—they were also Japanese civilians—
sometimes killed themselves rather than submit to capture. The
desperate struggle put up by the Japanese was one reason the
United States opted to drop atomic bombs on Hiroshima and
Nagasaki later. The thinking was that the destruction caused
by the bombs would be such a shock to the Japanese that they
would choose to avoid an invasion of the home islands and
months or even years of hand-to-hand combat.

The Marine Corps sergeant had just told Red that he was
at the Battle of Okinawa too. I asked whether he had heard
of the Japanese film or had ever visited the Tower of Lilies.
He shook his head. "Never heard of the Tower of Lilies,"
he said. He asked me what it was about. I told him. I was a
youngster, like so many youngsters, who wanted to make a

point and sometimes lacked finesse, Yukiko. About two-thirds of the way through my highly detailed account the sergeant walked out of the office without a gesture, without a word, and never came back. I saw him again a few weeks later at his retirement ceremony. He shook my hand. I was so glad he did that. It had occurred to me that I had no idea about what he had experienced in the battle.

The Battle of Iwo Jima was another one of those things that came back from the past to haunt me in my sixties. It reminded me, after many years of forgetting, of my connection with Japan that started in the White Rose bar when you walked up to me and said, with a tired smile, "Hello." That moment in the bar was really when my adult life started. I think you would be happy to know, Yukiko, that I followed your advice, almost to the letter. My university years began immediately after my four years in the navy. I majored in ancient Japanese history and language. My professional years, some of which I spent in Tokyo with *Newsweek*; my interests in the arts; even my personality, which includes a lack of patience for incompetents, can all be traced back through the tangled threads of life connecting them to that moment in the bar.

In early 1995, I got word that more than eight hundred surviving Marines (a Marine is always a Marine) who fought on Iwo Jima in 1945 were going back to the island for a memorial ceremony. A handful of former Japanese soldiers who opposed them would attend the ceremony too, which included the raising of both the American flag and the Japanese flag on top of the extinct volcano Suribachi. It was on this six-hundred-foot-high cinder dome at the south end of the island in February 1945 that photographer Joe Rosenthal snapped the photograph that will probably never be forgotten: five Marines and a Navy corpsman raising the Stars and Stripes after fighting their way to the top of Suribachi.

The newspaper in Phoenix I was writing for at the time went along with my suggestion that I sign up to travel with the Marine veterans. After all, one of the six flag raisers was Ira Hayes, a Pima Indian from Arizona. Hayes was long dead. He had a drinking problem and had passed out in the desert and died on a very cold day in 1955, depressed, according to his family, because he had survived and he could not handle fame. I interviewed his family members, such shy, modest people. They brought out a small box of letters from Ira. "Aye," they were saying, as if it were the first word of a lament. "Aye! Poor Ira." When they showed me the letters as if they were sacraments I suddenly thought of your letters, Yuki-chan.

On Iwo Jima I walked down to the beach with a half-dozen silver-haired Marines who had landed there in 1945. They stopped at the point where the ocean met the land and they turned to look up at Suribachi for the first time in many years. I could only guess what was going through their minds. The single question I asked myself as I stumbled through the deep black sand was, "Could I have done that?" Could I, at age nineteen, have dashed through the surf and crawled up the steep incline from the beach to the barren flat terrain above while bullets and shells were killing and maiming everyone around me?

Would I be as cheerful as these old men on this reunion day? They had come through the experience of combat, but what dreams did they have? What nightmares? They were such proud men.

I can never forget the scene at the airport in Honolulu, where our charter flight landed to refuel after leaving the West Coast. The Marine Corps had lined the corridors of the terminal with hundreds of young Marines in full dress uniform. They stood and saluted smartly. Some of them were crying, even as they held on for dear life to those stiff salutes. The old Marines, leaning on each other for support, were saluting and weeping too.

"Semper Fi!"—always faithful—someone shouted fiercely, not as if it were a motto, but as if it were a battle cry.

Chapter 15

WHAT IS MY JOY?

Love is not all: it is not meat nor drink
Nor slumber nor a roof against the rain

—Edna St. Vincent Millay,
from "Sonnet XXX,"
in *Collected Poems*

The *Shangri-La* sped south by southwest, past the main Japanese island of Honshu, past the smaller island of Kyushu, where Nagasaki was located, down the long string of tiny island jewels leading to Okinawa, and then to the Taiwan Strait, where the great mass of China loomed on one side and the island of Taiwan hid in the fog on the other. It was a journey of 1,400 miles. The People's Republic of China was fiercely, theatrically anti-American. Just a few months earlier in 1958, "Red China," as we called it, had unleashed deadly artillery barrages against Quemoy, Matsu, and other small islands within sight of its coast. The islands had been fortified by the Chinese Nationalist regime on Taiwan, which the Americans supported. It was the task of the *Shangri-La* to turn back any invasion by the mainland: that is why the ship had an arsenal of nuclear warheads. I did not have much sophistication when it came to understanding politics or making war, but you said, Yukiko, that I did know the difference between right and wrong.

Both the mainland and Taiwan claimed loudly to be China's legitimate government. Both governments were dictatorships. The mainland government called the Nationalist government "the running dogs of the US imperialists." The Nationalists called their foes "murderers" and "lackeys of the criminal Soviets." I struck a neutral pose and tried to keep an open mind—an attitude that infuriated most of my superiors. They said I was disloyal. I was naive. I was sleeping with the enemy. I was red, a Communist, for sure. But you said when we talked about China—because, after all, you were born there—"Do not believe in propaganda. Believe only in yourself. You can be a very young and nice boy. You don't have to be old and ugly to know what is true or false. And make sure you believe in me," you added, laughing.

Then you recited what sounded like a short poem, in Mandarin Chinese. And then you sang a little children's song in what sounded like Russian and while you did that you stared at your face in the mirror, tied your hair in pigtails, and said in English: "This is how I looked when my brothers were killed and my father was murdered. Yes. This was me. I was an innocent, like you. You will not always be innocent. Enjoy your youth, your glory, while you can."

The fighter pilots who flew F-8 Crusaders from the *Shangri-La* sometimes told me how, when their mission took them near the Chinese coast, small groups of MiG-17 interceptors with red stars painted on their tails would challenge them from a distance. Then, without firing a shot, the Chinese jets would wiggle their wings, spin round, and zip back to the mainland. One flier said a Chinese pilot once gave him a wave and that he was so shocked by the gesture he did not know whether he should return it, but fearing that he would be reprimanded if he waved back, he did nothing, and that still bothered him.

Every now and then, Yuki, we would see the black silhouettes of Chinese junks, their sails flying, nets out, scouring the ocean for shoals of fish. They took no notice of the *Shangri-La*. For them it was as if we, with our nuclear weapons and the power to obliterate whole cities, did not exist. One afternoon I heard strange sounds echoing across the open water. I borrowed some binoculars and climbed to the perch I often used for solitude above the captain and the bridge. There, far away, a group of men lay in the sun under an awning that shielded the junk's deck from the heat. I guessed they were listening to the gongs and drums and high-pitched voices of Cantonese opera, sung by stars whose identities were known only in China, a place in those days where not even Maria Callas was known. If there ever is a war, I remember thinking, it will be fought in the dark between two nationalities that know almost nothing about each other but that swallow the bait of mutual hatred and fear like swirling swarms of sardines.

We would be in Hong Kong in a few days. I would try to find Paul Feng again, I decided. I had not seen him since June, when he gave me the copy of *The True Story of Ah-Q*. I wanted to talk to him about the book.

I asked you about *Ah-Q*. I said, "Is this a comedy? Is it a farce? Was the author poking fun at the system?"

You put on your serious schoolteacher face, so I knew I

was supposed to listen carefully. You said, "You must decide for yourself.

"You are old enough to make important decisions. Your impression of that book may be different from mine. Defend your impression. Yes, do that. But listen carefully to what older people say. They may talk nonsense, which, in this case, sharpens your understanding of what is nonsense. That big officer on your ship who called me a 'spider.' Was that nonsense? Was that humor? I know what it was! You decide. If you do that you will become a wiser man . . . sorry, a very young man so wise."

I also was looking forward to replenishing my supply of *China Reconstructs*. I wanted to read about the progress of the Great Leap Forward, about which Paul Feng had been so enthusiastic. This was a plan, then in its second year, which Chairman Mao had decided would greatly boost industrial and agricultural production. The "masses"—not the bureaucrats—would make this possible.

Also, I had made two new friends on the ship: a tall German immigrant named Gunther Erlichmann, who was always looking over his shoulder, and a guy named Oscar Garcia Muñoz from Seattle, who said he was a pachuco (teenage member of a Mexican-American street gang). To prove it, he showed me a tattoo of a cross, crudely etched into the web between the thumb and the forefinger on his right hand. He said it was the mark of a gang member. Gunther and Oscar, who liked the fact that I was regarded by the overlords with suspicion, had almost convinced me to join them in visiting a genuine Hong Kong bordello. *The World of Suzie Wong*—Richard Mason's tale about a young British painter who falls in love with a Chinese hooker who wore dazzling, tight silk cheongsam dresses—was a big hit on Broadway in 1959. A Hollywood production company was already at work in the back alleys of Hong Kong's Wan Chai bar district, scouting locations to turn the book into a film. More than one hundred beautiful Hong Kong women had answered a casting call published in a local newspaper, hoping to star as Suzie Wong. Oscar was supernaturally excited about "slit skirts."

"What is a pachuco?" I asked him.

"A pachuco is a good Mexican. I spent time in jail. I read that book about Suzie Wong, man. That's all I could think about—slit skirts! Legs! Yeah! So I figured if I joined the navy I could meet girls in slit skirts. This is my big chance. I enlisted for four years so I could do this. And now God has given me the opportunity to get laid by a golden girl whose language I don't understand. Do you know what that means? Two people who don't understand each other, thinking their separate thoughts . . . me speaking my English and she speaking her Chinese. I would love imagining what she is saying, what she is thinking. Nothing can be as cool as that!"

He was already in a profound state of delight. He had dreamed about this for months, maybe years. Yes, he believed he had been "blessed."

"But, Oscar," I said, "we were in Hong Kong just a few weeks ago. Didn't you have liberty then?"

"No, man. They had me on report. I had to stand extra duty."

"But why?"

"You know . . . They make you take a rubber when you leave the ship, and no man I knew ever wore a rubber. That's for fags and mommy's boys."

"And this time?"

"This time I am gonna be smart. I'll take one of the damn things and then I'll give it to you for safekeeping. I can't stand rubbers. There is something about the touch and feel of them that reminds me of the dead."

One peaceful Sunday, while the *Shangri-La* was patrolling, I took out all your letters and I read them again one by one. I arranged them in chronological order. At that point you had written me fifteen times. During the entire summer, you probably wrote twenty letters. Half of those letters disappeared. I asked Red and Jim about them as they vanished one by one, but they just shook their heads and rolled their eyes. I began worrying that the missing letters had been confiscated by Chaplain Peeples. He had asked me to join him in Hong Kong to help distribute the toys he had gathered for Operation Handclasp. He seemed to know a lot about me when he interrogated me before. I began imagining that the letters were hidden inside one of his stacks of dirty books. He was probably waiting for the appropriate moment to use them when he lectured me again on the dangers of befriending women who worked in bars. Or maybe he would quote from them during one of his sermons about the power that sin has over the innocents of this world. We sailors on our first cruise overseas were sinful children, in his estimation, but not exactly lambs of God.

The chaplain wanted me to photograph the gift giving. I had asked him why there were so many plastic guns of all kinds in the bags of toys he showed me. I had this vision in my head of hundreds of small Chinese children brandishing their firearms and chasing the chaplain round and round the orphanage on a day when he had one of his migraine headaches. The arming of the children would take place near the

Happy Valley Racecourse, a favorite with the elite of the Hong Kong establishment. The kids came from one of the orphanages run by the Po Leung Kuk organization, which had for the last hundred years been housing hordes of abandoned children and fighting the abduction of women and kids who were forced to work as prostitutes or labor in sweatshops.

A new letter had arrived. I had not opened it yet. I was saving it until I could examine my state of mind and the meaning of our friendship, Yuki-chan. I felt increasingly uneasy. There was so much I did not understand. At times I felt as if I had plunged into an abyss. At times I felt an incredible longing. When I try to imagine your face—something that I still do—I felt the pain of something long denied: a kiss. I had just turned twenty. A young man that age really is still a child—I know that now. The kiss is an impulse. If we kissed then we would kiss again, and then September would come and we would both be desperate. We would be missing each other, and desperate. If I decided that I was in love, you would reject me. Yes, I know that now.

You would have said something like: "It is so easy for a child, boy or girl, to fall—yes, to fall—in love. For you, it is like jumping out of a window with flames at your back. But for an old woman like me who has scars and bruises, it is not so easy. In fact, it is impossible. So, don't fall in love with me, Paul-san. If you do, you will be disappointed and you might not want to love anyone else again." That is what you would say. I was sure of it. I had never told anyone that I loved her or him, probably not even my mother or father, both of whom gave evidence of disappointment about that. They did not kiss. They did not hold hands. They never embraced under a full moon. In correspondence this week with a woman whose books I carried to school when she was sixteen and I was seventeen, she told me I was "very romantic" but "brooding," and that she was afraid she had "hurt" me by cutting me off mostly because she wanted to dance and wanted to be kissed. I was not "gawky," she said, although that is how I saw myself. It was not until after I met you, Yuki, that I slowly started realizing there was no poetry in holding back, in refusing to admit to love. There was poetry only in declaring and celebrating love. I clearly remember that in England I asked my mother at the dinner table why so many of the songs on the radio were love songs, and she gave a little sigh—the sort of sigh you gave sometimes when you looked at me, your eyes piercing the gloom of the White Rose bar, your stare without any kind of expression and just a trace of a sad, sad smile on very thin lips, forcing me to stop breathing for that instant because I felt the first hint of desire.

The bond between us had grown and grown and grown until it had come to this moment when I sensed in your most recent letters a note of desperation. I read each letter several times. The more I read your question, "Do you remember me?" the more guilt I started to feel about leaving you. It was the first time I was aware of the burden. Or was it a responsibility? Or was it just a matter of a young man growing up who had not much experience when it came to love or, in fact, to sex without love? I did not even know there was such a thing. I was young enough to still believe, naturally and intrinsically, as if it were both a conundrum and a gift to humanity, that love was more powerful than sex. Or was it that love had to come first, before sex? Or was it that I was a weird kid, awash with hormones, denying myself the sexual marauding that just about every sailor did in our ports of call? Was I crazy? Did I not shiver the last time I was in Hong Kong when the Eurasian girl kissed my wound after the struggle over the *Outline History of China* in the Suzie Wong bar? That was just a peck on the cheek. What was a kiss involving the lips of a man and a woman like? I wondered. What was it like when they were in love?

All these thoughts chased each other inside my mind like dogs spoiling for a fight. I felt like throwing up. It was a moment of darkness. The stark neon light overhead did not help and provided no comfort. The moment I had not really thought about before was making itself known. The *Shangri-La* would leave Yokosuka for the United States on September 22 and arrive in San Diego on October 3. The *Shangri-La* would leave, and there was nothing you or I could do about it, Yukiko. I could not jump ship to stay with you. The difference in our years never was an issue. I was not even aware of that. Only my mother, in a follow-up letter to the one in which she called me an "idiot," brought up the matter of age, asking the question, "How old is she?"

How did I reply? "I am sorry, Mum. I don't really know. I never asked." Or did I say something like, "Yuki is probably about thirty," and nothing more because it never occurred to me in my naivety that it would be a problem?

I don't remember what I said to my mother. But I do remember she wrote me yet another letter full of contempt in which she said, "Don't be a fool," and I had not a clue what she meant.

The ship would leave, and then I would not see you again— *ever* again. That idea entered my mind like a spear. It was so frightening that I erased it immediately, put all your letters back in their envelopes, locked them in my desk drawer, and opened your new letter.

Dear Paul,

Thank you for your most recent letter and your interpretation of what I was trying to say. I was really surprised that you made the attempt to read my poor translation of the wonderful tanka of Saito Mokichi. When I am not at the bar I am researching this poet very late at night. I burn candles. When I read poetry the shadows and the light that flickers and the smoke from the candle flame improve my ability to appreciate what comes from a man's heart. Or should I say "soul"? Some unlucky men carry the burden of having a soul, I suppose.

Mr. Saito died not long ago. He was also a psychiatrist. His education gave him the special insight to write a collection of 59 poems about the gradual death of his mother. This was called Shinitamau Haha. In English, I believe, this means just My Mother is Dying. But I have told you many times until I am red in the face that English is such a stupid and brutal language. It does not have the delicate texture of Japanese. For example, in stupid English you say, I love you. This is like the sound of a stone falling into water. What do

we say? Kimi wo aishimasu. Maybe one day, if
you study Japanese well which I think you will
do because I demand it, you will understand
how delicious that very private thought you
will only say to one person in your entire
life. Yes, Paul-san. You will fall in love.
But only once . . . like me.

> What is my joy?
> I throw it into the air
> Like a ball no one can catch
> And then I chase it, bouncing,
> Bouncing, until I have it again.
> But not until it is safe in my hands
> Do I cry for joy once more.

I do not really have the ability to write
a poem like you do. All I have is the pretext
of writing poetry. I have the unexpected joy
of writing and then receiving your comments.
Your comments to me are like a splendid kiss
on my lips.

It is raining outside. I am thinking now
that I am typing that maybe I am interrupting
your happiness. I am sure that you are again
exploring Hong Kong. You are so fortunate
to be a man. I know from my own experience
that a woman is terrified of adventure. But
a man like you runs with open arms toward
the unknown. I looked up this word in my

dictionary . . . "uncharted" is better than "unknown," I think.

But here I am, still writing . . . gomen . . . I am so sorry. By the way, are you finding sensational news out there? Are you finding something like a poet of passionate love discovers, or is that trite? If you find it, please send it to me by some kind of news service. Oh! Oh! No! No! If you discover love and write about it and I read that, I will have to be burned at the stake. I will catch fire because of desire. Or maybe because of jealousy. Please let me enjoy, if you can, the pleasure of being an old woman writing to a beautiful young man.

I am very disappointed in my book store. I wanted to find a book for you. But it was not available. I wanted to see you, with my own eyes, reading it. I wanted to know how the paper of the book feels when you run your fingertips across the page. I have a good imagination, don't you think?

Oh well! I will close now before you are tired of my letter and before I say something I regret. However, I still want to be teacher's pet. Take care of yourself, sailor boy. Think of me, when you can.

Love,

Yukiko

Chapter 16

HALL OF FLOWERS

These Tan-ka people of the Canton river are the descendants of a tribe of aborigines pushed by advancing Chinese civilization to live on boats on the Canton river . . . These Tan-ka people were the secret but trusty allies of foreigners from the time of the East India Company to the present day. They furnished pilots and supplies of provisions to British men-of-war and troop ships when doing so was by the Chinese Government declared treason . . . They invaded Hong Kong the moment the Colony was opened, and have ever since maintained here a monopoly, so to say, of the supply of Chinese pilots and ships' crews, of the fish trade, the cattle trade, and especially of the trade in women for the supply of foreigners and of brothels patronized by foreigners. Almost every . . . kept mistress of foreigners here belongs to this Tan-ka tribe, looked down upon . . . by all the other Chinese classes.

—From *Correspondence Respecting the*
Alleged Existence of Chinese Slavery in Hong Kong:
Presented to Both Houses of Parliament
by Command of Her Majesty, March 1882

The *Shangri-La* was finally at anchor in the Fragrant Harbour, which is a generous English translation of Hong Kong. I stuck my hand in the bucket held by the officer of the deck and pulled out a required Durex condom, which stared like the eye of a large dead fish from the cellophane wrapping. I expected to rip open the wrapping in joyful ecstasy, and thus be struck from the list of virgin men maintained by God and His Angels. Oscar and Gunther were determined to have an adventure they would not be able to forget for the rest of their lives. We clutched our condoms as if they were gold sovereigns. Only after we hopped aboard a waiting sampan skippered by a cheerful pirate with a mouthful of twenty-four-carat teeth did we stash the condoms in our pockets.

We looked at each other and grinned. Excitement was turning the blood in our veins into fizzing soda pop. I had not really thought this out. I was acting on a mix of impulse and impatience, Yuki. We had ironed and starched our white cotton summer uniforms and had used lots of spit and bacon grease from our breakfast trays to put an astonishing sheen on our black leather shoes. We had had our flattops trimmed. I had remembered the advice given to me in boot camp by the chief petty officer in charge of recruits to make sure every millimeter of my genital gifts was scrubbed and pure. My new friends were roughly the same age as I was. They would therefore be around seventy-five years old now. Do Gunther and Oscar remember, I wonder, that day in Wan Chai, where the fable of Suzie Wong—the goddess with the slit skirt and golden legs—began?

"You like nice girl?" the pirate asked. We nodded yes.

"Wan Chai have very nice girl. You go to the Hall of

Flowers. Very nice. Many, many nice girls there. You drink, you go to Mermaid Bar. Very nice. You very nice young men. Many girls like you, for sure!"

We looked at each other and grinned again, Yuki. "I just know this will be such a wonderful day," Oscar said gleefully. He checked to make sure his rubber was still in his pocket. It was. He reached in, pulled it out, and gave it to me. "Souvenir," he said. "You may need this. Me, I don't want it."

Gunther was still looking over his shoulder. We were not being pursued. Then he looked at the Hong Kong skyline. In those days there were only a few high-rise buildings. A haze heavy with heat and moisture made the tops of the tallest buildings invisible. He was nervous, or spooked, or something. He looked again over his shoulder. Maybe he wanted to swim back to the ship. "I guess we going to make it, yah?" he asked, in his uncertain English. "I don't know how to swim!"

"I can't swim either," I said. "They told me in boot camp I had a large head and heavy bones. The only way I could pass the swimming test was to do it on my back, half underwater, round the pool. And then they had to pull me out with a long pole with a hook at the end as if I was a tuna."

We were about ten minutes away from the landing at Wan Chai. I could already see the frenzied neon signs of the bars and saloons and dance halls on the waterfront. Bar Neptune. Bar Mermaid. Bar Lucky. Bar Happy. In one of those places, I thought, a beautiful and accomplished girl—a university student of cello or of ballet, I hoped—was going to take my virginity on this day of destiny. The girl was probably already feeling the first thrill of arousal and anticipation. Should I let her know, I wondered awkwardly, that this was my first time? Maybe not. But maybe I should.

"Oscar," I said, "do you think . . . ?" And then I stopped. "Nothing," I said. "Nothing."

Oscar looked at me confidently, like any gang member would, I guess, when it came to backing up his *compañeros*. "No problem," he said. "Not to worry."

I looked down into the water, where refuse of all kinds bobbed and floated. Fishtails. Bits of noodles. Scraps of Chinese-language newspapers.

We were only yards away from the shore. I saw a smile on your face reflected in the water, Yukiko. Or maybe it was not really a smile. If it was a smile, it was the type that appears on the face of a Cambodian *apsara*, carved many centuries ago to be enjoyed by men forever. You were smiling, and then you looked as if you were going to ask me a question. You wanted to know whether I had remembered to write to you. Yes, excited though I was about going ashore, I had scribbled a short note. I said something like: "We have arrived in Hong Kong. I have liberty today so I will go ashore with some friends. I will be careful about the robbers you mentioned. I am sure I will have a good time." I had signed it, "Love from Paul." In earlier letters I had just signed my name. But now I added the word "love." I did so not knowing whether I should be truthful or whether I should be polite, and I did not know whether you were my "only" and whether the loyalty I felt to you was supposed to be complete, or whether our relationship somehow strangely permitted sex with someone other than you, given the fact we had not kissed or had sex, even though there was desire. Thus perplexed, and with no one to turn to for advice on a matter as confusing and personal as this, I enclosed another of my poems with the letter, which I hoped would reassure you that I was thinking about you all the time, even when I was about to step ashore with a rubber plus a souvenir rubber at Wan Chai.

> You will be a ribbon
> Caught in the hair of spring
> And you will sing and I will see you
> Tied, fluttering, and weary
> Bright among the black branches
> Sighing, fainting there.
> Yet I will not hesitate to free you,
> To trespass upon such unknown times
> That free spring's burnished hair
> From bright ribbons,
> Killing winter
> And loving summer's heated pride.

It was just after one o'clock in the afternoon. There was an incredible barrage of loud Cantonese exclamations from the wharf, where rickshaw men were jostling to give sailors rides. We three headed straight for the Mermaid Bar, which was jammed with sailors and Marines from several nations, mostly in good humor, but sometimes not. I felt an arm sliding round my waist and I turned to look into the eyes of a small girl in pigtails and blue jeans, who would not let go of me even when I wanted to sit down. I could not hear what she was telling me at first. There was too much noise in the bar, and the jukebox was cranked up so loud the floor was shaking. I don't know what it is like now for sailors, Yuki, but back then we were not conscious of or even privy to the notion that this was female slavery and that sex with women for money was exploitation. The girl with a python embrace was calling me "my honey." She was trying to drag me into a dark corner. Oscar and Gunther were laughing at me. She was laughing too. "Come, my honey. Come!" she said. "I know you like me."

At that moment, an older sailor cut his way through the crowd and yelled, "Cynthia. It's me. Your honey. Your money honey!" She threw herself into his open arms and curled up against his chest. A look of incredible contentment spread across the sailor's face as if he had just been admitted to paradise.

I zigzagged back to my friends and got in the back of the booth they had secured so I could watch the action but not be hauled off into the shadows again.

Oscar was talking to two squirming girls who looked as if they were trying to escape his clutches. "You gotta love the navy," he said. "They told me once that the navy is nothing but a bunch of rum, sodomy, and the lash." Many years later I came across that exact expression again, spoken by none other than Winston S. Churchill in a biography about his younger years when he was First Lord of the Admiralty.

I really wanted to see the Hall of Flowers. I had heard about this place before. What a beautiful name for a whorehouse, I thought. Beautiful. In fact, the name was so in keeping with the kind of language used in the sex instruction book given to me by Chaplain Peeples that I wondered whether a clergyman had given this establishment that name in gratitude (for who knows what). The Hall of Flowers. The Hall of Flowers. It was so exquisitely suggestive of a carnal paradise. I made a mental note to tell you all about this in ten days, when the *Shangri-La* dropped anchor for the last time in Yokosuka.

So we left the Mermaid Bar and passed in front of the grimy little Luk Kwok Hotel on Gloucester Road, where location crews were already filming street scenes for *The World of Suzie Wong*. (The hotel was redubbed the Nam Kwok in the film.) A tall Englishman, dressed in a rumpled light tropical suit, was talking to one of the members of the film crew. He had a long, somber face shaped like the figure 8. The fingers of his right hand were stained brown with nicotine. I heard a murmur going through the crowd of spectators, some of whom were pink-faced British residents of Hong Kong who had been drinking heavily.

"That's him," I heard a voice say. "Yes, that's him. Ian Fleming. Mr. James Bond. He's been doing one of his books here. Nice chap. Really nice chap. He drinks one bottle of the best gin every day! Holds the world record for drinking consecutive vodka martinis. Fourteen. Just like that."

We continued on until finally, up a wet, dank alley near the Wah Hong Healthy Center Spa and lots of other businesses stacked on top of each other five and six stories high and painted pink and gold and red, with names like High Class Beauty Parlor or Romance Club or Model Dancers, we came across the Hall of Flowers. It was not easy to see the small painted sign because of the dense arrays of laundry drying on bamboo poles projecting from each balcony. But this was indeed the Hall of Flowers, Yuki. I knew it was because I had been told by the same chief petty officer who strongly recommended clean genitals that a giant Sikh would be standing at the doorway with an elephant gun. Of course, I did not believe him at the time. But sure enough, there was the Sikh wearing a dark blue turban and khaki shorts and holding a massive shotgun in his hands. He gave us the glance of an eagle about to kill a rat or a mongoose about to bite into the neck of a cobra. His terrifying eyes were set impossibly deep in his face, and his skin had the patina of copper.

"Good afternoon, gentlemen," he said in an unexpectedly soft and gentle voice. "You will be wanting to see the young ladies?"

We nodded, vigorously.

"You have the required condoms?"

Gunther and I pulled condoms from our pockets and waved them. In fact, I pulled out two condoms. I hastily handed the souvenir rubber to Oscar, who was still staring up at the man as if he was never going to move a muscle again.

"Yes. I see you have come equipped," the Sikh said. "You are gentlemen. Very good. Very good."

He turned and whistled sharply.

Out from the shadows popped a tiny child about eleven or twelve years old. She wore cotton pajamas with a pattern of forget-me-nots on them. She had bare feet. She took my hand.

"I will show the way," she said in precise, British-accented English.

"What's your name?" I asked as we began to ascend the stairs in the vast antique building with whitewashed walls clad in molds of many colors.

"I am Cloudlet," she said.

I did not quite understand what she said. "You are what?" I asked. "Claudette?"

"No. I am Cloudlet. You know, like a tiny cloud floating across the sea."

"Really? Your name is Cloudlet? But why? How did you get that name?"

"I am not a sing-song girl," she said. "I am much too young. I am your guide. But all girls in the Hall of Flowers have special names. For example: Pine. Simplicity. Bright Pearl. Green Fragrance. White Fragrance . . . When we start working here the owner gives us a name from his favorite book."

"Oh. And what book is that?"

"It is *The Sing-song Girls of Shanghai*," the little voice said. "The owner says it is a very famous book much loved by men. But I am too young to read it and also I am a girl. Good girls should not read those kind of books. But a young man like you *should* read that book, I think . . . Maybe it is not in English. Do you read Chinese?"

"Read Chinese! Oh no. I am sorry. No. I wish I could."

"That is very good," Cloudlet said, shaking my hand. "Very good. Yes, please learn Chinese right away."

She told us, now that we had climbed three sets of stairs to a hallway heavily perfumed with jasmine and patchouli, that there were ten doors ahead of us, each with a large black number appearing on a white enamel plaque. Behind each door was a "one-woman brothel," so named because although whorehouses were illegal, it was not illegal for individual women to sell sex.

This was the kind of story I could not tell you back then, Yuki. You told me I needed to grow up and I suppose I thought that this was one way of doing it. Did you know I was a virgin? I feel embarrassed now because I do not know the answer.

Gunther was assigned to number 4. Oscar was given number 6.

The child turned to me. "You," she said, "will have a very special room. It is number ten. I decide which number goes with which customer. I have been trained. I look at the man's face. I read the face. You have a number ten face. Come with me, please."

"Wait a minute," I said. "Number ten? In Japan that means it is very bad. It is the worst possible thing. In Japan, number one is the very best."

"That may be," said the displeased child. "But here at the Hall of Flowers, number ten is Heaven. And I can see that you are a virgin. It is written in your face. V-I-R-G-I-N! V-I-R-G-I-N! I got top marks for spelling at Catholic school. Virgins are very important to Catholics. My English is good, I think."

Indeed, Cloudlet's English was good. Not only was it precise and daintily spoken, she was a profound child: small, yes, but also strangely and prematurely adult. I was startled. I felt like an idiot. My face turned bright red, and I brushed it with my hand several times, wondering whether I could erase what Cloudlet had seen there. Gunther was looking anxiously back at me over his shoulder. He paused in front of door 4. He knocked. The door, covered with mysterious stickers and red-and-gold good-luck charms, creaked open, and a thin naked arm shot out, grabbed Gunther's sleeve, and pulled him inside with a whoosh, followed by a series of high-pitched giggles.

Oscar rubbed his hands joyfully. "Now," he exclaimed. "Now!" He knocked at number 6. A thin voice came drifting out of the room like a puff of smoke—"Yesssss? Yesssss, please," the voice said—and again a hand appeared and pulled the eager Oscar, who was grinning so hard there were tears in his eyes, inside the room. There was a muffled crash. There was something that sounded like a bounce or a bump. And then there was silence.

Cloudlet gripped my hand more tightly and led me to the end of the hall to number 10. The child insisted that she be the one to knock on the door. She spoke in English. "Madame," she announced. "A guest for you."

Ooooh, I thought, my heart almost flying apart. Madame! Madame! Actually, I thought that would be a perfect form of address for you, Yukiko! Yes. I liked the sound of that and I was sure that Commander Crockett and maybe even Chaplain Peeples would be impressed.

The door opened slowly. Very slowly. I heard the shuffle of feet away from the door. I could smell cabbage being boiled and maybe a hint of onion. Some kind of highly emotional piano concerto was playing, almost drowning out a voice that I will never forget. "For me, a guest?" the voice said. The voice sounded Russian. The music sounded like Pyotr Ilyich Tchaikovsky, maybe. A homosexual composer! My father had always derided Tchaikovsky for that and for being "too emotional, like a girl." Now my heart was panicking. Russians! Communists! Spies!

"Is he a very nice young man?" the voice asked.

"Oh yes, Madame," Cloudlet said with a little dance. "I am holding his hand. He is a virgin, guaranteed."

"Come inside," the Russian voice demanded. "Let me see this virgin man."

I pushed the door open. Silk gossamer scarves in many colors were hanging from the high ceiling. They dangled all the way to the carpeted floor. To get to the sofa near the window I had to bend this way and that. The scarves felt like cobwebs.

"A spider," I thought. I was alarmed. "Another spider!"

I separated the scarves in front of the shape reclining on the velvet cushions of the ornately carved sofa. There, in the sunlight, was a woman in her forties or fifties in a billowing lime-green nightgown with a series of bright peach ribbons down the front. The nightgown was swollen with her enormous breasts. The woman's green eyes glinted in the merciless light. Her dyed blond hair was spread out on the sofa behind her head as if she were a corpse floating in a cold, cold pond. She extended an arm in my direction, nodded her head to me, and then lifted her hand for me to kiss.

"I am Veronika," she said in a whisper. "I will take care of you. Sit down with me. Close your eyes. Dream."

I did not close my eyes because they were fixed on a series of sepia-toned photographs taken sometime long, long ago. The portraits were hanging on the wall behind the old cast-iron bed whose mattress was so high off the floor I would have had to climb up there even though I was six feet tall. The women in the photographs wore large hats with ostrich feathers and were dressed in long high-necked gowns with very tight bodices. They had imperial looks on their thin faces. The men wore uniforms from another age bearing clusters of medals. Their faces were arrogant. They had waxed their long mustaches. Some of them wore monocles. The women in the photos sat on chairs and the men stood behind them, rigidly at attention, as if they had abducted these women from looted palaces.

"My ancestors," Madame Veronika said. "My uncles and grandfathers. My mother and aunts and grandmothers. We are White Russians. We fought for the czar against the accursed Bolsheviks. Now we live in exile in this shithole of a place. A shithole! And to think we were counts and countesses!"

There was sudden color in her otherwise pale, pale face, as if she had suddenly applied rouge to the layer of talcum powder dusted all over her body.

She rose to full height in front of me. She was taller than I was. She pulled me toward her. Her nightgown was floor length as if she had dressed to go to a ball. There was no warmth in that body. I did not get the same rush of mad heat and musk from her that I did when you were close to me, Yuki-chan. There was no sweat, no moisture at all on this body. She was using her long fingers to pull my sailor's jumper over my head.

I stared at her and she flinched. "Do not look at me with such eyes," she said suddenly. "Do not look into my eyes. Do not look at me. Do not look . . . Enjoy!"

This was not what I expected.

This was no sing-song girl. This was not a River Blossom or a Belle Tang or a Flora Zhan shyly tempting me. There was no slit skirt, no cheongsam, no golden legs, no teasing, no featherlike touching or sudden groping, no deep kissing, no rubbing, no writhing, no clutching, no ecstasy at all.

"I am sorry, Madame," I said. "This is not what I was looking for."

I expected her to be angry. But she looked forlorn and gave a smile of regret.

"I understand," she said. "You are polite. That is nice. Go quietly. Leave me now."

She went back to the sofa and arranged her body and her nightgown and her hair as if she were laying herself in her grave.

"One of these long, long days," she said, "after you get much older, you will know what it is like to lose your precious youth."

"This is not about youth," I tried to explain. "This is about something I wanted to remember forever, and that something does not exist. I guess I was looking for paradise."

I looked down at her.

I reached out to touch her hand. She flinched.

"No. Please," Madame Veronika said. "Don't do that. Don't be gentle with me. If you do that I will cry, and that will never do. I do a lot of weeping on bright sunny days like this when I am shut up in the Hall of Flowers."

Chapter 17

INAPPROPRIATE THINKING

I have said that all the reputedly powerful reactionaries are merely paper tigers. The reason is that they are divorced from the people. Look! Was not Hitler a paper tiger? Was Hitler not overthrown? I also said that the tsar of Russia, the emperor of China and Japanese imperialism were all paper tigers. As we know, they were all overthrown. US imperialism has not yet been overthrown and it has the atom bomb. I believe it also will be overthrown. It, too, is a paper tiger.

> —From a speech by Mao Tse-Tung
> at the Moscow Meeting of Communist and
> Workers' Parties, November 18, 1957

I made a quick exit from the Hall of Flowers. Cloudlet was not visible, but I could hear her singing somewhere, a cheerful children's song that found its way out through the iron bars over the open windows. It was a lullaby, maybe. But who would sing lullabies to a baby who would end up working in a place like this? What would be your opinion, Yukiko? I was left with such a strange feeling. What a world it is, I told myself. The song went on and on, and in the streets below young sailors were making pilgrimages to the Hall of Flowers, as we had done. They were laughing and shouting. None of the Chinese in the street appeared to pay any attention to them. They were too busy hawking their dumplings and pocketing coins. This was all commerce and profit. I vowed to try to find Paul Feng and to thank him once more for *An Outline History of China*, which examined the many humiliations China suffered at the hands of foreign powers but did not mention the existence of anything like the Hall of Flowers.

I was embarrassed and disgusted and intrigued, all at once. Was there an adjective for that triple combination? I wondered. If not, maybe it was my responsibility to invent one. What kind of human being would employ a child who got high marks at school to guide sailors at a place like that? I was hit by an involuntary shudder, mixed with guilt, thinking about it. Cloudlet, skilled at sizing up clients and selecting appropriate prostitutes, was in some ways more of an adult than I was. What would be her fate? Where were her parents? Would she get a scholarship to go to university? Or would she become a sing-song girl, and then a madam, and was this how capitalism worked?

I remembered something else Cloudlet had told me on the way up the stairs, Yuki.

"Sing-song girls are like the moon. Doesn't it make you feel good to look at that new moon? But then the moon becomes an old moon. No one wants to look at that. Do you know what I mean? Have you tried looking at the moon?" She said the girls looked at it all the time at the Hall of Flowers. They saw the moon when they looked in the mirror. A moon face stares back at them. It is a very long stare indeed.

Was Cloudlet talking of the impact that the wear and tear of a hard life had on one's beauty, or was she talking about the nature of beauty? I wondered. Was she talking about beauty and tragedy, or are those two things related, Yuki? Maybe I should have asked her. Child that she was, she probably would have known the answer. I thought of you and all those phases of your life I knew so little about, despite many hours of conversation, despite friendship, despite an intimacy I did not understand.

I was picking my way among a squatting swarm of street vendors who had steaming white dumplings packed with shrimp and other morsels of the sea laid out on huge bamboo trays. I was heading first for the Hong Kong ferry and the short trip across the harbor to Kowloon, where Chaplain Peeples had asked me to meet him at three o'clock sharp to help distribute toys from Operation Handclasp to orphans housed on the edge of what he called the Walled City. It was like the casbah of Pépé Le Moko, he said: a six-acre citadel of ten thousand people off-limits to foreigners and full of Communists and criminals who were so dangerous that the Hong Kong police did not dare to enter its densely packed hideouts where even sunlight did not penetrate. And yet Hong Kong was a British crown colony. The British—my countrymen—knew about the Hall of Flowers. They knew about the Walled City. They knew about the gambling, the opium, and the regular Triad gang killings done by the 14K and the Sun Yee On. But they welcomed our sailor dollars. They had their clubs, their privileges, their cricket pitch, their churches, their mansions. Some kept Chinese mistresses. They were comfortably pink and fat. They claimed to be champions of democracy. But it was all a house of cards, I decided in a fit of rage. It was a lie, as was the slogan used by the *Shangri-La* in the publicity for Operation Handclasp: "Man o' War with Men of Peace." I was so embarrassed by the fact that I dreamed up that slogan without much thought, not understanding that its contradictory nature could give comfort to those who might wage nuclear war. Maybe I should ask Chaplain Peeples about these facts of life, I thought. "These are moral issues, right?" I was in an indignant hurry now. "These issues are packed with moral contradictions." But who can define what is moral and what is not? The United States? Britain? China? Japan? Who could I ask about this? So far, no one was listening. If Chaplain Peeples could not enlighten me then I would turn to you, I decided.

The chaplain had given me some Hong Kong dollars to pay for a taxi ride to the orphanage. I arrived just before the appointed hour. The staff was gathered in front of the small brick building with about thirty of the children, who ranged from infants to teenagers. When I stepped out of the cab they began applauding, but then the applause stopped when they saw it was just a sailor, and the sailor was not hauling a big bag of candy and toys. A small man with a raisin-size pimple on the tip of his nose shook my hand. He was talking to me rapidly. I could understand only bits and pieces of his English. And I was distracted by the pimple. So I smiled and nodded and hoped that Chaplain Peeples would not be far behind.

A couple of the little boys were curious about my uniform, Yuki. Oh, you would have laughed, you would have laughed! They pulled at the white cotton legs of my pants. One boy lifted up the cuff and began pulling at the hair on my leg. I looked at the small man for help. He used the flat of his hand to whack the boy behind the ear, and the boy began howling. Then a lot of the children started crying. It did not seem to be a very auspicious start to what the chaplain believed would be a joyous occasion of great benefit to the public image of the United States and its navy. About thirty minutes went by, and I was becoming anxious. A young woman who appeared to be a nurse asked me in good British English if the gifts were really coming. She was annoyed.

"I told our director that this would be a publicity stunt," she announced. She looked at me. "False promises. Late. They don't telephone to say sorry . . . typical Americans," she said.

"I agree," I said.

"What do you mean by 'I agree'? You are one of them."

I shook my head. "I am wearing this uniform but I am not an American citizen."

"Oh," she said. "I am sorry. Well, look. I look as if I am Chinese and I am wearing this nurse's uniform. I am a nurse. But actually I am British."

"I am British too."

We started laughing. She threw her hands in the air and directed a stream of rapid-fire Cantonese at the small man with the pimple, who was obviously the director. He clapped his hands and laughed, and the children started laughing too.

"Would you like some tea?" asked the nurse, whose name was Lydia Wong. It was the first time I had tasted Lapsang souchong, which smelled of burned pine and tar. If I drink it nowadays I am reminded immediately of that day when I was a stand-in for the US Navy. "Do you like this tea?" the nurse asked. "This is a poor man's tea, made from the most inferior tea leaves. It is roasted, and that way the flavor is released. It is very good for sex. It is good for women before sex. I always drink it."

A horn honked at the approach to the orphanage. It was Chaplain Peeples, resplendent in his tropical whites and gold gilt and displaying an array of campaign ribbons across his chest. He paused to wipe a streak of dirt off his white shoes. He was purer than purity itself. The children were astonished but then they surged toward him when the taxi driver began extracting six sacks of those toy firearms and teddy bears out of the cab.

"Rogers," he bellowed. As usual, he was angry with me, for which there would be no explanation. "Get over here!"

I looked at the nurse and gave her a wink, Yuki. The wink made her blush. She was still sipping her cup of Lapsang souchong.

"Yes, sir," I said. I was grinning because I wondered, in a moment of fantasy, if he would ask me whether I had brought the sex manual with me when I went to the Hall of Flowers. But he said nothing about that. He was huffing and puffing, and I sensed he was displeased that I had arrived before him.

So, to embarrass him, I asked what had made him late. I made sure the director and the nurse were close enough to listen in. I also was wishing the director would unleash those two little boys again so Chaplain Peeples could have them pull at his hairy leg. "I am sorry you were late," I said. "What held you up, sir?"

Behind me, I heard Nurse Wong say, "Yes. Why are you late, Chaplain Peeples?"

The chaplain did not answer because the kids were swarming the sacks. He began gently pushing the children back, patting them on the head, which I knew from the cultural awareness class I had attended on the ship was an offense to human dignity in many Asian cultures, as was displaying the sole of one's shoe.

I wagged my finger at him.

"What are you attempting to do, Rogers?" he demanded.

I did not feel like explaining myself. "It is nice to see you here, sir," I said. "The children are very excited. We were all worried about you. Nurse Wong was very nice. She brought me a cup of amazing tea, which she said she also drinks because it is—" I caught myself and stopped.

Of course, Yuki, the children had a wonderful time chasing the chaplain and me around the school grounds. There must have been about twenty toy rifles as well as assorted toy handguns, guns that fired caps—*bang, bang, bang*—and even a BB gun or two that went *pop, pop, pop*. The chaplain was saying "Ho, ho, ho!" in a very loud voice, as if it were Christmas and not a very hot afternoon in late August. After the kids had ambushed and killed him several times, the chaplain made a speech. I knew what he was going to say because I had written it.

"Ladies and Gentlemen. On behalf of the United States of America and the United States Navy and also with the best wishes of the children of the United States, we hope you enjoy these gifts given to you as part of Operation Handclasp. These gifts came to you from freedom-loving boys and girls who hope you share their democratic values. I hope you have fun. Thank you to the director for inviting us to come here."

I heard Nurse Wong translating the speech for the director. The director was shaking his head and looking chagrined. I asked the nurse if there was a problem.

"No problem," she said quietly. "Except that we did not issue an invitation. If we knew he was going to make a speech like that we would have preferred to come to your ship ourselves to pick up the gifts. I said this was a publicity stunt, and it is."

The chaplain and I shared a taxi for the ride back to the ferry. He sat there, erect, his knees touching each other, his officer's peaked hat squarely on his head, his hands clasped in front of him as if he were the torchbearer for Operation Handclasp, which of course he was. I was just his minion.

"Nice speech," he said. "Good job!"

"Chaplain, I have a question," I said respectfully. "I need your opinion. I need guidance, I guess."

"Yes, son," he replied.

"Sir, I don't understand the contradictions I see everywhere here," I began. "This is a British-run colony. According to the material you gave us that was published in the ship's newspaper, this is a democracy. To me, democracy means moral government as well as personal freedom within the framework of the law. But let's face it: Hong Kong is a dump. It is full of vice. Children work in the brothels. The US Navy comes in and out of the harbor, and the guys go ashore and drink and spend their money—on vice. Even this toy thing doesn't sit squarely with me. We used a warship to bring toys. We talk about democracy and freedom. But isn't this really an attempt to buy the loyalty of people who are not necessarily America's friends?"

Chaplain Peeples stared at me. He looked deeply offended.

"Rogers . . . Rogers. You have a very cynical view of the world for someone so young and naive. Who have you been listening to recently? What have you been reading? You write a wonderful speech like that for me, but it sounds like you detested the whole thing. You detest the United States Navy! You are an immigrant . . . don't forget that. You enlisted in this man's navy . . . don't forget that. We are not perfect, but we really are the hope of the world."

"Yes, sir," I said. "Yes, sir. But I am confused."

"I can see that."

"Nothing makes sense. Nothing! I have just turned twenty and I thought I would not have these kinds of doubts anymore. But I do. One of my supervisors told me that the US Navy did not pay me to think. But I can't help thinking. I can't help noticing certain discrepancies, like this whole 'freedom' and 'democracy' thing. I don't know who or what to believe anymore, because these concepts don't match reality." I am sure we talked about this paradox, Yukiko, in one of those long conversations at the White Rose. I don't remember Mama ever telling you to serve other customers. She would lean against one of the columns festooned with plastic white roses, and she would stare, and stare, and stare.

"You are an honest person," the chaplain said. "But this is really inappropriate thinking. You need to get shipshape and get over it. What if there was a war? If you had to drop a bomb or fire a gun, would you engage in this kind of internal debate?"

We had arrived at the ferry near the grand old Peninsula Hotel, which had a line of Rolls-Royces parked in front and groups of foreign businessmen in pressed suits, and navy officers in full-dress regalia, milling about outside. I said good-bye to the chaplain and left the scene as quickly as I could to catch a ferry that looked as if it was close to departing.

The chaplain headed for the hotel, with the big loping strides of an athlete, not pausing to look this way or that but cutting across a street full of taxis and trucks as if he were a torpedo. Unexpectedly, I felt a twinge of sympathy for him. He was single-minded, like a torpedo. But was that bad? Was it pathetic? What had they taught him when he studied theology?

Thirty minutes later I was back in "The Wanch," as we sailors called Wan Chai, cutting through the streets to look for the bookstore where I had met Paul Feng in June. It took me a while to locate it. I was distracted by all my nagging doubts. But there it was. There was a display of the latest issue of *China Reconstructs* in the window. The yellow cover was decorated with black paper cutouts of butterflies, water buffaloes, men and women carrying burdens, peasants hoeing fields. It was almost dusk. I did not think that Paul Feng would be there but then I heard his voice from behind the cash register saying, excitedly, "Mr. Paul! Mr. Paul! Here you are again."

He rang up my copy of *China Reconstructs* and asked me whether I would like to attend "a meeting." He said he had told his friends about his "young American friend" and he wanted me to meet them. I expressed some concern, explaining that I would probably get into trouble if I did not head straight to the bars and get drunk but instead socialized with intellectuals. Paul Feng laughed at this. "It's very funny," he said. "You are developing an acute sense of irony. I think you will be appreciated."

I did not have much judgment, I suppose, at that age. You told me, Yuki, "A man should do what is right. Use your instinct. Use your mind. You don't have much experience. So you don't have much choice when it comes to making a decision.

Just do what you have to do, learn from your mistakes, and enjoy everything else . . . Go out into the world. Of course, if you make mistakes, I want to hear about them. I make many mistakes. I have many regrets. That is what makes me such an interesting woman."

You had given me once, written on a scrap of paper, the lyrics to "You Don't Know What Love Is," a song by Don Raye. Billie Holiday recorded a famous version of it. "Keep this and read it later, dear Paul, and read it and read it again," you said. I noticed you had that look on your face that told me this was a lesson I had to learn. "Sometimes in this life you have to risk *everything*, or else you will never know. Sometimes you have to crash, you have to burn. You have to cry out in pain. You have to experience something that cannot be understood just by reading books or writing poetry, like love. You have to go to the highest mountain. You have to go to the deepest valley. You have to search for the love that is waiting for you. And when you find it, please remember those who have gone before you to find what cannot be denied."

> You don't know what love is
> Until you've learned the meaning of the blues
> Until you've loved a love you've had to lose.
> You don't know what love is.

Yes, I did look at it, again and again, when we were at sea. And I had the sudden desire to run to you and cry out something that I thought was forbidden: "I do, Yuki. I really love you." Yet that would have been a simple risk to take. It was not even profound. It was true and not true that I loved you from the moment we first met. I know that to be true because here and now, more than fifty years after, I still remember and the memory makes me shiver as if it had happened in the dead of winter instead of in the heat of summer.

I was thinking about all this as Paul Feng guided me through the streets. People nodded to him as if they knew him. They looked me up and down as if I were a piece of offal. I began to feel unhappy, and it showed on my face.

"Don't worry, Paul," he said in a kindly fashion. "They are not used to seeing sailors in this part of the city. You are a strange sight to them. Sailors do not have a good reputation. Some of us look at sailors like you as the fist of American imperialism. But don't forget, this is 1959 and China is in chaos. Please excuse our anger and our despair."

"In chaos?" All I could see around me on the streets of Hong Kong was chaos, Yuki. Noise. Dirt. Rot. Decay. Masses of people foraging for what might help them survive.

"You should know that the Great Leap Forward, which you have been reading about in *China Reconstructs*, has failed," he said. I couldn't see his face. It was hidden by shadows. But I could hear the anguish of an idealism crushed. "Hundreds of thousands of people are dying in a very cruel famine caused by bad policy. Mainland China is only a few miles away. This crisis is happening all around you, right now. The Chinese government wants to arrest many thousands of young intellectuals, like myself, who were invited to put up posters that frankly aired our dissent. Yes. This really *is* happening now, at the end of what we Chinese call the Hundred Flowers Campaign. The government encouraged us to speak up and be critical, and then it turned on us like a mad dog. People like me ran away to Hong Kong. This is not my home. But here I am safe. I hate it here. But it is safe."

"You mean you took a big risk and now you have to deal with the consequences?" I asked. "You suffered and you learned something?"

"Yes. Something like that. We are both young men. I believe that young men in every nation share the same fate, even if they do not share the same experiences. We are the most vulnerable. We are the first to know fear. We are the first to die." I think you also told me that, Yuki.

Chapter 18

FRIENDS AND ENEMIES

To fall in love is easy, even to remain in it is not difficult; our human loneliness is cause enough. But it is a hard quest worth making to find a comrade through whose steady presence one becomes steadily the person one desires to be.

—Anna Louise Strong, American journalist and friend of modern China

There was a big round Formica table at the back of a restaurant that had unpainted concrete walls, a concrete floor, and a concrete ceiling. It reminded me of the inside of a giant sarcophagus. There were some modest pinup posters with impossibly innocent Chinese girls clutching pink parasols and ripe peaches. Long industrial neon lights buzzed from above, attracting swarms of insects. The flickering fluorescence made the faces of everyone bent over big steaming bowls of noodles look as if they had been freshly exhumed from their graves. This kind of light exaggerated everyone's expressions. Some of Paul Feng's friends gathered around the table looked harshly aghast. Other faces were blank, as if they belonged to someone who had spent months in solitary confinement.

Smiles became grimaces. Stares penetrated to the bone. There were eight of his fellow runaways. At least two of them gave me shy waves, and I headed toward those two after Paul Feng made a brief, earnest introduction.

I wondered, Yuki, if this was going to be the type of learning experience you recommended: an experience in which I would either succeed or fail. I sensed there would be no middle ground in a place like this.

"This is the young sailor I told you about," Paul Feng announced in English. "Please welcome him. He reads *China Reconstructs*. I gave him a history of China and the story of Ah-Q. Let's compare experiences and learn something. We are all human beings, after all."

Not everyone was happy to see me. One man, with the extraordinarily long fingernails of the classic literati that curved and twisted backward down to his palms, pushed his bowl forward. He sat back and spat his disgust on the floor. Three or four others were pelting Paul Feng with angry questions, and one man was shaking his fist at me in a gesture I had seen in news film clips that showed hundreds of Chinese, faces emanating an intensely personal rage, denouncing US imperialism.

Paul Feng stood there quietly, nodding his head slowly as he acknowledged their outbursts. He turned to me with a friendly smile on his face and said, in English again, "This, my friends, is what we were told is the enemy. This young man in his white uniform who sits down with us so peacefully . . . This young man is the enemy. Or is it possible he is our friend?"

A homely young woman to my left, who wore round reading glasses and had a small stack of books on the table, leaned toward me and whispered.

"I am Irene Chen and you are Mr. Paul, and you and I are not enemies."

I nodded. My face turned red. "Yes, Irene," I said. "We are not enemies. Our countries are enemies. Is it possible for you and me to be friends?"

"I would like that," she said, in a very tiny voice. In that unlikely moment, a slow ballad sung by Frank Sinatra drifted out of the semidarkness at the back of the restaurant where the kitchen was located. An emotion born out of a desire for impossible things gripped my heart and made me gulp. I imagined moving slowly across a dance floor with Irene Chen in my arms and then—in a flash—I recalled you, Yuki-chan, telling me that this was one of your favorite songs. And in that stillborn fantasy I was dancing with you, and you had your arms round my neck, and I bent down to kiss you.

But before that could happen, Miss Chen leaned over again and whispered in a breath made hot with chili sauce, "I really love this song. It's dreamy."

When she said that, she was suddenly transformed from plain to beautiful. "Dreamy?" I asked, not having much idea what it means to be a woman.

"Perchance to dream," she said. "Shakespeare. Hamlet! 'To die, to sleep. To sleep, perchance to dream.' Forbidden literature in China. Sinatra too, forbidden... So sad. No chance to dream."

She and I watched the battle of words around the table. Someone in the kitchen put on the recording, Sinatra's "All My Tomorrows" (lyrics by Sammy Cahn), again.

Today I may not have a thing at all except for just a dream
    or two,

But I've got lots of plans for tomorrow, and all my tomorrows belong to you.
Right now it may not seem like spring at all, we're drifting
and the laughs are few.

Irene Chen slid a book across the table to me. "Please read
this," she said. "It was written by a great American journalist, Anna Louise Strong. She is a powerful advocate for my
country. It is a book that will tell you about the success of the
Chinese revolution thanks to the leadership of the Chinese
Communist Party. My father took part in our revolution. He
was a writer who believed in the possibility of a new China.
This book is called *The Chinese Conquer China*." She looked at
me quizzically. "I think you understand. We took our country
back from the imperialists: the Americans, the Japanese, the
British, and all those other foreign countries that humiliated
us for two hundred years. We seized our country. We defeated
the corrupt dictatorship. It was a glorious moment. We were
so proud of being Chinese. And then . . . then . . ." Her voice
diminished, and she looked away. "Now I am in this British
colony and I have lost all contact with my family. My mother.
My father. My sisters. All gone, not knowing. And why?
Because I dared to criticize in public a national education
policy that I believed did not serve the people."

Irene, like everyone else at the table, had fallen victim
somewhere between 1956 and 1958 to the aftermath of a brief
period of liberalization authorized by Chairman Mao. The
Chinese leader had declared, "The policy of letting a hundred
flowers bloom and a hundred schools of thought contend is
designed to promote the flourishing of the arts and the progress

of science." But Mao reversed this brief period of free speech when unexpectedly strong critiques of Communist leadership and policy became commonplace. One million teachers and intellectuals were deported to the countryside to do forced manual labor, and many died of starvation and disease in the Cultural Revolution in the 1960s.

I picked up the small volume Irene Chen pushed toward me. "I would be happy to read *The Chinese Conquer China*," I said. "But my ship will leave soon and if I take it I can't return it to you. I am sorry."

"Don't worry about that. This is for you," she said loudly, so that the others at the table took notice. "Here . . . let me write inside . . . 'To my dear American friend from the land of Shangri-La' . . . There! Look, everyone! Look at this! I am celebrating a friendship." I thought that you would approve of that moment, Yukiko, although you and I had gone beyond friendship into another realm unfamiliar to both of us.

The Chinese Conquer China had been published in December 1949, two months after Mao Tse-tung proclaimed the establishment of the People's Republic of China from a balcony in Beijing's Tiananmen Square to a joyous multitude. Irene Chen would have been about fifteen at that time. What am I going to do with this book, I wondered? If I bring it back to the *Shangri-La* I am probably going to be arrested. I knew it would get me into trouble. The chaplain would say the book was forbidden. I looked around the table at the mix of fear, rage, and wonder. How is it possible, I asked myself, for two countries to be such ferocious foes at the same time Irene Chen was doing her best to make me feel welcome? Why had the dreams of millions of Chinese who had welcomed the revolution in 1949 been dishonored? Why do great notions crumble so easily? Why were the majority of Irene's companions still criticizing Paul Feng for bringing me to their table? What was it about Paul Feng that caused him to dare to make a friend out of this young foreigner in an American uniform? And why was someone playing that Frank Sinatra recording over and over again?

Paul Feng and Irene Chen escorted me back to the dock where sampans ferried sailors back to their ships. I had never been given a chance to say anything.

"I am sorry," Paul said. "It appears that some people—even good people like my friends—need enemies to make sense of their misery."

"Yes," Irene said. "Please do not be discouraged. We will not forget you. Make good use of your youth and get a good education. Remember who gave you that book and make sure you read it, please." She gave me a shy smile and shook my hand. She had a very strong grip.

Paul Feng did not speak. He looked as if he was still struggling with the idea that friendship has its limits, even if the offer of friendship is reciprocated. But he had courage, I thought. I envied him and his friends. I was experiencing the world from the comfort of a warship, where everything was planned and predictable. Paul and Irene could become dust, just like that, their lives snuffed out, and even if they lived they had no future.

I scrambled up the steel gangway to the deck of the *Shangri-La*, half expecting to encounter Oscar and Gunther there, or even Chaplain Peeples, prayer book in hand, full of loaded questions. Drunk and half-drunk sailors were stumbling or helping each other into the hatches leading to their bunks deep inside the ship, where the steel soaked up the heat from the tropical night. The heat was so intense it defeated the ship's rudimentary air-conditioning system and obliged swabbies, and maybe even officers too, to slumber in their skivvies and wake up feeling like slugs, soaked in the slime of their own sweat.

Waiting for me was a short note from you, Yukiko. I slipped into the hatch and descended to the compartment and to my bunk bed. I stretched out on the thinly padded cotton mattress laid on top of tightly stretched canvas. I slowly and carefully peeled open the envelope's flap. Inside were two sheets of paper, covered in handwriting and holding just a hint of your perfume.

A STARRY NIGHT

Dear Paul,

    Soon you will be leaving me. I will save my words and my thoughts until I see you again, hoping for such a special and beautiful happy goodbye. It will be enough for me if you hold my hand and sit side by side with me at the Mozart Café. I am going to ask Ito-san to play Debussy's so wonderful Nocturnes . . . his Nuages, his Fetes, his Sirenes . . . and also his La Mer—especially his Dialogue du vent et de la mer—because it is all about the deep ocean blue. You are a man of the ocean. You came to me from across the sea. And now you come back to me like seamen do, for just a few days.

Those days are your little gifts to me. In those days you may see me weeping. You may see me laughing. You may see a certain girl, a so ugly woman, look at you in a special way that you will never forget. No one will ever look at you like that again. When I look at you I want to have that memory of you in my mind forever. You will not forget how I studied your brown eyes, your thin lips, your poet's nose, and most importantly your smile when you know that I am watching you.

Yes, we can listen to Debussy. There will be no need to say anything. We will share the silence while the music plays. There is a women's chorus in Sirenes. There are no words. It is just soaring voices . . . those Sirens who made mariners afraid. As a Japanese woman, I believe those Sirens were just lonely, not bad, not dangerous. They were like a certain so sorry girl in Yokosuka who has been WAITING, WAITING, that's all.

Oh Paul-san, I so want to be able to sleep, remembering the way you looked in our last moments. I want to remember the morning your ship vanished over the horizon that God drew across the ocean so that a woman could say, "There he goes. I see him. I still see him. Oh no! Oh no! Now my love has gone." I want to remember how the sky looked, and the fog of the morning too, and the breeze stirring the flowers on the Paulownia so that the blue petals are falling.

Please do not be angry at me for this little note I send you. I can't help it. I have to write it. Maybe one day if you read this again you will have tears in your eyes. Those tears are my little gift to you. And let me tell you, sailor boy, if you have that emotion when you are an old man you will still know what love is.

Yesterday I was reading a very old scroll of poetry with Chinese characters drawn in ink by someone expert with the brush. I think a woman wrote those kanji because when I look closely I see that something, maybe rain drops, maybe tears, is still visible on the rice paper. This is from a collection of waka poems, written by Ariwara no Narihira in the Ninth Century.

> This is not the moon,
> Nor is it the spring
> Of other springs.
> But I alone
> Am still the same.

Love,
Yukiko

P.S. I had big trouble again. But now my problem is gone. I have room in my heart now so that I can say goodbye.

P.P.S. You remember that I like Franz Kafka? This is from my notebook. Please remember that Kafka wrote, "Now the Sirens have a still more fatal weapon than their song, namely their silence. And though admittedly such a thing never happened, it is still conceivable that someone might possibly have escaped from their singing; but from their silence certainly never." Yes, when we listen to Debussy, please remember that when we share the silence.

I put the letter back in the envelope and wondered. I laid the envelope on my chest.

After a couple of minutes I realized I had placed it on my heart. I could see the envelope moving slightly with each heartbeat and with each breath. I felt as if I was drifting, effortlessly, in the night breeze for destinations unknown.

I have lived a long time now, but I have never had that feeling again.

Chapter 19

WAITING WOMAN

Life in Japan may be compared to a scented bath which gives you electric shocks at unexpected moments. At least, I think that is as good a metaphor as any. . . . The first phase of sensuous and sensual delight is the tourist's inevitable reaction to a culture with a surface polish of utterly refined pretty-prettiness, smiling ceremonial, kneeling waitresses, paper-screen houses, dolls, kimonos, and, above all, an atmosphere with an erotic flicker like the crisp sparks of a comb drawn through a woman's hair—a guilt-free eroticism which Europe has not known since antiquity.

—Arthur Koestler,
from *The Lotus and the Robot*,
written after he visited Japan in 1959

The next morning I wanted to tell someone about my adventures ashore, which were now pursuing each other inside my head in a spitting and hissing blur. It was an exhilarating feeling. It was as if I had an excess of youth. The urge to pile one experience on top of the other and make sense of it all was too strong to resist now that I had completed my final liberty in Hong Kong. I had duty aboard the ship for the next two days as an on-call member of a firefighting team that had never aimed a high-pressure hose and would not know what to do if flaming gasoline poured into the hatches and corridors leading to our berths. My job was to man a simple handheld chemical fire extinguisher. The sorties into a series of port cities where my senses were overloaded had made me forget fire-drill procedures long ago. In two days we would be challenging our enemies in China again by cruising up and down and round and round just outside Chinese territorial waters, while on the mainland legions of workers, hoes over their shoulders, marched off to conquer the countryside and die in the many, many thousands.

I went to the chow hall to wolf down shit on a shingle—I had the most intense hunger. I heard the sound of Oscar's voice. He was being questioned by Chief Petty Officer Bobby Drybread, a navy yeoman with stupefying administration duties who had the ancillary job of being an enforcer on the ship's security detail. The chief, clipboard and pencil in hand, was telling Oscar in alarming language that Gunther had disappeared and that he might be dead. He wanted to know where and when it was that Oscar had last seen our friend. I held back and listened. I knew that trouble was coming and that would mean questions for me and maybe a summons from Commander Crockett or Chaplain Peeples.

"I didn't see him after we went to the . . . er . . . Hall of Flowers," Oscar said.

"What? What?" the chief asked. Clearly he had no idea what Oscar was talking about.

"The Hall of Flowers," Oscar said again. "It is famous, chief. The whole US Navy knows about that place, and if it has not been closed down it is because the chief of naval operations approves of it, don't you think?"

"What? What?" the exasperated chief demanded. He was wiping spittle from his cheek.

"Look, man—uh, sorry, 'chief'—the Hall of Flowers is the best-run educational institution for boys and girls on this side of the Pacific. I was happy to make a donation. Um . . . Gunther probably just missed the last boat—through no fault of his own, I am sure!"

Astonished because the chief was apparently buying into this explanation, I maneuvered forth to use my skills of deception and subterfuge. "He probably did not overstay his welcome," I said. "The Hall of Flowers is a very welcoming place. There is good security there too. I wouldn't worry too much."

"Well, look," the chief said. "Chaplain Peeples is very concerned about this, because Gunther is one of his assistants. He is going to put Gunther on report. The chaplain says that Gunther—like you, Rogers—is not an American citizen. He is a damned Nazi—I mean, he is German. And the chaplain says that any time a foreigner wearing the uniform of the US Navy is up to no good we can be sure he is vulnerable to exploitation and penetration by foreign espionage agents. All foreigners need watching, the chaplain says. And I am inclined to agree with him—not that I have any choice—because in my experience foreigners cannot be trusted. I don't care if the Hall of Flowers is a five-star university. If it is run by the Chinese, that school can't be trusted. If he is still at that place, they've put all kinds of Communist ideas in his head. You understand that, don't you, Rogers? Chaplain Peeples has already warned me about you, smart-ass!"

I cringed, Yukiko. You may remember how alarmed I could become when trouble was afoot and my fate was uncertain. I was thankful that I had tucked that copy of *The Chinese Conquer China* and the latest *China Reconstructs* into my pants when I got aboard the ship in the dark of night. I had hidden them under my mattress, saving them for those hours when I might sneak away to read them in my hideout above the captain's bridge. But I almost panicked when I began imagining Chaplain Peeples, or Chief Drybread, going through my possessions to search for un-American literature. I was sure they had already broken into Gunther's locker and had probably upended his mattress looking for documentation that Gunther was a spy or a degenerate or a dupe of the great Communist conspiracy to rule the world.

I told Oscar to stick around, and I raced back to my compartment, grabbed those items I knew would inflame the chaplain's imagination, and gave them to my pachuco friend, who took one look at them and said, simply, "Cool."

Later in the day there was still no Gunther. I was jumpy, an expression you thought was funny. I heard that a search party had been dispatched to Wan Chai. I also heard that certain members of the search party were extremely happy with their assignment: track down and apprehend Gunther Erlichmann at some kind of boys' and girls' school called the Hall of Flowers and make sure that you apologize to the schoolmistress for disturbing classes. That command, I knew all too well, had come directly from the chaplain.

Not much was happening on the firefighting front, so I decided to talk my way into the officers' quarters and head straight to the chaplain's chamber. The pilots who were also quartered there were familiar with me because of the work I did on the *News Horizon*, and they were always eager to lobby me for articles on themselves or their squadrons. They continued to ask if I knew any "college girls" ashore. Poor guys. They didn't have a clue.

I knocked on the chaplain's door. I heard him say, "Who is it?"

"It's Rogers, sir. Seaman Rogers."

There was a pause, a silence.

"R-e-a-l-l-y?" he said, dragging the word out slowly. "Come in here!"

I pushed open the door. Chaplain Peeples was sprawled in his green vinyl armchair. He looked exhausted and unhappy. Commander Crockett was standing behind the chaplain. He loomed over him with just a wisp of amusement on his rugged face.

"The Hall of Mirrors, Rogers," Peeples said. "The Hall of Mirrors!"

"Sir. Do you mean the Hall of Flowers?"

"The Hall of Flowers!" Crockett exclaimed. "I know that place." He silenced himself. But then he said, "The chaplain was under the impression that the missing seaman, your friend Gunther Erlichmann, had spent the night without authorization at an exclusive girls' school of some kind. Now we know! The Hall of Flowers! Goddamn it to hell, Rogers. Seaman Erlichmann is AWOL [absent without leave] and he is holed up, I am pretty damn sure, in a whorehouse, chaplain, a whorehouse!"

Chaplain Peeples inhaled deeply. He looked appalled. "My altar boy . . . Gunther?" he said. "I gave him so much good instruction."

Both men stared at me as if I were an agent of the devil.

"You," the chaplain said. "You, I expect such behavior from. But not Gunther. You, I suppose, fornicated at the Hall of Flowers. You defiled?"

"No, sir. Not I. There was this Russian woman and I didn't—"

"Russian! *Russian!*" Commander Crockett shuddered. His jowls shook. He smacked the side of his head. "Ha!" he exclaimed. "Russians. Goddamn Russians. Here we go again. Seaman Erlichmann is a dead man. A dead man! I am going to draw and quarter him myself, and you, Rogers, you! What will I do with you?"

Commander Crockett apologized to the chaplain for the profanity. And then, without saying another word and without looking at me, he left, slamming the door behind him so loudly that it sounded like a clap of thunder.

Chaplain Peeples shook his head in despair. "How is this possible?" he asked weakly. "How can a young man fall this low?"

There was a knock on the door. Chief Drybread burst in. "Chaplain! Chaplain!" he said. "We got him. He is in a Hong Kong hospital. He's in the nuthouse! He's sedated! They told me he is suffering from something called 'compassionate emotional exhaustion.' The poor kid! They said it is caused by a youthful mania or exuberance."

I had no idea what he was talking about.

Chaplain Peeples looked similarly confused. "So there is no crime?" he asked. "So Gunther is not exactly AWOL?"

"That's correct, sir," the chief said. "No crime. No AWOL. He is unconscious anyway. They gave him enough of a sedative that he's going to be sleeping for twenty-four hours. Too much of a good thing, according to one of the nurses. She said, 'He's just a boy.'"

"Did he say anything before they sedated him?" I asked.

"The nurse said he was speaking German when they found him, so they didn't know what he was saying . . . something about Wonder Bar."

By that evening the *Shangri-La* was smashing through huge waves somewhere northeast of Hong Kong and southwest of Taiwan. With each plunge of the ship, the waves exploded over the blunt bow. From my hideout above the bridge I could see spray ascending into the night sky, where the moon flickered every now and then through the clouds. I was listening for the chorus of the Sirens but all I could hear was the wail of the winds, now high, now low. Wedged into a corner of the tiny chamber, I thought about how you were preparing yourself for the last week we would be in port in Yokosuka. You wanted that to be a happy moment, Yuki. You wanted us to listen silently to Debussy.

You might cry. You might not cry. Your short life had been stalked by tragedy, but you had survived. A vast army of women—whole divisions and regiments of women—had lived through the war, even as their men died, their homes were destroyed, their families ripped apart. Two atomic bombs had been dropped on them, and they had done whatever was necessary to go on living. I remembered a news photo of an expressionless mother, the skin peeling off her face because of burns and radiation, breastfeeding her contented baby. The more I thought about this, rocked in my cradle by the storm, the more I was certain that these women of Japan were the heroes. In my mind, it did not matter if they were bar girls or *mamasan*s or prostitutes or factory workers or the 31,080 women who in the years between 1947 and 1959 became "war brides" of American servicemen, who were in love with them despite the damned regulations. In my mind, many women waited for a tender touch, a tender heart, a life worth living.

I thought of you at your house on the side of the mountain, waiting, waiting. I thought of you writing to me, sitting on the tatami matting, bent over the table with its very short legs, your typewriter positioned in front of you and your English dictionary close to your hand. I thought of all the effort you put into writing those letters and the absolute commitment you had made to have me as your purest love. I thought too of all the unanswered questions I had in my head, all the puzzles seemingly without solution, and of all the many things I had no hope of understanding or knowing because I did not speak Japanese.

I thought of Japan too. I thought of the sight of Fuji with the snowcapped peak that I could see through the mist each time the *Shangri-La* returned to Yokosuka. Fuji existed. It was not just something surreal. It was not just a mirage. It was not something imagined, something that only appeared in woodblock prints. I knew, even then, young though I was, how little Americans knew about this land they had occupied.

I thought of all the stereotypes that never acknowledged the possibility that you, Yukiko, and so many other Japanese, loved Debussy and Beethoven, loved jazz and Kafka and Sartre and, yes, even Kerouac. I thought also of your extreme finesse, and how you maintained it even in Honcho, with its bars and nightclubs promising cold beer and hot women. I thought of *enka*, the music you loved, and the singers Misora Hibari and Matsuo Kazuko and the lyrics we had shared as we became friends.

I thought of that afternoon when you were telling me about Manchuria and your certainty that although you were Japanese you were a different kind of Japanese and that your real home was not Japan but it was in Manchuria, and I could understand that a little because my real home was not the United States of America, it was England. We had both lost our birthplaces and our countries.

That afternoon, while you were explaining why you felt like an outsider, you told me excitedly that you had seen an early film by the great director Kurosawa Akira named *Shūbun* (*Scandal*, 1950). It starred the spectacular actor Mifune Toshiro, who was the bandit-rapist in *Rashomon*, and an actress with big eyes named Yamaguchi Yoshiko. In the film, Mifune plays a maverick artist on a motorcycle who goes on a painting trip to the countryside. He meets by chance Yamaguchi's character, a popular singing star looking for solitude. He offers her a ride. There is no romance, but a pulp magazine engineers a scandal after one of its photographers uses his trusty Leica to take a single picture of the artist and singer together.

"Well, Paul," you asked. "Do you know that Yamaguchi Yoshiko is from Manchuria, just like me?"

"Oh yes?" I asked.

"Yes, I am so proud of her. It makes me feel so happy. Do you know that just like me she speaks Chinese?"

"I did not know that."

"Yes. Like me, she had friends who were White Russians.

She had Jewish friends too. She is a coloratura soprano. Her father encouraged her musical talents, and she was taught how to sing by an Italian soprano married to a White Russian count—in Harbin!"

"Really?"

"Yes. If you watch that film you will see her singing Japanese songs. But do you know that during the war she sang Chinese songs and acted in Chinese films and that she truly thought of herself as Chinese, and the Chinese people believed that completely?"

I had to admit that was unusual.

"She became very famous in China. But she also became famous in Japan as the actress Ri Koran. It was another name she used. In China she was known as Li Xianglan. And now, after the war, she uses her birth name, Yamaguchi Yoshiko. When the war ended, in China they criticized her for being Japanese. But the Japanese criticized her for being too Chinese. Maybe you have heard the song 'China Night'?"

"Yes," I said. "Everyone on the *Shangri-La* knows '*Shina no yoru*.' You can't forget a tune like that. I don't know what it means but I have heard it so much that I can almost sing it in Japanese myself."

"Well, she is the one who sings that song," you said, laughing.

You reached into that notebook of yours. You pulled out a sheet of paper with an English translation you had done of the lyrics.

> What a night in China,
> I was waiting on the parapet

There was this girl in the rain,
The rouge on her cheeks
Like flowers was in bloom.
Forever, I will remember
Even after we separated,
Ah, China night,
A dream night.

Recently, Yuki, I came across "*Shina no yoru*" on an old Japanese LP probably brought back to the United States by a returning GI. The title of the album on the hot-pink cover, written in English in faux Oriental lettering, is *Japan Song: A Night of China and other GI Favorite Songs*. I listened to "Japanese Rhumba," "*Ginza kankan musume*," "Aloha Boogie," and "*Uramachi* Paradise." And then came "China Night," and immediately the conversation we had about Yamaguchi Yoshiko emerged from my memory as if it were my favorite scene from *Casablanca*.

I could hear you practicing with your *kokyū*—the ancient stringed instrument that came to Japan from China many centuries ago. You were seated cross-legged on the tatami with the *kokyū* held vertically in your lap. You were moving the taut horsehair bow slowly across the silk strings. You had a name for that tune, which for me was like no other. It spiraled upward into the night sky as if it were wind or a prayer.

"That is the old Chinese melody 'Stairway to Heaven,'" you said. "I like to sit alone, in the dark, like I did when I was a child in Manchuria. I use the bow like this, and the *kokyū* speaks for me."

Even all these years later I choked up, remembering that plaintive sound and how it gave voice to your loneliness.

"Memories and tears are locked together for all eternity, like lovers," you said. It is hard for me now to imagine one without the other.

Chapter 20

AM I OK?

I spent all my summer making plans for September. No longer . . . Now I spend the summer remembering plans I made that faded away, due partly to laziness and partly to carelessness. What's wrong with feeling nostalgic? It's the only distraction left for us with no faith in the future.

—The playwright Romano (Carlo Verdone) in the
film *La Grande Bellezza* (*The Great Beauty*, 2013)

I see myself as I was then with the supremely sweet sadness of old age, Yuki. I say "sweet sadness" because there is still so much yet to savor and so little I can forget. I am no longer innocent. However—and you would probably be delighted to know this—I am still just as intense. I spend hours considering every aspect of the issues confronting me now. If you could hear me having conversations with myself you might also wonder why sometimes I laugh out loud in delight when intensity results in inspiration, and why at other times I become reflective, especially when I have to pass my city's vast cemetery, with all that blinding white marble bearing so many fine words. Sometimes I remember one small thing you said. Yesterday I was laying out a gravel pathway in my cactus garden and I suddenly heard you declaring, as you did one day when you were showing me how to write kanji with an ink brush, "God did not intend for kanji to be straight." I looked. I could curve the path round a boulder and then again round the next boulder, so visitors would pay attention to each of the tiny cacti I have planted that otherwise would go unnoticed. I like to think that path is my kanji in the desert.

In my later years something I cannot define has happened to me, Yukiko. Maybe similar things have happened to you too. I pay attention to many things I formerly ignored or did not notice. Sunsets: I've begun looking up at the evening sky. Dew: I've started walking on the grass in my bare feet. The key smile that defines a person: I now remember that smile. The unopened book waiting to be opened. The music yet to be heard. The love song yet to be written. The two-mile walk around my block waiting to be walked. The woman staring up at the dead tree in her front lawn who suddenly asked me if it was true that she could get a kiss if she stood underneath the live mistletoe growing on a branch above her head. The little army of dark green seedlings in the black earth where last year I buried the yellow rind and seeds of a delicately flavored Vietnamese pomelo.

I also have welcomed memories of people long gone. I no longer shut them out: my father, who died in 1992 of a post-heart-attack operation gone wrong; my mother killed by Alzheimer's in 2006. I wait for my parents in my library. It happens late in the afternoon. They do not arrive together. They don't speak to me but I speak to them, out loud. Then there is the clan of sixty writer and photographer colleagues who were killed or vanished or were murdered in Cambodia and Vietnam in the 1960s and 1970s. Among them are Kyōichi Sawada; Sean Flynn and Dana Stone, who disappeared together and whose remains were never found; Larry Burrows and Welles Hangen; and Keizaburo Shimamoto, Claude Arpin, François Sully, and Kent Potter, who all were working for *Newsweek*, with which I spent ten years of my life. They form an unruly judgment committee from another realm observing the way I live my life. They materialize in my dreams, Yuki. They ask if I am enjoying my life and I never know how to reply. I share the guilt of those who survived. At other times, the dead are right there beside me, or so it seems, still young, still passionate, still magically talented with their black-bodied Nikons and Leicas. I now understand that those who died or who disappeared have an insatiable need to talk.

You used an old bellows camera to take my picture once on an outing to somewhere quiet and dark and green, a place of shadows now unknown to me.

The shutter went *click*. You laughed and you said, "There is no escape. There! I have you now."

I asked, not realizing that you meant you would possess me forever, "When we are old, will we also be young when we think about each other?"

And you said, "That is a very strange question. Do you mean when we think about each other will we see each other the way we are now? We will have to see if the life you live allows you to be forever young."

If you still have that photo, that will be your memory of me. I will be forever young. Until recently, I have been able to permit myself to say that I am becoming older much more quickly than I did ten years ago. Age is stripping away what remains of my youth with a cruelty that no young person, even my children, can understand. When they visit me they look, they nod, they smile, but what do they see? They see their "old man," Paul. That is the way I was with my dad. Toward the end of his life he was inside, looking out. I saw no further than what I gleaned from a glance. What would I see if I could see you now? Of course, I have not been able to watch you grow old. Every time I see a photo of a Japanese woman in her seventies or eighties I look, I peer. I study the face, the hair, the hands, and especially the eyes. I am searching for that woman's youth. Somewhere in the interior, behind those wrinkles and the shy smile, I know that you are still there. If we listened again to Puccini's "*Un bel di*" we would both weep a tear or two to celebrate a memory of us that never died. What a gift that was. What a gift that has been!

I am sometimes astonished when I wake up in the morning and discover that I am still alive. I am pretty sure this happens to you too because so many of my friends of a similar age say they experience this same shock. Yes, I am alive. It is still dark outside and the local mockingbird, having now built his nest, is in full chorus deep inside the dense stand of giant timber bamboo that serves as a battlement along the white stucco wall of my garden. That bird singing at four a.m. is evidence I am alive. I turn on the light and look in the mirror. This is the young man you knew? Not exactly. But I have the memory. I was too young when I knew you to be able to quote Thoreau. But here is how he saw it. Please enjoy his happiness:

Some birds are poets and sing all summer. They are the true singers. Any man can write verses in the love season.

I am reminded of this while we rest in the shade . . . and listen to a wood-thrush now just before sunset. We are most interested in those birds that sing for the love of the music and not of their mates. . . The wood-thrush's is no opera music, it is not so much the composition as the strain, the tone that interests us, cool bars of melody from the atmosphere of everlasting morning or evening. It is the quality of the sound, not the sequence. In the pewee's note there is some sultriness, but in the thrush's, though heard at noon, there is the liquid coolness of things drawn from the bottom of springs. The thrush's alone declares the immortal wealth and vigor that is in the forest. Here is a bird in whose strain the story is told. Whenever a man hears it, he is young, and Nature is in her spring. Wherever he hears it, there is a new world and a free country, and the gates of heaven are not shut against him

—*Summer: From the Journal of Henry David Thoreau*, Volume 6

I would much prefer to die in my sleep, even though there will be no weeping partner to find me. Some of us never wake up. Where do we go? Recently I have become preoccupied with accepting the fact that I will not be able to witness my own funeral. I resent that. As a chronicler of human behavior for half a century I have been to many funerals. I remember details from most of them: who turned up to mourn and who did not. What was said and what was not said. The blanched faces, the sidelong glances, the winces, the air heavy with the inevitability of decay, the small room in which the family members gather awkwardly around the open casket, not knowing whether they should shake my hand or embrace me, the surprising things said among those who have dressed up for the service as if they were at a wedding and not at a funeral, the priest or minister reciting a dirge with rehearsed sincerity that reverberates off the stark, bleak Sheetrock walls.

Six years ago, Yuki, I joined a "closed" Internet group called Vietnam Old Hacks. This site is moderated by the genial Carl Robinson, an American who married a Vietnamese woman and became an Australian after running the Associated Press photo desk in Saigon during the Vietnam War. It is an international online watering hole for reporters, photographers, TV crew, stringers, spies, operatives, actors (including the alluring Kieu Chinh and the dapper George Hamilton), former military advisers, ex-mercenaries, and various retired ambassadors and embassy personnel, plus a smattering of academics with an interest in the thirty years of combat in Indochina and, of course, veterans of the US State Department with intimate, unpublished memoirs of backroom deals and other skullduggery of the type beloved by John le Carré. Some Old Hacks have a futile and tiresome hatred for Jane Fonda because she visited North Vietnam in 1972, met there with American POWs, and posed for photos with an antiaircraft gunnery crew in Hanoi. She apologized. But even in old age, when it seems to me all should be forgiven, these Old Hacks need to hate.

The daily chatter among group members is entertaining at times but the group's most useful function is letting its members know who among them has dropped dead or is seriously ill. These men and women, who witnessed combat and survived that and all the associated drama of covering war nonstop, once regarded themselves as indestructible. "Who will be the last man standing?" I have asked a couple of close friends.

Within three weeks of my writing this chapter the illnesses or deaths of four Old Hacks had been announced and discussed.

They included Jacques Tonnaire, a.k.a. Jacques Thunder, former French paratrooper and freelance photographer who did courageous work along the DMZ in the early 1970s. Gutsy guy to the end, Jacques Thunder. Carl said a French friend told him, "I hate that doc who promised him [Jacques], and more than once, that he would have 'quite a few years of good-quality life' ahead. Normally this is the type of lie you get from politicians. Since when do docs behave like that? Today we learn that all his suffering, physical and moral, was useless. The chemo did not stop or contain his cancer."

Jacques died at the beginning of May 2014. The week before his death, his son, Chuong Duy, sent this email:

Good morning,

I'm Chuong, the son of Jacques.

Jacques is dying: I'll get on the train in an hour, to see and visit him in Figanières, South of France.

Please could you write him a message? I'll read it to him if he's alive. Thank you in advance.

Chuong

It is difficult for me to talk about war experiences with someone who was not there. Some people I've come to know have told me that when they met me for the first time they sensed I had "hidden history," and it made them feel uncomfortable. But when I meet up with those who were there, there is no stopping the memory surges and the sudden infusion of youth—as if youth were a serum and not an intangible.

Last week Van Thanh Lim, the former UPI combat photographer, suddenly called me from Los Angeles. I had heard that he had had major heart surgery. We had not spoken since 1975 in Saigon, when the war was shuddering to a close and I had had an encounter with a desperate upper-class Vietnamese woman at the venerable Continental Palace Hotel, who was trying to sell an exquisite necklace of emeralds and diamonds so she and her family could escape Saigon and flee overseas. Fear on the face of such a woman is truly frightening. It is an indication that the end is near.

"This is Van," my friend said when he called me, as if I would know who he was, as if we had just spoken yesterday. His voice was full of joy and excitement. "How are you, Paul? We are not getting any younger. Please have lunch or dinner with me sometime. Please try your best to visit me. Are you OK?" He talked about wanting to have dinner with me and Nick Ut, the AP photographer, also Vietnamese, who shot the photo of the burning girl running down a road away from her village just after it had been hit by napalm. "We should have dinner in Little Saigon," Van said. He meant Little Saigon in Orange County, California. A Little Saigon that did not exist in 1975.

Am I OK?

I notice that I make more errors than ever when typing, Yukiko. I sleep in two- or three-hour fits and starts. My eyes fill with tears a lot more frequently now. This happens, strangely, when I am confronted by beauty and kindness. For example, my joy early in the light of day comes from noting that everything in my garden is in bloom: roses and ginger and citrus and apples. In the morning, before dawn, when it is cool and tropical birds continue the loud songs they learned in the jungle, a layer of absurdly perfumed mist coats all those flowers and me in the nectar of youth. The other day I watched the recent Japanese film *Ame agaru* (*After the Rain*), made from a screenplay Kurosawa wrote before his death. I started choking up when the good-natured samurai Ihei and his sweet wife, Tayo, did their best to bring happiness to other guests at a country inn where they were all trapped by heavy summer rains. That would not have been my reaction in my younger years. The truth is that old age is duplicitous. It is the age of death. But it also is the age of rebirth. I am sure you understand, Yuki. Spring will soon be here and everything, including myself, will be in renewal. I sense it. For a few days, or maybe for a few weeks, I will be young again. I will pull out your letters once more. I have the moment planned for that. I have a chair set up among the roses, and on a certain hour of the day I am going to read your letters one last time. I am going to hold the paper in my hands, and then I am going to put it all away in a place known only to me.

For one enchanting second I feel that if I extended my hand I could take the hand of the other Paul you knew, the seaman, sailing from Hong Kong to Yokosuka with nothing more on his mind than how he will say good-bye. He has only a child's comprehension of that moment and how it will impact each stage of development throughout his life. He has only very limited understanding of what has happened during that summer. Watching the waves, he pictures your face and he smiles because he is happy. He is not wrestling with the puzzle of who you are, or what you were. For him, everything is simple. He is simply the virgin lover returning to the woman he barely knows, the woman he must leave, the love that can never be. He is thinking that the last good-bye will be one of many thousands of good-byes and kisses and embraces and, yes, promises and declarations of love. The *Shangri-La* cuts open the ocean as if the ship were a knife made of jade and the ocean the enemy. Orders go out from the bridge. The men do their tasks with a shrug, and the young Paul watches the rise and fall of his world and he thinks of you, Yukiko, somewhere out there thinking about him. In a moment of fantasy he thinks that if he called out to you, you would hear him. But what would he say?

I have been wondering about that for many, many, many years. I don't have a ready answer. I probably never will have an answer. The old Paul cannot speak for the young Paul. So I will go on wondering and not knowing.

I have been asked, always by men friends and never by women friends, if I was really as "green" as I have portrayed myself. Green, yes. I am not so jaded that I cannot happily admit that my green innocence was reality. It was the way things were in the late 1950s for many young men and women. It was in many ways, I believe, the last age of innocence. Sex was a mystery known to me only by rumor. Women feigned fainting when men touched their hands, or when they wrote sweet nothings in their high-school yearbooks that sound now as if they were written by children. Betty Friedan's *The Feminine Mystique* had not yet been published; it did not appear until 1963. The Beatles did not record their first hit—"Love Me Do"—until 1962, the year I got out of the navy, the year young women and men went collectively and joyfully insane.

In 1962, one night in a bar in Tokyo, I had a conversation with a young businessman named Nishida. I don't recall being astonished when he told me he had trained in 1945 at the age of nineteen to be a "divine wind" pilot—a kamikaze. The war had ended before he flew his mission. It did not strike me as odd when he described his teenage self as "sweet and innocent." He talked about the farewell letter he had written to his parents. I took some notes when he was talking: "I told them I would always remember their shining love for me. I understood that their love would vanish when I vanished. I told them I would regret not having their love but I had to do my duty. I told them to please give my thanks to everyone who had given me friendship. I told my sisters to take care of my parents and to always be worthy of being a Japanese woman. In that way, I said good-bye." He looked at me as if a chasm stretched between us that would not allow me to understand. Yes, I would have written that kind of letter, I told him. We drank sake. He filled my cup. I filled his cup. That was the custom.

The other day I came across an item at that great storehouse of video nostalgia, YouTube. It is a recording of "Barbara," a poem written by the French writer Jacques Prévert and adapted and sung by a very young Yves Montand, who was not much older than I was in 1959. In the song, Montand cherishes a memory of a woman he knew briefly long ago, a memory of just a look, just a smile, a single embrace that can never be forgotten. This poem was translated by the American beat poet Lawrence Ferlinghetti, who is now ninety-five years old.

[. . .] And you ran to him in the rain
Streaming-wet enraptured flushed
And you threw yourself in his arms.
Remember that Barbara
And don't be mad if I speak familiarly.
I speak familiarly to everyone I love
Even if I've seen them only once
I speak familiarly to all who are in love . . .

This afternoon, Yuki, the old Paul was watching for the eighth time the Italian film, from 2013, *La Grande Bellezza* [*The Great Beauty*], in which a sixty-five-year-old journalist whose past is riddled with rich experiences begins confronting the unpleasant truth that everything must change. The only woman he ever loved left him long ago without an explanation. Does this ring true? The journalist is a celebrated chronicler of bon vivant culture and excess. He has been to one too many parties. He has been celebrating his sixty-fifth birthday with characteristic decadence. He suddenly discovers that the woman has died. Her tearful and grieving husband, who he has not met before, comes to tell him that he has just read her private journals. She had written, the husband says, that the journalist—the seventeen-year-old boy she knew when she was nineteen, and who she never kissed—was the only man she ever loved. He becomes more aware than ever that beauty exists as he wanders through the film. All around him are friends and acquaintances whose lives are in disarray, whose loves and their urge to live are coming to an end. He thinks back to when he was seventeen and innocent, and his world is knocked off its axis. My sister Mary, quoting Oscar Wilde, told me recently that my

life—my wanderings—has been "crowded with incident."
She is correct. My life has not been a tranquil river flowing
to the sea. It has been a cataract. There have been whirlpools
and waterfalls. As the film images flickered and I knew the
narrative was taking turns that even on the first viewing were
strangely familiar, I started to become despondent. I was on
the verge of saying, "That man is me."

But then there was proof that the Great God of Surprises has
not forgotten me. This is the same God who, just like that, created
the universe, I suppose, and then left everything else up to us.

Ring. Ring. The phone was ringing. "Hello?"

A laugh. A young woman's voice, its accent from somewhere in Asia but also somewhere in Europe: "Do you know
who this is, Paul?"

"Ummm. No. I'm sorry. No."

Another laugh. "It's Flor."

"What? Flor! You are calling me from Paris?" I imagined
Flor—who is from the Philippines and is studying at a French
university and is always asking funny questions about French
men and whether they can be trusted—eating a doughnut and
drinking coffee in front of the Paris branch of Tiffany & Co.
Flor's command of spoken English and French has become
exceptionally good in the four years since I have known her.
She has a French Riviera sophistication to her now.

"Do you know Audrey Hepburn?" I asked.

"Who? You know, I may be too young to know who Audrey Hepburn is."

"Flor. Try to see *Breakfast at Tiffany's*. She was living the
life you are living right now, but that film was made in the
early 1960s."

"Oh," Flor said. "When you were young." That gave me something to think about.

Yes, the Great God of Surprises has been busy. I became more aware, as I was writing this book, that my knowledge of spoken Japanese and of Japan itself had become embarrassingly dated. I would be a Rip Van Winkle if I went back to Tokyo, I realized. Curious about what I would find, I had turned up at the 2013 Matsuri, a festival held annually in Phoenix that is America's second-largest celebration of Japanese food, drink, music, dance, and various arcane ceremonies. The experience was both familiar and—because of the enthusiastic presence of hundreds of American teens wearing the weird garb of Japanese anime (comic book) characters—unfamiliar to me. But while I was there, I was persuaded by one of its members to join the Japanese Culture Club of Arizona. It is a small organization that, I soon discovered, is dominated by women devoted to *chanoyu*, the severely formal Japanese tea ceremony, and to *ikebana*, the equally severe art of flower arranging. The club is led by Mae-jima Harumi, a woman in her fifties, who was dressed in a sleek kimono the color of mulberry leaves with hints of violet when I met her. For me, struggling with images from circa 1959 of a Japan that I know has undergone several transformations, many of which I have been told have obliterated the past, this was reassuring affirmation that in the new Japan not all is forgotten.

Somehow the unlikely subject of Alfa Romeos came up.

"Oh yes," the serene Maejima-san said. "The Alfa Romeo. My favorite car." She paused. "Do you have a Spider?"

Surprised, I nodded in the affirmative.

"I had a Giulietta," she said, referring to an older vintage of my car. "I used to race at Lime Rock [Connecticut]."

Bang. Just like that, she was in the lead. My car, a two-seater like her Giulietta, is a gentleman's cruiser, not a racing car. She had driven her Alfa in competition at the famed racetrack frequented by such daredevils as actor Paul Newman and professional racers Mario Andretti, Stirling Moss, and Dan Gurney. Maejima-san was not even born when my summer with Yukiko occurred. Here I was, in the quaint Souvia Tea shop in Phoenix, awed by a Japanese woman, again. Did this mean, I wondered, that despite rapid change, things are still very much the way they were: complete with poised, articulate, opinionated, reserved, demanding women actively living links to a culture and identity more than a thousand years old? I am sure you would have an opinion, Yuki.

Would I care to be the club's treasurer, Maejima-san asked? I balked.

"How about adviser to the club?"

I agreed.

She poured tea and not just any tea: a seasonal black tea to commemorate spring, with a dried pink cherry blossom peeking out of the tea leaves like pursed lips ready for kissing.

Chapter 21

NOCTURNES

In me nothing is extinguished or forgotten,
my love feeds on your love, beloved,
and as long as you live it will be in your arms
without leaving mine.

—Pablo Neruda, from *"Si tú me olvidas"*
("If You Forget Me"),
in *Los versos del Capitán*
(*The Captain's Verses*)

The hand-drawn sign outside the Mozart coffee shop read:
"Jour de Fête Debussy! Vive L'Amour! Enjoy Your Happiness!" I could recognize the hand of Mr. Ito in this. He always
had a surplus of smiles. I was a juvenile, still stuck with sneers.

As I approached the café, inhaling the delicious odor of
espresso that filled the alley from sunrise to sunset, I could see
the usual gathering of uniformed schoolgirls, clustered around
the entrance, waiting for something exciting to happen. I was
wearing the civilian clothes I had stashed at a locker club before
the *Shangri-La* left for Hong Kong: light-brown three-button
sports coat, dark-brown narrow necktie with discreet gold deco
zigzags, black pants with cuffs tight round the ankles, white

socks, and black loafers. I had a couple of paperback books of poetry tucked under my arm. A bent cigarette dangled from my mouth. I had that look of rebellion on my face that you liked. I was feeling very Belmondo. I was feeling French.

The schoolgirls parted to let me pass. They were definitely excited. A couple of them attempted to speak French to me, although I am not sure what a young Frenchman would be doing in shabby Yokosuka in an alley wet with the customary afternoon rain, even if he was lured there by the espresso sacrament. "*Bonjour, monsieur,*" one of the girls managed to say. "*Comment ça va?*" When I nodded, like a lout, as if I knew her but I had discarded her, she collapsed in a fit of red-faced giggles into the arms of friends staggering with the joy of unabashed embarrassment.

Earlier that afternoon I had stopped by the White Rose, but you were not there. *Mamasan* was not there. Reiko was not there. The remainder of the women who worked there were fluttering and twittering around the premises as if they were caged canaries.

Honcho was full of sailors from the *Shangri-La* headed to bars where they knew friendly faces. They acted as if they were children tasting their first chocolate milk shakes. Many bar hostesses stood in front of the places where they worked, showing off their cocktail dresses and newly permed hairdos and occasionally calling out names—"Bobby!" "Johnnie!" "Terry!"—when they recognized favorite swabbies.

Everyone knew that this was the Shitty Shang's last visit to Yokosuka. There was infection in the air. There was a fever, in fact, and everyone looked as if their body temperature had been elevated by at least two degrees. I knew that many members of the crew had unfinished business: some were ready to propose, some were determined to get drunker than they had ever been before, and some would be happy just to gather with their friends in a booth in the corner of a darkened bar so they could hold hands and maybe smooch a little with girls who they thought were their own.

I am sure at least one among them planned to make the one-hour train ride to Tokyo to propose marriage—thanks to the suggestion made by Commander Davy Crockett—to the most beautiful virgin woman in the world, Miss Kojima Akiko. Both Jim and Red were certain Miss Universe was a virgin, and so were Oscar and Gunther. Gunther had recovered now and was back to his old habit of looking over his shoulder. Oscar, a photo of Miss Kojima in his hand, had said to me before I went ashore, "Paul. You are a virgin. Look at her. You know. You can tell, right?"

We were all so young, thank God.

I had thought about Miss Universe as I picked my way through the streets and alleys to the Mozart. Her face was on the covers of many magazines in the newsstands. A few streets removed from Honcho I noticed that a couple of men wearing the white headbands of political protest, crouched on top of a sound truck festooned with what appeared to be anti-American slogans, were looking at a large foldout photograph of Kojima Akiko wearing a conservative one-piece bathing suit. One of the men gave me a comradely wave, and the other one handed me an English-language pamphlet from Nikkyoso—the Japan Teachers' Union—which denounced the 1951 US-Japan security treaty. That agreement allows American forces to retain bases, such as the naval facilities at Yokosuka, seemingly into perpetuity. I waved back, and continued down the street remembering the advice from on high, given to everyone, to stay out of politics, and the remark made by Chaplain Peeples that it was not just Japanese teachers who were Communist.

"Teachers in general tend to be Communists or homosexuals," he told me in Hong Kong after our visit to the orphanage. "Teachers everywhere are do-gooders and do-gooders tend to be un-American and homosexuals, unless they are Christian teachers. Do-gooders are definitely not Baptists. Baptists are reapers and sowers."

"But aren't there Christians who are do-gooders?" I asked. "And if a homosexual does good, what's wrong with that, sir? . . . And if Communists are do-gooders, why is Communism bad?"

He started muttering. "You need to go to college, Rogers," he said.

"And college teachers?" I asked. My thoughts were racing ahead. "Also, who are the do-badders?"

He did not reply. That was the way it always was with Chaplain Peeples. Everything was emphatic, doctrinal, black and white. There was no room for and/or, or for the color grey.

Mr. Ito was seated behind the big mechanical cash register, a prewar relic, no doubt. His fingers were racing up and down an abacus, the little ivory circles clicking away as he did rapid calculations almost without looking. But he did look up with a smile as I came through the door.

"Are you meeting someone?" he asked teasingly.

"I am not sure, Mr. Ito," I said. "I am looking for Miss Kaji."

"Ohhh," he said. "She *will* be pleased!" He began fussing—

straightening his bow tie and sucking in his belly—in a way that astonished me.

"Have you seen her today?"

"Oh no. Not today. But yesterday, yes." He straightened his bow tie again. His face went scarlet when the schoolgirls, entering in single file, began addressing him in babyish French.

"Well, maybe I should have coffee and wait for her."

"Yes. That is a good idea. Do you know that today is Debussy day?"

"I saw your sign."

"Good. Well," he began excitedly, "let me tell you, Mr. Anthony Perkins. Kaji-san told me this would be the most perfect happy day to play Debussy. So now, with pleasure, I present for you Debussy's *Nocturnes*." He clutched at his heart theatrically.

I laughed. The schoolgirls squeaked. Claude Debussy appeared to be smiling down at us from his portrait on the wall. Mr. Ito had ringed the portrait with pink paper cherry blossoms because, he said, Debussy had used the Japanese print master Hokusai's picture *The Wave* on the cover for the sheet music of *La Mer* when it was first published in Paris in 1905.

"Do you like Debussy?" I asked.

"Oh yes . . . I am homosexual."

I blinked and started sipping the espresso brought to me on a chrome tray by a shy young waitress who looked as if she were afraid I was going to bite her. I asked for cream. She looked alarmed. She bowed her head. "I am so sorry," she said in apology, backing away with a shuffle, as if I were some kind of potentate and not someone probably her own age.

"Do you know about homosexuals?" Mr. Ito asked.

"Well, as a matter of fact, my ship's chaplain, the priest—no, he is a minister—told me recently that homosexuals are Communists who are probably do-gooders."

Mr. Ito rubbed his crew cut rapidly with his hand in astonishment.

"I am sorry," he said in his halting English. "You mean, this . . . he . . . is a holy man?"

"Holy? You know, Mr. Ito, I never thought of Chaplain Peeples as 'holy.' I am not sure how to describe him."

Mr. Ito was still looking at me with amazement. I wished at that moment that Chaplain Peeples and maybe even Commander Crockett were there, seated at the table with me, so they could enlighten Mr. Ito and vice versa. But, of course, that was impossible. Officers never, ever socialized with enlisted men, although some officers made it clear to me they would like to socialize with college girls.

I did not know much about homosexuals when I was twenty. They were do-gooders. They were Communists. They liked Debussy, apparently. Like Debussy and Mr. Ito, they wore bow ties. They made delicious espresso. The espresso made them extraordinarily fastidious. They had a unique and memorable way of writing signs in English, and they also seemed to be polite and very interested in the subject of happiness.

I also knew that if someone aboard the *Shangri-La* was rumored to be a homosexual, the rumor expanded overnight by leaps and bounds to excruciating heights. One of my friends developed a serious stutter after the rumors began. Some of the rumormongers asked me about him. I told them that as far as I was concerned, his girlfriend was—next to Kojima

Akiko—the most beautiful woman in the world, and as for Jim being a homosexual, what did I know?

"Take a look at the photos his girlfriend sent," I told them. "What do you think? Can you match that?"

I was confused, Yuki. Mr. Ito was confused. The waitress, who now appeared with a little white ceramic pitcher of cream, also looked confused. She held the pitcher out in front of her, walked slowly to my table, gave a quick bow, and said again in a voice like a child's, "I am so sorry." This is a charming expression frequently used in Japan and is said politely by people intruding into another person's presence.

"Don't worry about it," I told her in a careful and kindly manner. "It is not important. What is your name?"

"I am so sorry," she said. "Just I know, 'I am so sorry.'"

Debussy's *Nocturnes* was playing, but I could clearly hear the sound of high heels clattering across the concrete floor toward me. Mr. Ito was laughing out loud and straightening his bow tie again as if he were about to stand inspection. It was you, Yukiko, wearing a dark red beret to go with your lipstick. You had buttoned your trench coat to your neck, as was your custom. The belt was cinched tightly round your waist. "Oooh, oooh, oooh," you were saying, and, "Ooh la la!" As you moved your body, it had a slight sway to it. You did not often wear high heels and you had explained to me that when you walked you had to move your body as if you were some kind of goddess of love, to help you balance.

"My marching shoes," you called your high heels. "If only I could dance tango."

You were coming closer. I could see that you had not forgotten to enjoy your happiness. I remembered in that Debussy moment how one day when we were walking, and you were swaying in your heels so that your hip touched my hip again and again, you told me you had a record of "Tango Uno" from the 1940s that you said "inflames the beating hearts of women." You played it for me a couple of times, but the lyrics were in Spanish so I could only imagine what they meant. Only recently have I translated it. It is from Buenos Aires, Argentina, world capital of high heels, elaborate lingerie, highly evolved despair, and manic melancholy. A Brazilian woman poet languishing in a Buenos Aires apartment with moldy plaster falling off the walls once told me (in Portuguese): "*Num deserto de almas tambem desertas, uma alma especial reconhece de imediato a outra* [In the desert of souls also deserted, a special soul immediately recognizes another]."

> One seeks full of hope
> The road that dreams
> Promised to one's anxiety.
> You know the road is tough

You sat down. You moved your chair closer to my chair and leaned in my direction. You had been walking quickly—I knew because I could feel your heat. When I finally breathed in, I could smell your Ancient China perfume, which you daubed behind each ear before you uttered a little cry of joy. You straightened my necktie and then brushed my forehead with the palm of your hand so that I closed my eyes.

"Don't open your eyes, sailor boy, until I tell you," you said. "I am going to look at you now."

Two or three minutes went by. I had not moved. You had

not moved. But then I heard you inching your chair even closer to mine. I felt your hip touch my hip. Your breath was hot and was flavored with pomegranates. You held my hand. You said something to Mr. Ito and he turned up the volume to *Nocturnes*. You told me to open my eyes, and when I did I saw that your face was only inches from mine and that you were still staring at me. Your eyes were slightly crossed. What did you call being cross-eyed? *Ron-pari*. London-Paris. Yes, you were sometimes *ron-pari* because, you explained, it was as if one of your eyes saw London and the other saw Paris at the same time. *Ron-pari* was one of your qualities that I have never forgotten.

I am still fascinated by women who get cross-eyed when they look at a man. It is as if, without knowing it, they are making magic that cannot be resisted.

You put your finger on my lips to silence me. You rolled your head back a little like you did when you were listening to Ludwig van Beethoven. Sunlight coming through the window made it look as if the beret you were wearing was a halo, but a blood red one, not a golden one. No, gold would not do, I thought. Gold is for angels, for ethereal creatures not of this world. Blood red is for a woman like you, with a heart beating fast and a passion for life and love she is not able to share.

I squeezed your hand, and you did the same to mine. And then we listened to the three passages, each about eight minutes long, while Mr. Ito brought us scoops of vanilla ice cream and sugary wafers whose taste reminded me of the wafer popped into my mouth during Holy Communion in those days long ago in England when my mother imagined herself to be a Catholic.

We said nothing. I hardly dared to breathe.

Every now and then, Mr. Ito looked at us as if what he saw was impossible.

The waitress looked at Mr. Ito, and she looked at us like a dragonfly not knowing whether it should alight or pass on by.

After the last portion of *Nocturnes*, the *Sirènes*, had ended, and the chorus of their voices without words had melted away, you finally said something. "This is the moment I waited for so long. This is my happy time. When you leave me I will have this to remember. Thank you."

You looked so astonishingly sincere.

Then we started talking. We were still seated very close together. I had never seen a Japanese woman sit that closely to a man in a public place.

Grown women and the high-school girls scattered around the coffee shop could not take their eyes off us. They did not say anything. They watched us talking. They watched the way you were still looking at me.

You were studying my face, as if I had just told you "I love you" and you believed me.

They watched me too. It was as if you had kissed me for the first time because I had said "I love you."

Chapter 22

WHAT MEN FIND BEAUTIFUL

All my life through,
These eighty-one years
I have done what I wished
In my own way:
The whole world
In one mouthful.

—Death Poem left
by Kenzan Ogata*

The next afternoon I started walking the familiar route to
your house. I made a mental note of every landmark, every
small store selling mysterious candies and saucy girlie magazines, every shrimp-fried-rice place pumping the smell of
cooking out onto the street, every one of the small sake bars
competing with every other with colorfully designed signs
that clamored for attention in a language I could not read.

---

* Kenzan Ogata was a genius of Japanese ceramics and master of Zen who
died in 1743. This poem was found the next day by a lodger at the tenement
house they shared on the Sumida River near Tokyo. The translation is from
Kenzan and His Tradition, by the British potter Bernard Leach, on whom the
Japanese bestowed the title of the Seventh Kenzan in 1913.

I knew the visit would probably be the last I could make to your retreat on the hill. Sometimes you called it "my fortress against vicissitudes." The world could change around it, you said, but as long as you were the tenant, the serenity it provided would remain exactly the same. There would always be your guardian, the paulownia, scattering its blue petals on you when you sat outside to write me letters. There would always be the array of cawing crows standing witness, malevolent, reminding you that you were "doomed," you so often said. There would always be the 101 steps to Heaven. "This is the end of the road for me," you sometimes said. But you never explained what you meant, although you did tell me on the trip to Kamakura that you would like your ashes to be scattered on the hill because no one would grieve for an "ugly woman with no family to call her own."

One day, as you were peering intently into the mirror at your house, I had asked you why you insisted on calling yourself "ugly."

"When I was a young woman," you said, as I watched you apply lipstick, "I was told my skin was as pure as the finest porcelain laid in a bed of snow. My breasts are not large because in my childhood I was encouraged to bind them tight with cloth so I would be able to offer myself with modesty. I was told frequently that big breasts are the curse of a loose woman. I was encouraged to glide graciously like a passing shadow. I discovered that when I read books late in the day, and the light is fading and my face has strong character, men are drawn to me. This encouraged me at an early age to read the most complex of the ancient classics." You knew by heart, you said, the key passages about lost love in the *Kagero Nikki*

journals (*The Gossamer Years*), written by an unknown woman
of the tenth century. You knew the best commentaries written
by a woman about men in Lady Murasaki's diaries. You turned
to your notebook, always so close at hand. "For example,"
you said, "here is a very small poem from the *Gosenshu* [*The
Six Collections*, A.D. 951]."

> Dreams, listen, my dreams!
> Do not bring me together
> With the man I love . . .
> When once I have awakened I would feel so lonely.

"I can recite, like that, in a pleasant voice that will fascinate an
intelligent man," you said, after you had put me in a trance.
"Or, at intimate moments, I will speak as if all I can do is
whisper, so that men have to listen closely to every word,
knowing that if they fail to understand me they will not know
if I am willing to submit."

I was watching you from the shadows of your room as
if I were your captive. On some occasions over the years I
have watched closely as women apply makeup and attempt
to define their beauty with various degrees of success, or no
success at all if they have the fatal flaw of being modest. You
were speaking as if you had been born in another age, as if
you had been the mistress of a court noble—but then, that
was just my interpretation. I was learning to write poetry. You
can't blame me for being a dreamer, seduced, without even
a kiss, by your charm. You can't reprove me for mentioning
that you were the only woman I knew who was so conscious
of her beauty that she called herself "ugly."

You looked closely at the apparition I was to make sure I was paying attention. "I use a combination of ancient Chinese and Japanese techniques when I feel it is possible for me to feel beautiful," you said carefully. "I feel beautiful today because you are here and I thank you for that. I smooth on very lightly this *bintsuke* wax as a foundation and then gently dust my face and my shoulders and the back of my neck with rice powder," you said. "I use a pomade rouge on my cheeks to bring them to life, like this. I use a vermilion balm for my lips and a mix of dried flower petals and beeswax to make my eyebrows curve, like that. Not all of my lips should be colored with the balm because I wish to stress the fullness and pout of my lips, like this. Then, after I am satisfied with that, I emphasize my nose and the corner sockets of my eyes with gentle touches of rouge, like this.

"On my nails, I have a red tint made of gum arabic, egg whites, beeswax, and gelatin. Last month, my nails were tinted in the purple color of a beating heart, but I decided to change to the most brilliant red today, just for you. I use a perfume I make myself that only releases its fragrance whenever I make love, or whenever I walk after making love, so that there is a trace of me that briefly lingers even after I disappear. I pretend that these jade earrings are a gift from the emperor and why not? Why shouldn't I pretend?

"All this is what men find beautiful, I was told when I was a young girl and still a virgin. But you know, when I became older, and my body became rounder, men were not interested in white jade skin or secret perfumes. For them, I was like a piece of ripening persimmon. They were eager to bite into me, but like the fruit I kept them waiting, waiting, waiting until that moment when I was sweet. If I had allowed them to taste me earlier, the taste would have been so bitter. It is like that with persimmons. It is like that with certain women who are no longer girls. That was my technique. These men could hover around me and offer money and gold. But I made them wait until they became acceptable to me. They found it irresistible. They found it incredible that they could not have me. They were not like you, Paul-san. But you are not yet a man."

All of this was on my mind on that breezy, cheerful day as I made my way to your house.

Almost everyone I passed appeared to be busy. They were not just acting busy. It was as if the whole population of Yoko-suka was pulling together to restore something lost: a moment from youth, maybe, or a vision of the village they abandoned. Millions of country folk had moved to the cities to look for work after the death and destruction caused by American bombs. This was not a day for thinking, it occurred to me. This was a day for doing. Schoolchildren were scampering home with their leather satchels bouncing up and down on their backs to study algebra and trigonometry and to one day start companies like Sony or Honda. Housewives were hanging out newly washed clothes to dry in the sun, and some were using bamboo paddles to whack dander out of the cotton-packed futon mattresses they used for sleeping. One woman with a big smile on her face called out *konnichiwa* (good day) to me and then walloped her futon in rhythm with a jaunty song on the radio that made her happy.

I picked up the pace of my walking. I was worried about how you were going to react when I sailed away. At times in your letters you had sounded almost frantic, asking—demanding—that I remember you forever. When I said good-bye, would you cry and cry and cry even though you told me you would not? Would you? I felt apprehensive about those final days and yet I felt good about this day on which you suggested that we meet.

We had walked out of the Mozart with Debussy filling every emotional void in our senses, and you had pulled on my sleeve and stopped me in the alley. Under the streetlight you had said, almost in a whisper, as if you were sharing one of your secrets: "Paul, I want to dulcify these days."

"Dulcify?"

"Yes, Paul. If you are going away, I want to celebrate our brief life together. I want to dulcify every moment we have together. Do you understand?"

But I did not understand "dulcify." When I told you that, you looked so disappointed. It was as if my inability to understand that word had reduced me in a flash from being an almost-man to a helpless child again.

You pulled hard on my sleeve and looked up at me with those *ron-pari* eyes and you asked, "Do you ever read the dictionary? Do you ever look for words that can make your ugly English language sound beautiful? If you don't do that, you will have a miserable life, sailor boy, and you will forget me. But you will remember me if you remember that this one word, *dulcify*, means sweetness and gentle and agreeable. That is the memory I want you to have when I say good-bye."

A huge flood of emotions surged up inside me. I could not speak. My voice was locked, paralyzed. You used a finger to wipe a tear from my cheek. It had never occurred to me that despite the longing in your letters, you would be the one planning the last of our good-byes, and I, who had spent the summer desperately trying to grow up, would be the one struck down with grief.

But that was yesterday.

Today I had my own list of things to do, the first of which was to do my best to help you dulcify. I had decided during the night that I was not going to be in mourning. Yes, that was it. I was going to be kind and generous and considerate and make these last days bearable for you because I was almost certain that your determined approach to the end of our affair was a charade and that you, a woman who had shuddered with joy when I gave you that "embrace of a lifetime," would be on your knees begging me not to go. That thought frightened me. But it was a sunny day. Everyone was whistling and sweeping and dusting. At one household, a young woman had placed an easel in her tiny garden and was using oils on canvas to paint a likeness of your hill. She had already daubed the blue flowers of the paulownia and she had painted the steps, twisting and curving like a writhing snake upward into nothingness. I stopped to look and I smiled at her. "Hello," she said in really pretty English. "I have seen you before. You are such a gentle boy."

How strange it was, I thought, to be able to tell such things just from a man's quick smile, or the way he stands to look at her. What a gift. No wonder Japanese women were the poets in ancient times. No wonder I, as yet still a boy, could be called "gentle" by a woman I did not know.

In the background I could hear the sound of Misora Hibari singing "*Ringo oiwake*" (Apple Folk Song) coming from an open window. I have to tell you that when the woman painter told me the name of the song I wrote it into my notebook so that one day (and that day happened just last month) I could hear it again and know what the lyrics meant. Once the music begins like a soaring bird in a dark sky, it is impossible for me to move. When it starts, I have to sit down. If there is a cushion, I have to grip it. If I let myself go, that sweet summer unfolds again as if it were a record playing on the turntable. Listening to "*Ringo oiwake*" causes the same reaction I have when I listen to Butterfly sing "*Un bel di*" (One Fine Day). Here are the words to the song, the translation courtesy of my Japanese friend Ogawa Wakako, who says she would have enjoyed knowing you, Yukiko.

> Then early apple flowers bloom.
> It is the happiest season for us,
> But rain without mercy falls
> and scatters their white petals . . .
> Which reminds me of mother who died in Tokyo then.
> [the singer gasps] . . . I . . . I . . .
> I heard a girl of Tsugaru crying,
> Crying because of a painful separation.
> Petals of apple blossoms
> Are falling with the wind, ah-ah-ah.

You might like to know, by the way, because you so love to laugh at the little eccentricities of life, that the "*Ringo oiwake*" melody somehow found its way to Jamaica, where it became the foundation for the classic ska hit "Ringo Rock," sung by all kinds of Rastafarians. Until recently, after a Jamaican musician visited Tokyo and heard "*Ringo oiwake*" on the radio, everyone in Jamaica had believed it to be a Jamaican tune. "Everything of consequence in this world is a fable, and if you live in that world you become a fable too," you once said. I did not reply then. But now I am going to tell you that you were correct.

I was dulcified by the song. I was saddened too. You told me that every Japanese knew that the mother "who died in Tokyo then" had been killed by American bombs, and that "then" referred to a war in which so many people had lost someone. You said this without any bitterness. You said it with kindness. I was thankful for that. Despite my worry about leaving you, and how to leave you, and the stark truth about war, I still felt good about that day on which we had agreed to meet.

But then, just as I was approaching the steps to your house, I came across Detective Nazaka sitting on a park bench with his shabby raincoat unbuttoned and his thin black tie loosened. He was looking deceptively relaxed and confident as he took a drag from a broken cigarette. He squinted at me. His mouth twisted as if he had bitten into the sourest of *umeboshi*. He coughed and spat something horrific onto the pavement before sticking his hand up to signal vigorously for me to stop as if I were a speeding taxi.

"Excuse me," I said gingerly. "I am on my way to meet Miss Kaji." I was desperate to get past him and climb the hill.

"Yes, I know," he said. His voice was the usual harsh croak. He did an imitation of a smile. "The police know everything!"

"It's nice to see you, sir. But I don't want to be late," I told him.

"Yes, I will make this quick," he said. "I understand that you met Kaji-san at the Mozart café yesterday. She is Japanese, you know. We Japanese do not necessarily have to discuss certain concepts or subjects, even though you might have wanted that to happen. We can remain silent in our conversations and use our senses to know what the other person is thinking. We can talk silently. Foreigners cannot do that, you know. It is the Japanese sixth sense. We Japanese are especially sensitive people. The crimes I investigate excite the senses. Those are the type of crimes that cause poetry to be written."

I had no idea what he was talking about. But I showed interest by nodding in agreement. It was a mistake. He continued.

"For example, here is a crime I wish I had investigated but which I could not do because it happened in 1936 in Tokyo and I was living in Manchuria at the time. There was a woman, Abe Sada, who had been a prostitute. But then she started working as a maid in a cheap hotel. Kichi, the owner of the hotel, foolishly molested her and that caused the two of them to start a love affair in which they engaged in sexual experiments that were bizarre even for Japan. Miss Abe became more and more possessive and jealous. The hotel owner did everything he could to please her, but Miss Abe murdered him after he confessed to her that the sensation of strangling excited him. She cut off his penis and she used it to write in blood on his chest, 'Sada and Kichi: together, forever.'" Nazaka looked closely at me for some kind of reaction. But nothing in my experience allowed me to speak. I thought how little I knew about your life, Yukiko, and the relationship you had with the man who became a bear. He raped you: that I knew. You became his woman: that I knew. Would you kill him, I wondered?

"Well," Nazaka said. "You can see that we Japanese are so

288

very sensitive when it comes to matters of the heart. I think you know now we are a special people. Even without battleships we are a superior people. I believe Jewish people have this special sixth sense too."

I told him I did not know that. Since I started writing poetry because you required it, I thought I had developed the skill of knowing and sharing thoughts without speaking. But that was a skill, not a sense. If it was a sense, it would have been a *wu wei* thing—not planned, not considered, but done.

"People who write poetry," you told me with a chuckle, "are not normal at all. We are like messengers from somewhere. We are angels. Remember that, please, and always make sure that your private thoughts when you are with a woman are poems that you do not have to recite to her."

"I am sure you had a good conversation with your friend," Detective Nazaka said. "You don't have to answer me. I can sense that you did."

No wonder that in Japan the police know everything, I thought.

"Well, Mr. Paul, there is some news that Miss Kaji did not announce to you because it is old news. It has gone. It is the past. She did not tell you about it because, being Japanese, she thought you would realize it already. But of course, you are a foreigner, so you don't know . . . Do you?"

I shook my head. "Can you please give me the news?" I asked before sitting down on the bench because I sensed there was going to be a shock to my nervous system.

"*Saaaaa*," he said, as if he was struggling with something. "*Saaaaa.*" There were a few seconds of silence.

"You were gone for three weeks. The week after your

ship left there was an incident. During the night, a certain Japanese man who was drunk attempted to attack Miss Kaji. He threatened to kill her if she refused to go with him. Do you understand?"

I did not understand. I saw that he could tell from the look on my face that I was incapable of visualizing scenes of violence, even after I had witnessed Nazaka's struggle with Shinoda Yusuke, the bear of a man on the train station platform.

"I am sorry," he said, coughing. He banged his fist against his heart. "Excuse me, please. My doctors tell me that every day I am practicing the art of dying."

Then he cleared his lungs with more spitting and he said, "You will never understand this explanation I give you, even when you are an old man and you have had much experience with life. But I have to tell you this because you are a nice young man. This is Japan. Remember, Miss Kaji and I are both Manchurian Japanese, and it is true that because of that we are different. But we are still Japanese even if we can speak English and we like classical music and Western literature and philosophy. You know, I like Mickey Mouse and Donald Duck and Betty Boop. At the cinema, they make me laugh, and it is unusual for me to laugh at anything. I do not have children of my own and I am a bachelor, you know. When I hear children laughing at those cartoons it makes me sad, so I have to laugh."

I was astonished by these revelations. I am sure that I must have looked on that sensually warm afternoon as if I had just stepped on a nail. I looked on anxiously at Nazaka Goro, Kanagawa Prefectural Police detective, who was having another coughing and spitting fit. Was he ever going to tell me the truth about what happened to Kaji Yukiko while I was experimenting with being a feral male in Hong Kong?

"There is an ocean of misunderstanding between us, Mr. Paul," he said after regaining his composure. "You call it the Pacific Ocean. But for we Japanese, it is not 'pacific.' It is not a peaceful ocean. You send your ships of war and your aircraft with nuclear weapons across that ocean. You come across that ocean from far away like children, playing with your toys that kill. Do you know that in two nights in 1945 your bombers firebombed Tokyo, and one hundred thousand men, women, and children were burned alive? Your country is drunk with the sensation of power. That makes it the Dangerous Ocean—the *abunai* ocean—dangerous." There was a pause while he scratched the stubble on his chin. "Oh, my apologies," he said. "Of course, you are a British citizen. You are English. You are a 'gentleman.' I am sure all the girls at the White Rose tell you that. You are a *shinshi*!"

"Excuse me," I said, producing my notebook. "I am a *shishi*?"

"No. *Shishi* means lion. *Shinshi* means you are a proper gentleman. We Japanese believe that all Englishmen are gentlemen. They are noble!"

"Like a lion they are noble?" I suggested.

"Excellent," he said. "I see your intelligence that Miss Kaji appreciates."

"Thank you, sir," I said with desperation. "But what about this attempted attack? The *Shangri-La* is leaving soon for the United States. I will be so worried about my friend. She says she has a sword. I can't imagine what she would do with it if she felt threatened."

"Ah, Mr. Paul," the detective said with some amusement. "When that man stood at the bottom of the steps leading to Miss Kaji's house he shouted up at her in a very loud voice. He demanded that she come with him. One of our patrolmen who lives nearby was playing mah-jongg with his friends. He heard the commotion even over the sound of the tiles. He heard the man saying he would kill your friend if she did not come down. But Miss Kaji stood at the top of the stairs with that sword in her hand and said nothing. She was wearing a *yukata*. It was one of those days . . . hot, hot, hot and very humid. She rolled up her sleeves and she stared down at the man in the moonlight. Our patrolman could see the moonlight reflecting off her sword in a very dignified manner."

I could not believe this. It was 1959, not 1859. Surely such things could not happen. I told the detective that it seemed too fantastic.

But he said it all worked out for the best. The patrolman arrested Shinoda because the police had already warned him against making more trouble. Nazaka contacted the man's big gangster boss, the *oyabun*, back in Hiroshima and told him to release Shinoda from his obligation to bring you back so that you could resume your duties as a favorite of elite patrons. The police and the yakuza organizations communicate regularly, Nazaka said, especially if gangsters behave violently in public and without honor, and if their crimes become headlines. He reminded the boss that publicity would be embarrassing. Both Shinoda and the *oyabun* would lose face. How could they live with stories in newspapers read by millions of people that told how a woman they had enslaved as a prostitute had escaped their clutches and had faced them defiantly and successfully,

292

armed with a sword, from her castle on the mountain? The *oyabun* had thought about that for a while, Nazaka said, and then he agreed to call off the mission that had brought Shinoda to Yokosuka.

In fact, the boss had acknowledged his admiration for your discretion and your demeanor, Yukiko, and he had confessed that he had always had respect for you.

"She has the Yamato spirit," the boss said, using the proud term for ancient Japan. As for Shinoda, the *oyabun* said he would deal with him privately.

"Miss Kaji is, in effect, free," the detective said with a grimace that could also have been a smile. "Please enjoy your friendship."

Chapter 23

THE GARDEN OF GRAND VISION

Having mastered the instruction booklet, Shingo gave the [electric] razor a trial. . . . He moved his chin over the razor, the instruction booklet in his other hand. "It says here that it does well too with the downy hair at the nape of a lady's neck." His eyes met Kikuko's. The hairline at her forehead was very beautiful. It seemed to him that he had not really seen it before. It drew a delicately graceful curve. The division between the fine skin and the even, rich hair was sharp and clean. For some reason, the cheeks of the otherwise wan face were slightly flushed. Her eyes were shining happily.

—Scene from *Yama No Oto* (*The Sound of the Mountain*),
by Kawabata Yasunari, in which an affectionate
father-in-law feels desire for his son's wife, Kikuko*

I fled from Detective Nazaka after he pointed the way up the mountain in a sudden gesture as if I were going to leap up the 101 steps like an Olympian. This is going to be the last time

---

* Kawabata won the 1968 Nobel Prize for Literature. He killed himself four years later in Kamakura.

I ascend the steps, I thought. I knew that if I paused on the steps on the way up, I would gulp and then I would cry. So I ran all the way to the top, two steps at a time, not knowing what lay ahead.

You said we should meet at your house, but there was no set time. That was normal. There was never any set time when we encountered each other. Time was set in terms of afternoons and evenings. They were concepts that made a mockery of schedules aboard the *Shangri-La*, which were set to the exact hour and minute, very much like the timing mechanism, I suppose, that would cause the nuclear weapons on the ship to detonate if we ever dropped them on Paul Feng's friends and family in China. You told me how much you hated having to start work at exactly seven in the evening and how you dreaded watching the minute hand move round the face of your windup alarm clock with the dual bells on top that scared the crows in the trees outside your house when the little hammer hit them, *clang, clang, clang*.

But three-quarters of the way up the steps, which were now slick with lichens and moss because of the summer rains, I heard your alarm clock ringing. And then, when I reached the top, I heard the cursing of a sleepy woman and the sound of the alarm clock tumbling across the floor after you slapped it. At the doorway to your house I heard you muttering to yourself, as if you were cross or annoyed. You sounded as if you were murmuring a song without even realizing it, which you often did when you were preoccupied with greeting me or gathering your favorite books around you for what you called "a delightful afternoon in the Garden of Grand Vision."

When you first told me that, I remember saying, "But I thought this place was your castle on the mountain."

"If I was a man, this would be my castle," you said. "If you want to look at it as my castle or my fortress that is understandable . . . after all, you are almost a man." You laughed as if you had just said the most wicked thing in the world.

"But I am a woman," you said. "This is the Garden of Grand Vision. I have decreed that this is my pleasure dome.

"Read Samuel Taylor Coleridge, sailor boy. Learn about Xanadu. Xanadu was no Shangri-La. It was a refuge for drug addicts and dreamers. I am a constant dreamer."

You were pouring the green tea now. A look of pleasure came across your face as you inhaled the fragrance of the brew.

"Intelligent people know that Xanadu was a vision from a dream . . . 'In Xanadu did Kubla Khan a stately pleasure dome decree . . .' I don't mean to be cruel, and I don't want to be critical of you, Paul-san, and I especially don't want to offend Mr. Coleridge by stating that opium made him have that dream. None of us know if that is true. But get an education for Heaven's sake!"

You gave me a big mug of tea. I reminded you that I still had to do three years of my enlistment in the navy. College would have to wait.

You waved your finger at me slowly.

"No! No! No!" you said. "Read! Read! Read! Listen! Listen! Listen! Question! Question! Question! Think! Think! Think! I work in a bar and I read. I work in a bar and I write. I work in a bar and I have to listen to stupid men talking to me in pidgin English as if I was a baby. And then I ask them to buy me a drink because I earn money from that, and they always do, of course. But I would never ask you to buy me a drink. Oh no. Do you know why? It is because from the first day we met you talked to me as if I was a woman."

Oh! I remember now how spectacular you looked when you first woke up after a profound afternoon nap awakened not by kisses but by a windup alarm clock manufactured in the People's Republic of China! The clock face was a picture of a woman People's Liberation Army soldier hoisting a rifle in one hand and clenching her fist with the other. "Be happy, happy!" you sometimes teased, addressing the stern-faced soldier.

Your hair hung down over your face and your eyes were swimming in what you called "wake-up water." You are one of the few women I have known who looked far better without makeup. Without it your face showed so much of your history, at least I thought it did when I looked at you closely. The faint web of lines around your eyes and mouth were like faint images of a road map. There was no hint of white powder on your face, and no vermilion touches.

You never minded me looking that way at you. In fact, you usually stared right back.

It was humid, which meant that your *yukata*—maybe the one you were wearing when you defied Shinoda Yusuke—was damp with sweat. It clung to the outline of your body. You told me once that the Japanese typically wear nothing under a *yukata*. That did not surprise me because you also told me that Japanese men and women loved to go to community hot baths together to soak in unbearably hot water where they gossiped naked and without shame.

You began searching in the gloom of your kitchen for the

tin container in which you kept your precious green tea leaves. I heard you speaking by name to obstacles getting in the way of your search: "Shoo, Mr. Tea Cup. Shoo, Mr. Radish. Shoo, Big Fat Coffee Maker . . . Shoo . . . Out of my way!"

You suddenly realized that I was standing just inside your wide-open door, studying you dealing with disorder. "Shoo!" you said sharply. "You too, sailor boy!"

But when I turned away as if I was going to leave, you came running.

"Wait! Wait! Wait," you demanded. "This is the Garden of Grand Vision. I didn't give you permission to leave. You don't have my permission to go, even if you want to go. Do you understand, sailor boy?"

I laughed and I saw a wonderful smile break across your face. You were standing about three feet away. "Oh, oh, Yuki-chan," you said. "Is this thin young creature really the man you love?" And then you laughed again because you knew you had hurt my feelings and because you also knew that I was not going to hold it against you because I loved you too.

"I am really happy to see you," I said. My face was earnest, I am sure. You took my hand and let me pull you toward me. I could smell the special smell of your body after you had been dreaming and making tea. You looked up at me. I brushed those strands of hair out of your eyes. You leaned your head far back as if we were a couple dancing tango.

"How nice," you said. "How nice you are to me!"

Your little brass-tinted kettle was belching steam again. It was time for another cup of *ocha*. After you had poured the scalding water over the leaves, we went outside to sit with our hips touching on one of the steps to your porch. We stared at the sun, as if it were something to worship. You draped an arm round my shoulder and rocked me a little. You were murmuring again. It was the plaintive, simple, sad folk song "*Itsuki no komoriuta*" (Lullaby of Itsuki). It is a song traditionally sung by very young female descendants of the Heike clan, which fought a bitter war for supremacy in the twelfth century and lost, prompting many Heike warriors to throw themselves into the sea rather than surrender. These girls were now living in poverty and earning money as babysitters among the descendants of their victorious rivals. When the Bon festival, commemorating those deaths, occurs each July, the babysitters are given a few days off to return to the poverty of their home villages in the distant mountains. It is a lullaby dipped in sadness that in 1959 every Japanese mother knew.

> As soon as the Bon festival arrives, I will leave for my
>   hometown.
> The sooner Bon comes, the sooner I will go home. I am
>   no better than a beggar.
> They are rich people
> With good obis and good kimonos. Who will cry for me
> When I die?
> Only the locusts in the mountain behind the house. No,
>   No! It's not locusts,
> It's my little sister who cries.
> Don't cry, little sister, I will be worried about you. When
>   I am dead,
> Bury me by the roadside. Passersby will lay flowers for me.

What flowers would they lay on me? They would lay
fresh camellias.
Their tears will fall down on me from above.

That afternoon at your house, in which we did nothing but
sit with each other as day slowly became night, resulted in
my most vivid memories of who you were. It was as if I had
been treated to a box of the finest Belgian chocolates, and I
was unwrapping the silver foil from them, one by one, to
discover what was inside.

For a while I tried talking to you about how you had faced
down Shinoda Yusuke, but you were having none of it. You
would not show me your sword. You would not accept any
praise or admiration from me. You just shrugged, and tightened the grip of your arm round my shoulder. "Hush," you
said. "Hush."

I also tried talking about the fact that we would be saying
good-bye tomorrow. But you dismissed that too. It was as if
for you there would be *no* final good-bye.

"Will you be sad?" I asked with no accompanying words,
like a child.

"Don't ask me, please. You will not want to hear that I
will be happy when you go."

"Happy?" I asked, startled.

But you would not explain. You only hugged me tighter.
For the first time I got a sense of the roundness and weight
of your hips and the smallness of your waist and the straight
strength of your back. Your small breasts were pressed against
my arm. I did not dare to move for fear of losing you. The
night breeze that always started on your hill when the sun

began going down was rustling the paulownia. It responded by showering us with petals, as if we were betrothed.

I knew I soon had to report back to the *Shangri-La*, but I could not move. I did not want to move. I wanted to dream where I was and fall asleep with you, but that was impossible. The surface of the sea around the ship was sparkling in the moonlight, and all across the dark sky stars were signaling to us from the heavens.

You said to me: "If you go now, you will break the spell."

I put my arm round you, and we sat like that for a while. You were still humming songs. A dense mist was descending on your hill. The trees and the shrubs and the grass began glistening with dew. There was a chill that now blew in from the sea, as if to remind us that I was being called. We stood up and looked at each other with just traces of a smile. I thought I heard a chorus of voices somewhere far off. It was something like the fabled song of the Sirens. It would start and then fade in and out as the breeze stirred your Garden of Grand Vision, which you told me existed in your lost city of Harbin.

"What kind of garden was it, Yuki?" I asked, once again the child.

"Well. It was a garden with a wall around it, and there was a plaque high above the entrance gate identifying it as the Garden of Grand Vision. The Chinese writing expressing that name was very beautiful. It was built to celebrate the grandeur of five thousand years of Chinese civilization. But the truth was that when we Japanese came and created the Manchukuo Empire [Manchuria], something terrible happened. We Japanese grew rich. The Chinese people became poor. That wonderful garden filled up with drug addicts and prostitutes and drifters. Someone told me later there were two thousand prostitutes living in the garden. They would pick the red roses and put them in their hair. Those poor women felt secure inside those walls and the garden shared its beauty with them so that it made their life more bearable while they were struggling to survive or giving up to die."

You stopped talking for a few moments. The mist was now moistening your hair, giving it a sheen and a look of wildness, as if you had just ridden into Harbin on horseback, straight from the wastes of Mongolia where Kublai Khan once ruled. Now the tears were coming. You could not stop the tears.

"I remember that when I was a little girl, I asked my father to show me the garden. It was on an afternoon—a long, hot, and humid one, just like this one. He did not put on his uniform but he slipped a pistol into his pocket before he took me by the hand . . . How old was I? Maybe seven or eight years old . . . I had on a white dress and my mother had tied my hair in pigtails. We set off walking toward the Garden of Grand Vision. The shopkeepers were greeting my father with a great deal of respect, but here and there from other people—Chinese people—on the streets I could hear hissing or the whispering of words that I could understand because I spoke Chinese. They were cursing my father but they were doing it discreetly. I told my father I was frightened, but he told me we were Japanese and we should hold our heads high. We were proud. We were invincible.

"We passed through the gate to the garden and my father pointed out the plaque, which was painted in gold. It looked so elegant. But do you know that just a few meters beyond the gate there was a dead person. My father said he died from the famine. I asked him how it was possible that people did not have enough to eat if we had a dinner table piled high with fresh fruit and big bowls of pure white rice and all the chicken and pork you could imagine. My father said it was because we were Japanese. He said it as if being Japanese was so special, which of course it was, because *we are* a special people. After a while we saw more dead people in the garden, and I told my father I wanted to go back home. And do you know what he said? He said that we could not do that because we were Japanese, and if we ran away it would show that we were afraid. We can never be afraid, my father said. That was the way it was, I believe, on the day that he was killed soon after the Soviets seized the city without firing a shot."

He was killed, you said, after Emperor Hirohito of Japan went on the radio and announced the surrender. He called on all Japanese "to bear the unbearable" ignominy of defeat—the first defeat in their two-thousand-year history.

"I believed he was killed because he was hated for torturing Chinese people," you said. "My mother always said his death was an accident. But I have heard that even when they were hacking him to death with kitchen cleavers he refused to show fear. Some witnesses told my mother that he stuck his chest out and took the blows in silence.

"I am his daughter. This is why I say I am a bad woman."

There was silence. I hoped your daughter was looking down on you from the stars. I hoped that she would kiss your forehead and call you "Mama." I wish now that I had told you that.

"Do you know where your father died?" I asked.

"In the Garden of Grand Vision, under a huge acacia tree covered with golden flowers."

I had to pick my way carefully down the steps to reach the street below. A light rain had started that chilled me. I began shivering. I had a long walk ahead of me. I glanced back and I could see that you were standing at the top of the steps, probably much as you had done when Shinoda Yusuke turned up to try to drag you back to Hiroshima. I knew that he had been sent to make you return. I also thought there might be more to this story. Maybe he was in love with you even though he had forced you to work for him as a prostitute. Maybe he was one of those men you would not give yourself to even if he showered you with gold and diamonds. Maybe in some strange way you loved him too. But I knew I would never know.

You had faced him with a sword in your hands. But when you watched me descend the stairs there was no sword. It was just you, standing there as if you were the statue of Kannon, the much-loved Buddhist goddess of mercy, her head bowed modestly, her hands clasped under her breasts, that had once graced Harbin's Garden of Grand Vision.

I walked quickly through the wet streets toward the lights of the city, the umbrella you gave me over my head. The sound of men laughing drifted out of the small sake bars. I caught glimpses of the warm scenes inside as I passed by. There was room for no more than eight or ten customers at the typical sake bar. Behind the bar was a *mamasan*, but she was not like the typically older ones who ruled the sailor bars on Honcho with compassion and an iron fist. These *mamasan*s looked as if they were in their midtwenties. They had done their best to appear glamorous. As I passed I heard several of them call out a loud "*Irrashai!* [Welcome!]," followed by a chorus of giggles and drunken male comments because they realized they had invited an unwanted US Navy sailor to step inside. There was a sudden power outage, and all along this street of bars I heard the hostesses shouting out in English, amid laughter in the dark, "Chance! Chance!"—an invitation to patrons to steal a kiss.

If only I could speak Japanese, I thought. I would step inside and be funny and cheerful. It was my duty to study Japanese, I decided there and then. It was an idea that thrilled me and inspired me to whistle a happy tune that I made up as I went along.

Tomorrow, you told me, I should meet you at the White Rose at exactly eight p.m. That was unusual. You had set a time for something. But you gave me no clues. You set the hour almost as an afterthought, in fact. Yet another subtle version of your "happy" smile passed over your face.

Chapter 24

WE ARE VERY SORRY

Echoes of my shadow, the memory of you wanders through
　　the alleys of my thoughts.
Your life and mine are two opposite paths, two silhouettes
　　cast by the same poetic light.
Lost in a delicate romance that never begins, a romance
　　unfulfilled in silence conveyed.
Luck sends us on different paths:
I, unseen by you, you unseen by me.
Our lives shall meet on the same horizon to await the
　　glowing light of our own love.

　　　　—From the song "*Sombra de Mis Sombras*"
　　　　(Echoes of My Shadows), circa 1934,
　　　　by the Mexican musical genius Agustín Lara*

Nazaka Goro had shocked me with details of the dramatic
confrontation at your house. But then he had told me you were
free and he had signaled me with a heroic gesture—in the way

---

* Translated for this book by Carmen Barnard Baca. "This is the opposite
of waiting for the dawning light of love," Carmen notes. "It's waiting for
the glow of that light of love, after it has gone over the mountains."

of an officer in the heat of battle urging his men forward—to climb your steps. You had told me tearfully about the horror of the Garden of Grand Vision in Harbin, but as a result we had never been as close as we were that day, sitting side by side on your mountain. What was that you told me? Oh yes: "We are two lost souls who are now united." Violence and sweetness. Sweetness and violence. I would encounter the coupling of those two opposites all my life, through wars and marriages, again and again and again.

As I settled into my rack—which is what we called our bunk beds—deep inside the *Shangri-La*, I realized that you had at last been able to open the vault where you kept your deepest secrets. I was sure you had never told anyone that story before. My body felt cold. I gripped my pillow for warmth and then I realized that it was wet with tears. Happiness and sadness. Sadness and happiness. I was leaving in two days. It would be impossible to know more.

Fortunately, while lost in those regrets I was not old enough to realize that the way was now clear for us to become actual lovers. But that could never be. I was still a child, mourning my loss—that I would no longer have you looking over me, urging me with a mix of forcefulness and tenderness to make something of myself in this life that had robbed you of the opportunity to have a love that would last forever. As I now look back through the years, the love I had for you is still as ardent as it was back then. "Do you remember me?" you often asked. "Do you remember me?"

In the morning there was a blur of activity on the ship. Sailors had been making last-minute purchases ashore: excellent cameras by Canon and Nikon made in Japan that far outclassed anything manufactured in the USA, early reel-to-reel tape recorders by Akai and Sony, chinaware by Noritake to keep the wife happy, and dolls with downcast eyes dressed as geishas to give to mothers. Jim Fowler had bought a bolt of purple silk for his girlfriend and he had surprised me by presenting me with a copy of *Anthology of Japanese Literature: From the Earliest Era to the Mid-Nineteenth Century* by Donald Keene. I still have the book, which is signed by Jim: "Let this from the past be a window from which you can see the future." Red Downs had been worried because his girlfriend in Jackson had not written him in recent weeks, and then, suddenly, there was a letter from her telling him she had been bitten by a police dog as she was being arrested in a civil rights demonstration. He was a proud man. I had not seen much of Oscar and Gunther but I had heard from tittering girls at the White Rose that those two guys were "skivvy honchos"—a vulgar Japanese expression for lotharios.

In the afternoon Chaplain Peeples stopped by the *News Horizon* office to tell me I had passed the written test to become a JO3—a third-class petty officer with a special rating in journalism—one of the rarest of all categories for enlisted men. There was a woeful look on his face, but he shook my hand.

"You have been a difficult handful this summer," he told me. "You have a big responsibility now. I only hope that you behave wisely." I thanked him. But it occurred to me at that same moment that promotion from gnat to wasp might enable me to apply for a transfer from the *Shangri-La* to someplace else, maybe even here in Japan, where there were lots of US Navy facilities needing someone who could spell and write speeches for ambitious commanding officers.

The clock was ticking toward evening. I searched my locker for a farewell gift. I discovered that other than books and a shamisen—an elegant three-stringed instrument with a sound akin to a banjo and a body covered in snakeskin that I had bought from a startled music-store owner on the island of Okinawa—I had not acquired much in those port cities during the seven-month cruise of the USS *Shangri-La*. I had been too busy writing to you and editing and mailing your letters. I had been preoccupied with long nights in which I attempted to write poetry. I had gone ashore and I had wandered much farther afield in those cities than any other sailor I knew. The ship made five visits to Yokosuka between April 15 and the third week of September. I had spent virtually all my time getting to know you in those forty-four days the ship was anchored in your harbor. I got to the bottom of my locker and I realized that I really did have nothing for you. I tried writing a letter and enclosing some of my poetry, but I could not find the words to express how I felt about you and our friendship. These feelings were too profound. I had not experienced them before and I could not think of anything to say except "beautiful" and "thank you." I was not equipped with the language to dazzle a woman. I was myself, newly twenty, bedazzled.

Night was approaching. Commander Crockett came by the office to ask me whether I was going ashore. I gave him a quick explanation of what had happened at your house and I told him I did not have a gift for you. "What young man would have such a gift?" he asked with a snort. He told me to wait a few minutes, and then he returned with a record that included Lena Horne's 1941 recording of the Rodgers and Hart song "Where or When."

"Son," he said, "I do believe from what I know about your lady friend that she would appreciate this. You are a very fortunate young man." And then he gave me one of his big Texas grins and exited quickly, disappearing before I could even give him a salute or say thank you.

I clicked on the power to the record player, and I listened. I listened again, and then again. I realized that all those inexplicable emotions I was feeling at that moment, which were almost halting my beating heart, were happening because, suddenly, I was no longer a boy. I was a man.

It seems we've stood and talked like this before
We looked at each other in the same way then
But I can't remember where or when.
The clothes you're wearing are the clothes you wore
The smile you are smiling, you were smiling then
But I can't remember where or when.

There was a notice attached to the door of the White Rose. It read: "We Close Tonight 2000 to 2200 Hours. We Are Very Sorry."

I had a moment of panic. I looked at my wristwatch. It was almost eight o'clock. Twenty hundred hours in navy-speak meant eight p.m., but why was the White Rose closed? I approached the door and then noticed Mama's nose and eyes peeking through a little sliding hatch, head high to the average Japanese.

I stuck my nose forward to where it was almost touching Mama's nose, and she let out a series of giggles. I heard her voice. "Mr. Anthony Perkins is here." She unlocked the door and slowly pulled it open. She was dressed in her customary white apron and baggy pants and sandals but she had newly permed her hair and she did something she had never done before: she hugged me and kissed me on the cheek.

I heard the excited voices of the hostesses inside the bar.

Suddenly all the lights came on. I could see you waving wildly in the background. Reiko was skipping toward me with her country-girl laugh and her rosy cheeks aflame. Everyone was shouting, "*Irasshai! Irasshai!* [Welcome! Welcome!]" That scene and that cry now so familiar to me was one of the many reasons I have always had a special place in my heart for things Japanese.

Inside the bar, attached to the pillars, the mirrors, the balconies, the booths, and even around the doorway to the *benjo* (toilet), someone had hung scores of bright pink balloons, each one of which bore the words "Happy. Happy." Nowadays, I suppose, balloons like that would have smiley faces.

I especially liked the large, crudely painted silhouette of the *Shangri-La* hanging over the cash register. Whoever had done the work had painted the ship pink and on the hull of the ship, which everyone knew had a cache of nuclear weapons, had spelled out, in deep red, the word "Happiness."

The girls were clapping. And then they joined in a spirited Japanese-language rendition of "Auld Lang Syne," which I realized was more familiar to the Japanese than it was to me, followed by a chorus of affectionate exclamations and smiles so sentimental I had to gulp to keep from bursting into tears. The jukebox was not playing country and western: it was loaded with Japanese pop tunes for dancing. It was slowly dawning on me that this was a good-bye party that you and Mama and Reiko had organized. But for me? Just for me?

I placed myself in front of you and I gave you the record with the cut of "Where or When."

"Oh, déjà vu!" you exclaimed. "I love that song that you and I never heard together."

We stared at each other for a long, long time. "Yuki," I said. "When I am gone and you listen to that song, remember me."

There were tears in your eyes, but you did not weep. The tears made your eyes flash. You were more *ron-pari* than ever before. You were wearing a tight black dress with a pattern of small sequins that glittered as your body slowly moved to the rhythm of the music. Long black hair. Eyes the color of coal. Scarlet lipstick. Black high heels. I was dressed in my white US Navy uniform, which emphasized the thinness of my frame and my youth. You took me by the hand and led me to the dance floor while everyone clapped. You nestled your head into my chest as we slow danced to *enka* blues that as far as I was concerned had been written especially for sweetheart moments like this.

Reiko watched, a hand clutching her heart. There were tears—when I think back now, they were happy tears—trickling down her cheeks. Mama was blowing her nose, and several of the hostesses ran to her to give comfort. The dancing, the applause, the weeping and sobbing: all of it continued until Reiko came forward to lead you and me to one of the booths.

We sat there, a spotlight over our heads, our bodies touching.

You reached out, straightened the little finger of my right hand as if doing that was the most normal thing in the world, and without offering an explanation you tied a length of red string to that finger before connecting the other end to the little finger of your left hand.

The girls, even gayer now, were dancing with each other. It seemed as if we had exchanged only a couple of dozen words since the evening began. And then you untied the string and shook my hand, smiling in a way that I had never seen before, as if tears would give you comfort but smiles would break your heart. You shot a quick look at me and then you faded into the background, slowly moving from one table to another until shadows hid you from me.

It took me several minutes to realize that you had not gone to get drinks. You had gone. You were completely gone and I had not had a chance to say good-bye. I leaped up in alarm and started for the door, but Reiko blocked my path.

"Mr. Paul," she said. "Sit down with me, please. Yuki-chan gave me this letter. It is for you. She said it is only for you. She told me to tell you, 'Be happy.'"

Dear Paul,

Now that you are almost gone like a shadow disappearing from my life, it is appropriate for me to say I love you. I am writing this letter inside my house. It is the night before the party. It is dark in my room. I have been watching a beam of moonlight retreating slowly, so slowly from my bed to the window. At the moment that moon ray vanished I thought, I love you. There will be no other.

I am not afraid to send you my love, sailor boy, knowing that there will be silence. I know that you will not come back. You will not reply and I am so happy. I am proud to

be telling you this, beautiful young man,
because you have grown up. You loved me too,
I think. It is true, isn't it? You don't have
to tell me. I know it is true. How wonderful
and precious that feeling is for me to know
that I can love again.

You have seen and heard many things this
summer. Those were things that most people
cannot imagine. Now you will live a long and
adult life. You see clearly. Your mind is like
a sharp sword. You have strong opinions. You
have good judgment. Because you know what a
lie is, you know how to use truth.

When you are old you can look back through
all the events this summer when you helped
me with your innocence to be free. Remember
that you so kindly gave me the embrace of a
lifetime? That embrace will sustain me until
I die. That one strong embrace so gentle and
yet so strong that made me a happy woman again
instead of a desperate and unhappy creature
with no one to love. I will remember you.

Forgive me for disappearing, Paul-san.
One day I believe you will understand why I
shook your hand before I vanished. I hope you
can understand this very bad written letter.
I worked many hours with my dictionary. I
made many cups of tea. What I want to say is
that we are brother and sister. We are like
mother and son. We are like man and woman

bound together by their love and charity.
We are from opposite ends of the world, but
we will be together for eternity even in
this existence where love affairs amount
to nothing more than frost on the ground in
late spring.

A Chinese poet from the T'ang Dynasty
once told his beloved when he was losing her:
"Promise that at the end of every summer
when I look up at the inexhaustible night
and watch the seasons change, you will be
a star looking down at me . . . and if I
die before you die, I will wait for you in
Paradise."

Loving You Forever,
Yukiko

Many, many years later (fifty-four years later, in fact), I finally
understood. When I typed those words—red string—into my
computer's Web browser, a virtual meteor shot across the sky
as I looked at what Wikipedia had to say.

The red string of fate, also referred to as the red thread
of destiny, red thread of fate, and other variants, is an East
Asian belief originating from Chinese legend and is also used
in Japanese legend. According to this myth, the gods tie a red
cord around the ankles of those that are to meet one another in
a certain situation or help each other in a certain way. Often,
in Japanese culture, it is thought to be tied around the little
finger. According to Chinese legend, the deity in charge of "the
red thread" is believed to be Yuè Xià Lǎo ([月下老], often

abbreviated to "Yuelăo" [月老]), the old lunar matchmaker god who is also in charge of marriages.

The two people connected by the red thread are destined lovers, regardless of time, place, or circumstances. This magical cord may stretch or tangle, but never break. I know why you never gave me an explanation. It was a good-bye and yet not a good-bye. As far as you were concerned, we would be linked until the end of time.

Please enjoy your happiness.

Chapter 25

CAN YOU FIND IT
IN YOUR HEART?

What the finer nature of the Japanese woman is, no man has
told.... It would be too much like writing of the sweetness
of one's own sister or mother. One must leave it in sacred
silence—with a prayer to all the gods.

—Lafcadio Hearn,
from *Some New Letters and Writings**

It was mid-September 1959. We were back in San Diego. At the
dock, ecstatic families were waiting to greet the *Shangri-La*.
There was no one there for me, of course. I was single and
uncomplicated, not single and complicated as I am now. Three
thousand four hundred and forty-eight of us stood at attention
in our navy blues in formation on the vast flight deck led by
Davy Crockett and Charlie Peeples. Only the chaplain marched
nervously around and around and up and down, searching
for someone—his wife, maybe—in the shrieking and leaping
crowd of women with kids in tow on the quay far below.

---

* Lafcadio Hearn married a Japanese woman, Koizumi Setsu, in 1891. He is
buried next to Setsu and their son Kazuo in Zōshigaya Cemetery in Tokyo.

There had been one more letter from you the day before we arrived. The mail plane flew out from California and touched down on the ship. The aircrew kicked out a dozen canvas mailbags. A few hours later the words "Mail call! Mail call!" came over the intercom and, surprise, there was the letter. It took me a while to summon up the courage to open it. I was still bruised, I suppose, by the abrupt farewell and by my inability to say what I had wanted to say, but which I did not remember now that I was opening your letter.

Dear Paul,

How are you? Are you still in the Shangri-La? Are you in America? Maybe someone will let me know. This little bird singing in the tree is half expecting someone to come to the bar to tell her what you are doing and how you are thinking now that you have gone. Are you well? Are you happy? Oh no. I am sounding like an old woman now. Forgive me for writing to you again, but when we parted that last evening we did not say the word "goodbye."

And that last time, when we parted, we did shake hands. When our hands touched, my thoughts were saying you were going and yet my heart was hoping that you were not because I did not want to be losing you. I did not dare to cry. Reiko told me I had to be a happy strong woman. How hard that was for me! In films there is always one last incredible embrace. But Mama was a very strict schoolteacher that night and like a good Japanese woman she wanted to make you happy.

I am really joyful now to say that we had so many happy times enjoying every tiny second of every minute of every long day . . . and now we have such a beautiful relationship built from our memories. Yes, no matter what happens to me, I will always cherish the truth about what we were. My father and mother, my brothers, my dear daughter, have all been telling me in my dreams that we were beautiful together.

Tonight I listened to my favorite record. I am sure you remember that I sometimes played it for you. It is an old scratchy record which is why I love it so. Since you have gone, I have played it so many times. Billie Holiday sings the song so slowly, no faster than her breathing or her beating heart, I think. That record is from 1944, you know. I was yet a young girl in Manchuria, and you were only 5 years old. But like the memory of you and me, this song will live forever. So, now I will let the record speak.

I'll be seeing you
In every lovely summer's day,
In everything that's light and gay,
I'll always think of you that way [. . .]

You know, sailor boy, I can tell you now that it is not easy to get an experience like we had when life becomes poetry. I know that because I am an old woman who has been knocked down many times. All around me I see unhappy people. But now when I see women cry I think, "Yuki! You are such lucky ugly woman. You are so lucky to find such a nice man whom you could love and who loved you in return." That is why I need once more to say to you, thank you very much.

I know one day many years from now, when you see the morning light on the garden of roses you said you want to have, that you will remember me. I have full confidence that we will meet again. I'll be seeing you in that small café and in all the old familiar places that this heart of mine embraces.

All my love,
Yukiko

I wrote back, bleating like a lamb, but there was no reply.

EPILOGUE

I had been in love with you and I had not fallen out of love. You had stopped writing to me but you lingered, at first a presence, and then a fragrance I sensed in shadows, and then a faint voice carried on winds that crossed the sea. I also was in love with your country in a giddy way, almost as if I was in love with a woman. You had urged me to study Japanese. But how would that be possible? I had been promoted and soon word came through the grapevine that I would probably be transferred to the Great Lakes Naval Training Center in Michigan to write press releases sent to the hometown newspapers of recruits training at boot camp there. This was supposed to be a choice posting. But as soon as I stepped ashore in San Diego I immediately went to the Pacific Fleet personnel office to plead for a transfer to any navy facility in Japan that might have a job opening for a petty officer with a journalism specialty like me. I spoke to a veteran clerk who had clearly once been bitten by a spider because he never asked me why I wanted that transfer. Instead, a hint of a grin came over his face as if he had just reverted to his youth. "Japan," he said. "Yes, Japan." And he said it with such longing that he might as well have been talking about sending me to Shangri-La itself.

During the week of Christmas 1959, Yuki, I learned that I

would be reassigned to the navy base in Yokosuka. I had beaten the odds, Red Downs said. He invited me to go with him to San Diego's old College Avenue Baptist Church the following Sunday when the African-American congregation raised its voice in song to give thanks. I did not know the words to the spirituals, but Red did, and he looked at me and said, "Let yourself be lifted up!" We sang "Oh Freedom" and "Eyes on the Prize." Black America was rising up and Red would soon be part of it. He was taking a train to Jackson to ask his hero girlfriend to marry him. My trajectory was different. I was joyful. I was dazzled by the prospect of returning to Japan, and who knows what else. In truth, I knew that my time with you was over and I was positive you would wish me to lead a life as a man—to work, to get more promotions, to study, to have adventures, to write poetry, to meet women, to get knocked down and get back up again.

I went with the *Shangri-La* when it left San Diego to dock at Bremerton, Washington, a few weeks later for a refit. Before I said my good-byes, I read several poems I had written for you in coffee shops in Seattle, appearing a couple of times with the late Allen Ginsberg and with Gary Snyder. I read with a new sense of maturity. There was applause. Jazz records were spinning. Several people were reading paperback copies of Kerouac's *On the Road*. This was my brief incarnation as a beat and I enjoyed it.

The ship would be Atlantic- and Mediterranean-based for a few years, but it would never cruise the western Pacific again except as a hulk. She was towed to Taiwan to be cut apart after she was sold for scrap in 1988.

Early in 1960, a navy plane flew me and forty or so other

young fortunates to Japan. I remember that almost everyone was talking about a woman they had met there. But not me, Yukiko. My summer with you was yours and mine alone and how could I possibly describe what had happened when I did not know the answer to that myself? I had taken a few days of leave but I did not tell my mother any more about you and she did not ask, which was good because we would have argued and she would have made me feel as if I had done something wrong. I began resisting the urge—the need—to think about you. But I was keenly aware that I had changed because of the gift of yourself that you gave me. I had your letters too.

I could have become melancholy, I suppose. I did miss you. But I focused all my energy on my new job writing news releases at the admiral's headquarters in Yokosuka. Kip Cooper, a navy chief petty officer fond of cigars, kept a grip on me as if he was my father and if I stepped out of line I would hear about it. He could be gruff and caring at the same time. Kip liked it that when I began venturing out of the base I took a notebook with me that I was filling with newly learned Japanese words and phrases. I bought a small, primitive, portable reel-to-reel tape recorder that I used to record conversations with Japanese men in sake bars.

For several weeks I avoided going anywhere near the Mozart café. I bypassed the bars in Honcho. There was something, just something, holding me back. You had slipped through my fingers and that final night at the White Rose had been so special and so perfect that I did not want to do anything to spoil that moment by revisiting it. And then one day I heard that "*Un bel di*" aria again from *Madama Butterfly*. It was as if the voice of Maria Callas was the voice of one of Claude Debussy's

Sirènes. The aria wafted down an alley where store workers and apartment tenants were putting out their rubbish in small cans and children were noisily playing *ken-ken-pa*—Japanese hopscotch. I suddenly heard a woman shout, "*Urusai!*" It was not your voice, Yukiko. But that shout caused me to wheel about and, in an instant, become determined to find you.

Honcho was different, somehow. This was midday on a Saturday. Not much was happening. The light was harsh. The facades of the nightclubs and bars looked shabby, forsaken, forlorn, garish. The White Rose had closed, although I discovered some months later that it had reopened in a different location. The door was locked. There was no notice there explaining what had happened. I asked at neighboring bars for you, for Reiko, for Mama—but nothing. I climbed the 101 steps, but you were not living there. There were no crows in the trees. The paulownia looked forlorn. Your prayers written on neatly folded pure white paper were gone. I spent some frustrating hours with my limited Japanese trying to ask questions. This was the nightmare I experienced in the aftermath of you. That summer of innocence and rain we shared now seemed so remote, almost not real. I searched for Nazaka Goro and discovered that he had been reassigned because of poor health. Mr. Ito was still running the Mozart café but he said, regret clouding the usual cordial smile on his face, that he had not seen you for weeks. The sign outside was still there: "Please enjoy your happiness."

And so you became the woman who occasionally, and then less occasionally, haunted me. We were sharing that beautiful memory you spoke of in your letter and you were happy, happy, happy with that memory. I hoped you were somewhere, maybe almost within reach. I sometimes had the thought that if I turned such and such a street corner, you would be there, clad in your *yukata*, clip-clopping along in your wooden geta, with a bag of books slung over your shoulder, and that you would look at me with a strange nod and pass on by without a word. But the premonition was false. Maybe it was wishful thinking. As the weeks went by and the rainy season of mid-summer, 1960, came and went, you became less of a presence and maybe even less of a memory.

I only spent a few months in Yokosuka, Yuki. There was a second promotion and it meant that I would be living as a virtual civilian in Tokyo. *Pacific Stars & Stripes*, the daily newspaper written and produced by a mixed team of young military guys and their mentors—a hard-drinking, scrappy, cigarette-smoking, and liquor-drinking gang of characters who had mostly been in Japan since the start of the US occupation in 1945—snapped me up and made me a reporter. I am sure my escapades would have amused you. They were evidence of manhood. There were two bar fights that resulted in reprimands. I was yanked back from Taiwan after being sent there to cover the official visit of Robert F. Kennedy: I wrote that his aggressively driven limousine knocked several Chinese off their bicycles instead of writing about diplomacy. I also was pulled back from the Philippines because the *Stars & Stripes* Ford sedan I had parked outside the home of an American missionary couple who put me up overnight was stolen.

The man you helped create had his share of early loves. Do you remember the sultry singer Matsuo Kazuko? I met her at Club Rikki in Tokyo. I have been playing her records, hearing her voice again, and remembering her tobacco kisses flavored with cognac and how she slapped an astonished gangster's face in the club when he tried to buy her. Koga Yasuko, a shop girl who looked so good in pink angora sweaters, read *Romeo and Juliet* out loud in English on the subway as a way of flirting with me without embarrassment. And then there was Asaoka Michiko, who was really not Japanese but Korean. I called her "Michi." She sang blues in cheap nightclubs reeking of spilled beer and foul cigarettes. One day—after I spent the night with her while a typhoon rattled the shutters in her tiny apartment—she led me proudly to a pro–North Korea rally where everyone was denouncing the United States. She won my admiration that day, and I bought a bottle of sake that we drank later. I told her she was brave and pretty and bold and wonderful, which made her cry because no one had told her that before. I could have so easily fallen in love with her. But one day Michi simply disappeared, with no hint and no note and no trace except for a comb on the floor thick with a tangle of her long black hair. That image has remained with me for all these years. It is only recently, after I mentioned the scene to Japanese friends, that I learned that among the many thousands of Japanese superstitions is a truly ancient one involving combs. A comb falls—for some women that is a bad omen. They will not pick up the comb. If you break the complex kanji (櫛) used for the word *kushi* into its as-sociated parts, one part (*ku*) means bitter and the other part (*shi*) means death. Also, *kushi* sounds a lot like *kushin*, which means trouble or pain.

After my four years in the navy were up in 1962, I studied Japanese history and language at the University of Illinois, and I received a Woodrow Wilson Fellowship to study ancient Japanese history and culture at Harvard. Between 1968 and 1970, my poetry was appearing in prestigious literary journals alongside work by the likes of W. H. Auden, Thomas Kinsella, Anthony Kerrigan, Stanley Cooperman, Joyce Carol Oates, and Dilys Laing. I turned down Harvard's offer of an additional grant and selected instead a summer internship with *Newsweek* in Chicago. That internship resulted in ten years of writing for the magazine, including two more years based in Tokyo and several years in and out of Cambodia and Vietnam doing war coverage. That is where my poetry writing ceased, Yukiko. My sister Mary blames the magazine, arguing that, "it should never have sent a poet to cover a war." In the early 1970s, when I was based in Tokyo for *Newsweek*, I made one personal visit to Yokosuka. But I went there only because I was curious to see how the city had changed. I did not have an expectation that I would find you and so I made no attempt to look for you.

I have related how in these later years of my life, in the midst of conversation about lost loves with friends in Costa Rica, I remembered that somewhere I had your letters. I found them, I had an epiphany, and I began writing. There were immediate questions asked by people interested in the story. Where are you, Yukiko? Are you still living? Who were you? Am I going to try to find you?

Because I do not know what happened to you after we last saw each other, I do not know if you moved to Tokyo or some other city or if you went back to the Hiroshima area: the city from which you had escaped. You had no reason to return, I believe. The yakuza gang in Hiroshima had washed its hands of you. I suppose that it is possible that a relative, maybe from your ancestral town, may have emerged. I will never know, probably, whether you and Shinoda Yusuke really were lovers and if you might have chosen to be with him again.

According to Detective Nazaka, you were a courtesan to the Japanese elite in Hiroshima. You were a woman of culture because you were brought up in Manchuria. You were not a prostitute in Yokosuka. You were not a geisha. You poured drinks, listened to sobbing sailors, danced with them too, and earned money from tips and your cut of the drinks they ordered. Geishas are not prostitutes. They sometimes become the lovers of wealthy patrons but they are artistes and highly trained in all of the arts. They were a national treasure really, and are still regarded as such in Japan, where to have the pleasure and prestige of an important geisha's company for one evening can cost a man as much as round-trip airfare between Los Angeles and Tokyo.

Many people ask why I kept your letters. They sometimes say that was unusual. After they read the letters they ask if it was really possible that a woman like you, working in a grim occupation for the Japanese mafia in Hiroshima, would read Kafka and Rilke, be familiar with the ancient Japanese women poets, appreciate Maria Callas, Debussy, and Beethoven, and speak Mandarin Chinese and Russian? Why didn't you teach school, or work in a library, or marry a college professor? they want to know.

A few young people ask why I did not use email to keep in touch with you after I left Japan in 1959. A woman in her thirties said to me, "Come on, Paul. You mean you didn't put the moves on her?" I am not going to bother to talk about the email notion. The answer to the other question is a simple "That's right!"

Is it possible that you are living? If you are alive, you are not living as Kaji Yukiko, the name I gave you in this story. You are under your real name. Last year, Ogawa Wakako, my friend in Tokyo, who is in her late sixties, said when we were exploring the possibility of tracing you, "Paul, eighty-five is pretty old. But Japanese women are young and strong!" That wonderful statement came about after Ogawa-san became so intrigued that she took a train from Tokyo to Yokosuka in the hope of finding you. I had not asked Ogawa-san to make that trip. She talked to the police. But there were apparently no records that would give clues. Ogawa-san then made a second trip to Yokosuka to see a nostalgic photography exhibit at the city's Museum of Art titled *Memories of a City*. Many of the photos showed Yokosuka as I remember it, and the catalog from the show enabled me to identify the White Rose.

Later, Ogawa-san suggested that I look for you in the United States. Your English was excellent. You did not have family ties in Japan. You may have met an American serviceman and emigrated to the US, Ogawa-san suggested.

There are many online search engines in the United States. You sign up. You pay a small fee. Then there are often multiple choices of identical names. I was shocked when I found a woman, in the right age group, using your real complete first and last name attached to an American surname: in other words something like "Yukiko Kaji Williams." I telephoned her. She said she was hard of hearing and asked me to "type" a letter, which I did, enclosing with it an original carbon copy of one of your 1959 letters. There was silence. Ogawa-san was absolutely convinced that this was you and even I, usually skeptical, began to believe. The woman had used the word "type," which is what you and I did when we used typewriters to write letters. And that voice on the phone—telling me, in measured, beautifully phrased English, "I am so sorry that I have this hearing problem. I can't quite understand what you are telling me about yourself. But if you believe that this is important, please type me a letter. And thank you very much . . ."—that voice rang true. But eventually a niece of the woman called me to say that her aunt was already in the United States in 1959 and that she could not, therefore, be you, Yukiko. She added that her aunt already had an American Social Security card in 1959. I am still not 100 percent convinced that she is not you. I was ready to drive cross-country to meet you. I was crushed. I lost you once. If you are she, I don't want to lose you again.

American-style online searches for people are not really possible in Japan, Ogawa-san explained. Privacy laws are restrictive. And besides, she said, there are several different ways of writing the kanji characters for your name. I have the kanji for your first name because on one occasion you chose to sign your letter in kanji. But I did not keep the envelopes that your letters came in. I did not have any idea then that having your address might be important one day.

I should mention, also, that Ogawa-san had a conversation with an official of the Japanese government's social services agency to ask whether there was an association of repatriates from Manchuria, which might have membership lists useful in locating you. She was told that such an association had existed, but because of the passage of time, and the aging of that generation of 1.5 million people who were able to return to Japan from Manchuria between 1945 and 1948, there did not seem to be any reason to keep the organization going.

What became of the others I met in 1959? Paul Feng? I don't know. Nurse Lydia Wong? I don't know. Irene Chen? I don't know. Cloudlet? I am sure she is a good Catholic. Mr. Ito? I don't know although I suspect he is still living, a man in his early eighties cheerfully saying, "Please enjoy your happiness." Detective Nazaka? I am sure he is smoking cigarettes and drinking cognac and chatting up barmaids in a Japanese version of Heaven, which is where he belongs. Shinoda Yusuke? Long gone, for sure. Chaplain Peeples? He passed away in 1997 and his grave can be found in the Lawtonville Cemetery of Estill, South Carolina. He is probably preaching in a Baptist version of Heaven. Red Downs died in 2012 and is buried in the Veterans Memorial Cemetery in Newton, Mississippi. Jim Fowler, Oscar, and Gunther? I have made attempts to track them down, but no luck. Commander Crockett? He rose to the rank of captain and died peacefully in 2005 in Dallas, Texas, where he is "entombed" (according to an obituary) at Hillcrest Mausoleum. I am sure he is ballroom dancing or piloting jet fighters in a Texan version of Heaven.

The names of *Shangri-La* crew members are real, as is the name of the ship itself. Fortunately, I have the amazingly detailed "cruise book" from the ship's voyage to the Pacific in 1959, which lists the ship's crew and has photos of many individuals. These names may sound contrived, but Davy Crockett, Charlie Peeples, and Bobby Drybread all are authentic, as are the names of my shipmates. The names of the Hong Kong characters appear in books they gave me or are listed in one of my notebooks. I wrote the names of Mr. Ito, Detective Nazaka, Reiko, and other Yokosuka personalities in the Japanese phrasebook in which I made entries as you began teaching me fragments of your language. Many other Japanese names are in the notebook, written there by men and women who befriended me. My efforts to find you and my old friends in the Far East even resulted in a well-intentioned but misleading article that appeared in some Taiwanese newspapers when I began writing this book. You were not mentioned in the article. But a reporter from Taipei who visited me in Arizona confused the friendship I had with a Chinese widow who tutored me in classical Chinese poetry in 1962, with the friendship I had with you.

Looking through my notes of our conversations that I made in 1959, I see that you often reached into your journal so that you could express certain thoughts in English that had been translated from the Japanese. One of your favorite statements was a line from Lady Murasaki's long novel *The Tale of Genji*. Murasaki started writing the novel at the end of the tenth century and continued writing it into the beginning of the eleventh. You often told me that line inside the Mozart café, a smile rippling across your face. "There are as many sorts of women as there are women," you would say with a knowing chuckle, as I laughed, still the child.

Another of your favorites from *The Tale of Genji*, which you recited in the week before I returned to the United States, was: "Did we not vow that we would neither of us be either before or after the other even in traveling the last journey of life? And can you find it in your heart to leave me now?"

Last year, I made a working trip to Las Vegas with my

younger son, Alexander, who is an attorney geographer, and I brought your letters with me. I read some of them to my son while we were driving—especially those in which you predicted that I would write—and I told him, "You know, when I am gone please make sure these letters are not thrown out, so that if you have children your kids can read them and learn something about their grandfather and what a woman who was pure of heart saw in him when he was a young man."

A Note on the Text

The reader should know that I have changed Yukiko's real first and last name so that if she reads this someday she can chuckle privately and enjoy her cup of green tea.

More than fifty years have passed since Yuki and I first met in 1959. I have had to invent most of the dialogue. I have tried to remain true to Yuki's manner of speaking, a task actually not that difficult, because she was unique and because she was my teacher, and we listened carefully and we talked and talked until there was moonlight and midnight. I do remember key expressions and phrases Yuki used. While not fluent in English, she delighted in using a level of speech that had a striking intelligence and uniqueness. She loved to quote lines from Japanese, English, and Chinese poetry. She kept in her purse a large notebook with a black cover full of translated poetry and song lyrics. When she was not pouring drinks at the White Rose, she spent hours studying at the city library or listening to educational programs and jazz and classical music on Tokyo radio stations. The reader can hear Yuki's voice in her letters, many of which are presented here verbatim. Other letters include the editing changes she asked me to make. I have had to use the same inventiveness with other characters in the book, again trying to stay as true to the events as I remember them.

Acknowledgments

Many friends helped me throughout 2013 with the writing and also refreshed my memories of Japan in 1959. Thank you to my sister Mary Finke and my friend Kimberly Rice for reading each chapter diligently and making important suggestions. Thanks to Zona Tropical natural history publisher John McCuen in San José, Costa Rica, who spent one year in Japan himself, for endorsing my idea for the book one morning in his office in April 2013. Thank you to my agent, Michael V. Carlisle of InkWell Management in New York City, for a phone call that startled me one day and for his guidance thereafter, and to Carole Tonkinson, publisher of Pan Macmillan's Bluebird imprint in London, for insightful editing that led to the publication of *Please Enjoy Your Happiness* in the UK in January 2016. Thank you also to Tara Parsons, editor-in-chief of Simon & Schuster's Touchstone imprint, for making this American version of the book a reality. A photograph taken of Tara's mother, in Japan, is used on the cover to the book. Special thanks to Ogawa Wakako in Tokyo, my classmate at Columbia University, for attempting to track Kaji Yukiko and for sending films and books that helped me remember Japan circa 1959, and also for her translation of the lyrics to *"Ringo oiwake"* (Apple

Folk Song). Hearty thanks to Patricia Trumps in Florida for excellent editing suggestions and for her enthusiastic support. Special thanks also to writer Emily Benedek in New York City for the generous amount of time she spent reading the manuscript and for the idea of going to YouTube to listen to music mentioned in the book. Thanks to two California author friends: Geoffrey Dunn in Santa Cruz, for his wizardry; and the late Larry Engelmann of San José, author of *Daughter of China*, and Linda Lee, for their hospitality. Like me, Larry had a habit of recording much of what he saw and thought about in notebooks. Thank you very much to Amy K. Hughes of New York City, who edited a late version of the manuscript in September 2014.

Thanks to former Yokosuka nightclub hostesses Fujiwara Mie and Koreyama Hanako in California for their vivid memories of 1959. Thank you to Michael W. Donnelly, who served with me in Yokosuka and who later became a political science professor specializing in Japan at the University of Toronto, for commenting on Yuki's letters. Thank you to Michael's wife, the writer Lynne Kutsukake, whose novel about postwar Japan titled *The Translation of Love* was published by Doubleday in April 2016. Thank you to Roger Goodman, Nissan Professor of Modern Japanese Studies at Oxford University, for his encouragement after reading the manuscript on a long flight to Asia. Thanks to Christopher Bauschka in California, son of Mieko Niishi Bauschka and the late US Navy Captain Patrick F. Bauschka, for an email I quote in the book. Thank you to my old friend Shawn Hubler in Los Angeles for giving the book a sensitive reading in the month I completed writing the story. Thanks to Janelle Rossignol of Phoenix, a frequent visitor to Tokyo who is an authority on Kabuki, for helpful comments on the story.

A big thank-you to avant-garde composer Cédric Lerouley in Paris, France, who is an *enka* fan, for mailing vintage LPs recorded by torch singer Matsuo Kazuko and also by Misora Hibari. Thank you to "Muppet" of Oldskool Japanese Music Thread (1920s–1980s) at forum.jhip.com for the translation of "*Dare yori mo, kimi wo aisu*" (More Than Anyone Else, I Love You). Thanks to writer Linda Style and screenwriter Marvin Kupfer (who, like me, is a former *Newsweek* correspondent), both of metro Phoenix, for important critiquing and advice given at crucial moments. Thank you to Ryan Seki of Phoenix for help with translations of book, film, and music titles, and to Vivian Seki for detecting errors. Thanks also to the remarkable Mehta family of Phoenix—Ajay, Momoe, and Sumi—for their comments and encouragement, and to Barbara Urso in Illinois, who every January, together with her husband, Paul, celebrates a special happiness. Thanks also to Phoenix residents Bob Golfen of classiccars.com and Ed Bergman of cruising66.com, and to San Diego resident Eduardo Aenlle, MD, all of whom understood why I wrote the book and my obsession in old age for Alfa Romeos. Special thanks to an avid Arizona reader, Melody Shouse, for a friendship that helped complete the book.

Thanks to two dynamic Mexicanas. The first is writer and bolero singer Carmen Barnard Baca in California, who visited Japan in her youth, for identifying so passionately with Yukiko and for translating Mexican composer Agustín Lara's lyrics to his "*Sombra de mis sombras*" (Echoes of My Shadows). The second is editor and music lover Elvira Espinoza in Phoenix, who said that the lyrics of *"Tango Uno"* from 1943 could well have been written for Yukiko, "who loved you in her own way inside her own very small and private soul."

Thank you to photographer James Caccavo of Los Angeles, who worked with me during the Vietnam War, for reading the manuscript and immediately understanding everything. Thanks also to the grizzled denizens of the Blue Marlin Bar (Arnold and Dexter especially) in San José, Costa Rica, and to my neighbor Mrs. Gloria Loeser for their encouragement, and for frequently feeding me and offering wine and liquor when I neglected to provide for myself.

Thank you to the many scores of Japanese—*mizu shobai mamasan*s, salarymen, bar hostesses, cops, and gangsters big and small—who listened with interest, and often with tears, when I first started telling bits and pieces of this story in small sake bars across Japan during the 1960s and 1970s. Thanks to the gracious residents of Hong Kong, especially Paul Feng, who befriended me in 1959.

Finally, thank you to Kaji Yukiko, wherever you are, for writing the letters more than fifty years ago that appear in this book. I changed your name. But if you read your letters again you will know that almost everything you predicted came true. I would enjoy so much having coffee with you again at the Mozart café.

MUSIC AND FILM REFERENCES

Chapters 1, 20, 22 Maria Callas sings "*Un bel dì*" [One Fine Day] from Puccini's *Madama Butterfly*: http://www.youtube.com/watch?v=AR0SlCTjlBo.

Chapters 3, 6 Ludwig van Beethoven, Ninth Symphony in D Minor, "Ode to Joy": http://www.youtube.com/watch?v=XFX8S9aAgvw.

Chapters 3, 5, 14 George Gershwin, *Rhapsody in Blue*: http://www.youtube.com/watch?v=eFHdRkeEnpM.

Chapter 3 Matsuo Kazuko and Wada Hiroshi sing "*Dare yori mo, kimi wo aisu*" [More Than Anyone Else, I Love You]: http://www.youtube.com/watch?v=BOt9lHjOtIE.

Chapter 4 The Genies sing "Who's That Knocking": http://www.youtube.comwatch?v=SXlRbXhvFIA&list=RDY3Wgs KEDg5Q.

Chapters 4, 8 Erik Satie, *Vexations*: http://www.youtube.com/watch?v=dBhjGIdL5cM.

Chapters 4, 8 Erik Satie, three *Gymnopédies* and six *Gnossiennes*: http://www.youtube.com/watch?v=dtLHiou7anE.

Chapters 4, 22 Misora Hibari sings "*Ringo oiwake*" [Apple Folk Song]: http://www.youtube.com/watch?v=U9D0sDgY2eU.

Chapter 4 Matsuo Kazuko sings "Again" in English: http://www.youtube.com/watch?v=7xrJsjJrEwI.

Chapter 4 Puccini, *La Bohème*, "*Si, Mi Chiamano Mimi*" [Yes, They Call Me Mimi]: http://www.youtube.comwatch?v=6tFGGPYlAEs.

Chapter 5 Fats Domino sings "Whole Lotta Loving": http://www.youtube.com/watch?v=nOONKeSTlDM.

Chapter 8 Yamaguchi Momoe sings "*Hitonatsu no keiken*" [Experiences of Summer Youth]: http://kayokyokuplus.blogspot.com/2013/03/momoe-yamaguchi-hito-natsu-no-keiken.html.

Chapters 8, 19 "*Ginza kankan musume*" [Ginza Street Girl] on 78 rpm record: http://www.youtube.com/watch?v=GNfdH9nockE.

Chapter 11 Franz Schubert, *Impromptus Opus 90*: http://www.youtube.com/watch?v=QDVJkxGz_Tc.

Chapter 12 Kurosawa Akira, trailer for the film *Rashomon*: http://www.youtube.com/watch?v=xCZ9TguVOIA.

Chapter 14 Trailer for the film *Sands of Iwo Jima*: http://www.youtube.com/watch?v=NZoRnZ6Jw0w.

Chapter 14 Final scenes of Imai Tadashi's film *Himeyuri no Tô* [*Tower of Lilies*]: https://www.youtube.com/watch?v=Vhg_SBGKgz8.

Chapters 15, 16 Trailer for the film *The World of Suzie Wong*: http://www.youtube.com/watch?v=jnepiAcqb_g.

Chapter 17 Billie Holiday sings "You Don't Know What Love Is": http://www.youtube.com/watch?v=6P96s6bIeQk.

Chapter 18 Frank Sinatra sings "All My Tomorrows": http://www.youtube.com/watch?v=WNzlDI0ph0s.

Chapters 18, 21 Claude Debussy, *Nocturnes*: http://www.youtube.com/watch?v=AtL_enacFn8.

Chapters 18, 21 Claude Debussy, *La Mer*: http://www.youtube.com/watch?v=FOCucJw7iT8.

Chapter 19 Kurosawa Akira's film *Shūbun* [*Scandal*]: https://www.youtube.com/watch?v=sVVaPCP6lc.

Chapter 19 Misora Hibari sings "*Shina no yoru*" ["China Night"]: http://www.youtube.com/watch?v=63mZal2YNO0.

Chapter 19 *Kokyū* recital of "Stairway to Heaven": http://www.youtube.com/watch?v=sDXyjUVl2ak.

Chapter 20 Yves Montand sings "Barbara": https://www.youtube.com/watch?v=AW8kS7zjpyU.

Chapter 21 Libertad Lamarque sings "*Tango Uno*": http://www.youtube.com/watch?v=3JZwXiwSIjY.

Chapter 23 "*Itsuki no komoriuta*" [Lullaby of Itsuki]: http://www.youtube.com/watch?v=PrKESru3550.

Chapter 24 Agustín Lara's "*Sombra de mis sombras*" [Echoes of My Shadows]: http://www.youtube.com/watch?v=die006Q0rQ.

Chapter 24 Lena Horne sings "Where or When": http://www.youtube.com/watch?v=FnRSM3dLSTk.

Chapter 25 Billie Holiday sings "I'll be Seeing You": http://www.youtube.com/watch?v=zDlKb2cBAqU.

Selected Readings, Films, and Music

Books and Magazine Articles

Adelstein, Jake. *Tokyo Vice: An American Reporter on the Police Beat in Japan*. New York: Vintage Books, 2009.

Allen, Louis. *The End of the War in Asia*. London: Hart-Davis, Mac-Gibbon, 1976.

Anderson, Joseph L., and Donald Richie. *The Japanese Film: Art and Industry*. Tokyo: Charles E. Tuttle, 1959.

Bacon, Francis. *On the Interpretation of Nature*. Whitefish, MT: Kessinger Publishing, 2010.

Bashō, Matsuo. *A Haiku Journey: Narrow Road to a Far Province*. Translated from the Japanese by Dorothy Britton. Tokyo: Kodansha International, 1980.

———. *The Essential Bashō*. Translated from the Japanese by Sam Hamill. Boston: Shambhala, 1999.

Baumgardner, Randy W. (ed.). USS *Shangri-La CV/CVA/CVS-38*. Paducah, KY: Turner Publishing Co., 2002.

Benedict, Ruth. *The Chrysanthemum and the Sword: Patterns of Japanese Culture*. New York: World Publishing Company, 1967.

Bernardi, Daniel (ed.). *Classic Hollywood, Classic Whiteness*. Minneapolis, MN: University of Minnesota Press, 2001.

Borges, Jorge Luis. *A Personal Anthology*. Translated from the Spanish by Anthony Kerrigan. New York: Grove Press, 1994.

Bornoff, Nicholas. *Pink Samurai: Love, Marriage and Sex in Contemporary Japan*. New York: Pocket Books, 1991.

Bourdaghs, Michael. *Sayonara Amerika, Sayonara Nippon: A Geopolitical History of J-Pop*. New York: Columbia University Press, 2012.

Bradley, James. *Flags of Our Fathers*. New York: Bantam Books, 2000.

Buruma, Ian. *Behind the Mask: On Sexual Demons, Sacred Mothers, Transvestites, Gangsters and Other Japanese Cultural Heroes*. New York: Meridian, 1985.

———. *The China Lover*. New York: Penguin Press, 2008.

Busch, Noel F. *Fallen Sun: A Report on Japan*. New York: D. Appleton-Century, 1948.

Bush, Lewis. *Japanalia*. Tokyo: Sanseido, 1938.

Chan, Sucheng. *Asian Americans: An Interpretive History*. Boston: Twayne Publishers, 1991.

Chan, Yeeshan. *Abandoned Japanese in Postwar Manchuria*. London: Routledge, 2014.

Constantine, Peter. *Japan's Sex Trade: A Journey Through Japan's Erotic Subcultures*. Tokyo: Yenbooks, 1993.

Dazai, Osamu. *No Longer Human*. Translated from the Japanese by Donald Keene. New York: New Directions, 1958.

———. *The Setting Sun*. Translated from the Japanese by Donald Keene. New York: New Directions, 1956.

De Barry, William Theodore, and Richard Lufrano. *Sources of Chinese Tradition*. New York: Columbia University Press, 2000.

Dore, R. P. *City Life in Japan: A Study of a Tokyo Ward*. Berkeley, CA: University of California Press, 1958.

Enright, D. J. *The World of Dew: Aspects of Living Japan*. Tokyo: Charles E. Tuttle, 1956.

Ericson, Jean E. *Be a Woman: Hayashi Fumiko and Modern Japanese Women's Literature*. Honolulu: University of Hawaii Press, 1997.

Fairbank, John King. *The Great Chinese Revolution, 1800–1985*. New York: Harper & Row, 1986.

Feifer, George. *The Battle of Okinawa: The Blood and the Bomb*. Guilford, CT: The Lyons Press, 2001.

Galloway, Patrick. *Stray Dogs and Lone Wolves: The Samurai Film Handbook*. Berkeley, CA: Stone Bridge Press, 2005.

Gold, Alison Leslie. *A Special Fate: Chiune Sugihara, Hero of the Holocaust*. Danbury, CT: Scholastic Corp., 2000.

Golden, Arthur. *Memoirs of a Geisha*. New York: Alfred A. Knopf, 1997.

The Gossamer Years: The Diary of a Noblewoman in Heian Japan. Translated from the Japanese by Edward Seidensticker. Boston: Tuttle Company, 2001.

Han, Bangqing. *The Sing-song Girls of Shanghai.* Edited by Eva Hung. Translated from the Chinese by Eileen Chang. New York: Columbia University Press, 2005.

Harden, Fred. "Yokosuka: Joyful Kingdom of the Orient." *Our Navy* (October 1957): 20–21, 36–37.

Hattori, Ryutaro. *One Hundred Japanese Folk-songs.* Tokyo: Ongaku-no-tomo sha, 1960.

Hayashi, Fumiko. *Floating Clouds.* Translated from the Japanese by Lane Dunlop. New York: Columbia University Press, 2012.

Hearn, Lafcadio. *Some New Letters and Writings.* Tokyo: Kenkyusha, 1925.

Hibbett, Howard. *The Floating World in Japanese Fiction.* Oxford, UK: Oxford University Press, 1959.

Historic Decade (1950–1960). New York: Year Inc., 1960.

Hoaglund, Linda. "Protest Art in 1950s Japan: The Forgotten Reportage Painters." Cambridge: Massachusetts Institute of Technology Visualizing Cultures, 2012.

Hucker, Charles O. *China's Imperial Past.* Stanford, CA: Stanford University Press, 1975.

Ishiuchi, Miyako. *Club and Courts: Yokosuka Yokohama.* Tokyo: Sokyusha, 2007.

———. *Sweet Home Yokosuka, 1976–1980.* New York: PPP Editions and Andrew Roth, 2010.

———. *Yokosuka Again, 1980–1990.* Tokyo: Sokyusha, 1998.

———. *Yokosuka Story.* Tokyo: Shashin Tsushinsha, 1979.

Iwasaki, Mineko. *Geisha: A Life.* New York: Atria Books, 2002.

Johnston, Lt. James D. *China and Japan: Being a Narrative of the Cruise of the U.S. Steam-Frigate Powhatan in the Years 1857, '58, '59, and '60, Including an Account of the Japanese Embassy to the United States.* Philadelphia: Charles Desilver, 1861.

Kafka, Franz. *The Complete Stories.* New York: Schocken, 1971. (The passage quoted in the letter in chapter 18 is from "The Silence of the Sirens.")

Kant, Immanuel. *Critique of Pure Reason.* Translated from the German by J. M. D. Meiklejohn. Buffalo, NY: Prometheus Books, 1990.

Kaplan, David E., and Alex Dubro. *Yakuza: Japan's Criminal Underworld*. Berkeley: University of California Press, 2003.

Kawabata, Yasunari. *Snow Country*. Translated from the Japanese by Edward Seidensticker. Tokyo: Charles E. Tuttle, 1957.

———. *The Sound of the Mountain*. Translated from the Japanese by Edward Seidensticker. New York: Knopf, 1970.

Keene, Donald (ed.). *Anthology of Japanese Literature: From the Earliest Era to the Mid-Nineteenth Century*. New York: Grove Press, 1955.

Kinkelaar, Freek. "Michi Aoyama and the Hardship of Enka." *Record Collector (UK)*, no. 428 (June 2014): 70–73.

Kirkup, James. *These Horned Islands*. New York: The Macmillan Company, 1962.

Koestler, Arthur. "The Lotus and the Robot." *Horizon: A Magazine of the Arts* 3, no. 4 (March 1961): 4–11.

Kuramoto, Kazuko. *Manchurian Legacy: Memoirs of a Japanese Colonist*. East Lansing: Michigan State University Press, 1999.

Lamont-Brown, Raymond. *Kempeitai: Japan's Dreaded Military Police*. Stroud, UK: Sutton Publishing, 1998.

Lawson, Capt. Ted W. *Thirty Seconds over Tokyo*. Edited by Robert Considine. New York: Random House, 1943.

Leach, Bernard. *Kenzan and His Tradition*. London: Faber and Faber, 1966.

Le Carré, John. *The Honourable Schoolboy*. New York: Alfred A. Knopf, 1977.

Levine, Hillel. *In Search of Sugihara*. New York: Free Press, 1996.

Liu, James J. Y. *The Art of Chinese Poetry*. Chicago: University of Chicago Press, 1962.

Lu, Xun. *The True Story of Ah-Q: Bilingual Edition*. Taiwan: Jiliu Publishing, 1953.

Maruyama, Paul K. *Escape from Manchuria*. Bloomington, IN: iUniverse, 2010.

Mason, Richard. *The World of Suzie Wong*. London: Collins, 1957.

McCain, LTJG John R. (ed.). *Sir Shang Goes West: Introducing Far East Cruise of USS Shangri-La and Carrier Air Group 11, March–October 1958*. Tokyo: Toppan Publishers, 1958.

Mellen, Joan. *The Waves at Genji's Door: Japan Through Its Cinema*. New York: Pantheon Books, 1976.

Memories of a City: Yokosuka in Photographs and Contemporary Art. Yokosuka, Japan: Yokosuka Museum of Art, 2013. Exhibition catalog.

Michaelson, John Nairne. *Morning, Winter, and Night*. New York: Berkley Books, 1958. (Michaelson was a pseudonym of the journalist and playwright Maxwell Anderson.)

Michener, James. *Sayonara: A Japanese-American Love Story*. New York: Random House, 1954.

Millay, Edna St. Vincent. *Collected Poems*. New York: Harper & Row, 1956.

Mishima, Sumie Seo. *The Broader Way: A Woman's Life in the New Japan*. New York: The John Day Co., 1953.

Mishima, Yukio. *Death in Midsummer and Other Stories*. Translated from the Japanese by Donald Keene, Ivan Morris, Geoffrey Sargent, and Edward Seidensticker. New York: New Directions, 1966.

Murasaki, Lady. *The Tale of Genji*. Volumes 1–6. Translated from the Japanese by Arthur Waley. Boston: Houghton Mifflin, 1925–33. (The author is also known as Shikibu Murasaki.)

Neruda, Pablo. *The Captain's Verses*. Translated from the Spanish by Donald D. Walsh. New York: New Directions Books, 1972.

———. *New Poems (1968–1970)*. Translated from the Spanish by Ben Belitt. New York: Grove Press, 1972.

———. *100 Love Sonnets: Cien sonetos de amor*. Translated from the Spanish by Stephen Tapscott. Austin: University of Texas Press, 1986.

O'Donnell, Joe. *Japan 1945: A US Marine's Photographs from Ground Zero*. Nashville, TN: Vanderbilt University Press, 2005.

Oe, Kenzaburō. *A Personal Matter*. Translated from the Japanese by John Nathan. New York: Grove Press, 1968.

Ohbayashi, Takashi. *Musuko e: Matsuo kazuko no yuigon fuinsarete ita hyakujukyutsu no tegami* [To My Son: 119 Letters Written by Matsuo Kazuko to Her Son]. Tokyo: Taeiaiesu, 1999.

Okakura, Kakuzo. *The Book of Tea*. Tokyo: Charles E. Tuttle, 1956.

An Outline History of China. Beijing: Foreign Languages Press, 1958.

Pagnamenta, Peter, and Momoko Williams. *Sword and Blossom: A British Officer's Enduring Love for a Japanese Woman*. New York: The Penguin Press, 2006.

Paine, Robert Treat, and Alexander Soper. *The Art and Architecture of Japan*. New York: Penguin Books, 1960.

Patric, John. *Why Japan Was Strong*. New York: Doubleday, Doran & Co., 1943.

Pedigo, M. L., and J. E. Torino (eds). *USS* Shangri-La *CVA-38: Far East Cruise 1959*. Tokyo: Toppan Publishing, 1959.

Poems of Solitude. Translated from the Chinese by Jerome Ch'en and Michael Bullock. London: Abelard-Schuman, 1960.

Prévert, Jacques. *Paroles*. Translated from the French by Lawrence Ferlinghetti. San Francisco, CA: City Lights, 2001.

Price, Willard. *Journey by Junk: An Adventurous Voyage Through the Inland Sea*. New York: The John Day Co., 1953.

Random, Michael. *Japan: Strategy of the Unseen; A Guide for Westerners to the Mind of Modern Japan*. Translated from the French by Cyprian P. Blamires. Wellingborough, UK: Thorsons Publishing Group, 1987.

Reischauer, Edwin O. *The Japanese*. Cambridge, MA: Belknap Harvard, 1978.

————. *The United States and Japan*. New York: Viking Press, 1962.

Richie, Donald. *The Films of Akira Kurosawa*. Berkeley: The University of California Press, 1984.

————. *The Inland Sea*. New York: Weatherhill, 1971.

————. *The Japan Journals, 1947–2004*. Edited by Leza Lowitz. Berkeley, CA: Stone Bridge Press, 2005.

————. *This Scorching Earth*. Tokyo: Charles E. Tuttle, 1956.

Rilke, Rainer Maria. *Selected Poems*. Translated from the German by C. F. MacIntyre. Berkeley: University of California Press, 1964.

Rossiter, Dr. Frederick M. *The Torch of Life: A Key to Sex Harmony*. New York: Eugenics Publishing Co., 1939.

Saga, Junichi. *Confessions of a Yakuza: A Life in Japan's Underworld*. Translated from the Japanese by John Bester. Tokyo: Kodansha International, 1991.

Saikaku, Ihara. *Five Women Who Loved Love*. Translated from the Japanese by William Theodore De Barry. Tokyo: Charles E. Tuttle, 1956.

Sann, Paul. *The Angry Decade: The Sixties*. New York: Crown Publishers, 1979.

Scott, George Ryley. *Far Eastern Sex Life*. London: Gerald G. Swan, 1943.

Senryu: Japanese Satirical Verses. Translated from the Japanese by R. H. Blyth. Tokyo: The Hokuseido Press, 1949.

Shōnagon, Sei. *The Pillow Book of Sei Shōnagon*. Translated from the Japanese by Arthur Waley. London: George Allen & Unwin Ltd, 1928.

Spence, Jonathan D. *The Search for Modern China*. New York: W. W. Norton, 1990.

Strong, Anna Louise. *The Chinese Conquer China*. Garden City, NY: Doubleday, 1949.

Sugihara, Yukiko. *Visas for Life: Chiune Sugihara*. Sacramento, CA: Edu-Comm Plus, 1995.

Tan, Daniela. "Literature and the Trauma of Hiroshima and Nagasaki." *The Asia-Pacific Journal* 12, issue 40, no. 3 (October 6, 2014).

Tanizaki, Junichirō. *Naomi*. Translated from the Japanese by Anthony H. Chambers. New York: Alfred A. Knopf, 1985.

———. *Seven Japanese Tales*. Translated from the Japanese by Howard Hibbett. New York: Knopf, 1963.

Tōmatsu, Shōmei. *Chewing Gum and Chocolate*. New York: Aperture Press, 2014. (Photographs of the US occupation, including Yokosuka, 1959.)

Turnbull, Stephen. *Samurai Women, 1184–1877*. Oxford, UK: Osprey Publishing, 2010.

Valley, David J. *Gaijin Shogun: General Douglas A. MacArthur, Stepfather of Postwar Japan*. San Diego, CA: The Sektor Company, 2000.

Watts, Alan W. *The Way of Zen*. New York: Pantheon Books, 1957.

White, Theodore H. *China: The Roots of Madness*. New York: W. W. Norton, 1968.

Whiting, Robert. *Tokyo Underworld: The Fast Times and Hard Life of an American Gangster in Japan*. New York: Pantheon Books, 1999.

Wildes, Harry Emerson. *Typhoon in Tokyo: The Occupation and Its Aftermath*. New York: Macmillan, 1954.

Yapp, Nick. *1950s: The Hutton Getty Picture Collection*. Cologne, Germany: Könemann Verlagsgesellschaft, 1998.

FILMS

After the Rain [*Ame Ageru*]. Koizumi Takashi (dir.). Asmik Ace, 1999.

Black River [*Kuroi kawa*]. Kobayashi Masaki (dir.). Shochiku, 1956.

Black Sun [*Kuroi taiyo*]. Kurehara Koreyoshi (dir.). Nikkatsu, 1964.

Crazed Fruit [*Kurutta kajitsu*]. Nakahira Kō (dir.). Nikkatsu, 1956.

Delinquent Girl Boss: Blossoming Night Dreams [*Zubekō banchō: zange no neuchi mo nai*]. Yamaguchi Kazuhiko (dir.). Toei, 1970.

Desperado Outpost [*Dokuritsu Gurentai*]. Okamoto Kihachi (dir.). Toho, 1959.

Even Parting Is Enjoyable [*Wakare mo tanoshi*]. Naruse Mikio (dir.). Toho, 1947.

Floating Clouds [*Ukigumo*]. Naruse Mikio (dir.). Toho, 1955.

Gate of Flesh [*Nikutai no mon*]. Suzuki Seijun (dir.). Nikkatsu, 1964.

Girl Boss Revenge [*Sukeban*]. Yamaguchi Kazuhiko (dir.). Toei, 1973.

The Great Beauty [*La Grande Bellezza*]. Paolo Sorrentino (dir.). Indigo Film, 2013.

A History of Postwar Japan as Told by a Bar Hostess [*Nippon sengo shi: Madamu Onboro no seikatsu*]. Imamura Shohei (dir.). Toho, 1970.

The House of Bamboo. Samuel Fuller (dir.). Twentieth Century Fox, 1955.

The Human Condition, Parts 1–6 [*Ningen no joken*]. Kobayashi Masaki (dir.). Shochiku, 1959–61.

I Am Waiting [*Ore wa matteru ze*]. Kurehara Koreyoshi (dir.). Nikkatsu, 1957.

The Inland Sea. Lucille Carra (dir.). Travelfilm Company, 1991.

The Insect Woman [*Nippon konchūki*]. Imamura Shohei (dir.). Nikkatsu, 1963.

Intentions of Murder [*Akai satsui*]. Imamura Shohei (dir.). Nikkatsu/ Toho, 1964.

In the Realm of the Senses [*Ai no koriida*]. Oshima Nagisa (dir.). Argos Films, 1976. (The story of Abe Sada and Kichi, chapter 22.)

A Japanese Tragedy [*Nihon no higeki*]. Kinoshita Keisuke (dir.). Shochiku, 1953.

Japanese War Bride. King Vidor (dir.). Twentieth Century Fox, 1952.

Late Chrysanthemums [*Bangiku*]. Naruse Mikio (dir.). Toho, 1954.

The Makioka Sisters [*Sasameyuki*]. Ichikawa Kon (dir.). Toho, 1983.

The Naked Island [*Hadaka no shima*]. Shindo Kaneto (dir.). Toho, 1960.

Navy Wife. Edward Bernds (dir.). Universal/Allied Artists, 1956.

Pigs and Battleships [*Buta to gunkan*]. Imamura Shohei (dir.). Nikkatsu, 1961.

Rashomon [*Rashōmon*]. Kurosawa Akira (dir.). Daiei, 1950.

Red Silk Gambler [*Hijirimen bakuto*]. Ishii Teruo (dir.). Toei, 1972.

Rusty Knife [*Sabita naifu*]. Masuda Toshio (dir.). Nikkatsu, 1958.

Sands of Iwo Jima. Allan Dwan (dir.). Universal Studios, 1949.

Sayonara. Joshua Logan (dir.). Warner Brothers, 1957.

Scandal [*Shūbun*]. Kurosawa Akira (dir.). Shochiku, 1950.

Story of a Prostitute [*Shunpuden*]. Suzuki Seijun (dir.). Nikkatsu, 1965.

Street of Shame [*Akasen chitai*]. Mizoguchi Kenji (dir.). Daiei, 1956.

Sugihara: Conspiracy of Kindness, How a Heroic Japanese Diplomat Saved Jewish Refugees in World War Two. Robert Kirk (dir.). WGBH/ PBS, 2005.

The Thick-Walled Room [*Kabe atsuki heya*]. Kobayashi Masaki (dir.). Shochiku, 1956.

Tower of Lilies [*Himeyuri no Tō*]. Imai Tadashi (dir.). Toei, 1953.

To Whom It May Concern: Ku Shen's Journey. Brian Jamieson (dir.). Virgil Films, 2010. (Docudrama about the actress Nancy Kwan, star of *The World of Suzie Wong*.)

Visas and Virtue: A Short Film Inspired by the True Story of Chiune Sugihara. Chris Tashima (dir.). Cedar Grove Productions, 1997. (Winner of the Oscar for Live Action Short Film in 1998 at the seventieth Academy Awards.)

Wandering Ginza Butterfly [*Gincho nagaremono*]. Yamaguchi Kazuhiko (dir.). Toei, 1971.

The Warped Ones [*Kyōnetsu no kisetsu*]. Kurehara Koreyoshi (dir.). Nikkatsu, 1960.

When a Woman Ascends the Stairs [*Onna ga kaidan wo agaru toki*]. Naruse Mikio (dir.). Toho, 1960.

A Woman Called Sada Abe [*Jitsuroku Abe Sada*]. Tanaka Noboru (dir.). Nikkatsu, 1975.

Women of the Night [*Yoru no onnatachi*]. Mizoguchi Kenji (dir.). Shochiku, 1948.

The World of Suzie Wong. Richard Quine (dir.). Paramount, 1960.

The Yakuza Papers: Battles Without Honor and Humanity, Parts 1–5 [*Jinji naki tatakai*]. Fukasaku Kinji (dir.). Toei, 1973–74.

Yakuza Wives [*Gokudō no onnatachi*]. Gosha Hideo (dir.). Toei, 1986.

Yakuza Wives: Burning Passion [*Gokudō no onnatachi: Jōeni*]. Hashimoto Hajime (dir.). Toei, 2005.

Yakuza Wives II [*Gokudō no onnatachi II*]. Dobashi Toru (dir.). Toei, 1987.

MUSIC

CDs

Ariagno, Cristina. *Satie: Complete Piano Works*. Brilliant Classics, 2010.

Boulez, Pierre, and the Cleveland Orchestra. *Debussy: La Mer and Nocturnes*. Deutsche Grammophon, 1995.

Callas, Maria, and the Orchestra and Chorus of La Scala, Milan, conducted by Herbert von Karajan. *Puccini: Madama Butterfly*. Major Classics Company, UK, 2012.

Callas, Maria, and Teatro alla Scala, Milano, Italia. *Puccini: Madama Butterfly*. Membram Music, Germany, 2005.

Vinyl Records

Eri, Chieme. *Chiemi's Folk Song Collection* [*Chiemi no minyōshu*]. King Records, 1958.

Hashi, Yukio. *Outstanding Song Collection 3* [*Keisaku shu 3*]. Victor, 1961.

Ichimaru. *Sings Japanese Emotions* [*Ninon no jocho wo utau*]. Victor, 1976.

Matsuo, Kazuko. *Hi-Light* [*Stereo hi-light*]. Victor, 1964.

———. *Husky in the Night 2* [*Yoru no husky 2*]. Columbia, 1960.

———. *I Don't Want to Know* [*Shiritakunaino*]. Victor, 1967.

———. *Sighs and the Night* [*Tameiki to yoru*]. Victor, 1970.

Misora, Hibari. *Complete Collection* [*Zenshu*]. Denon Columbia, 1963.

———. *Golden Hit Album: Songs That Live* [*Gōruden hitto arubamu: uta wa ikiteiru*]. Columbia, 1965.

———. *Hibari Sings Folk Songs* [*Hibari minyō wo utau*]. Denon, 1966.

———. *Hit Song Collection 1: Apple Folksong* [*Ringo oiwake*]. Columbia, 1954.

———. *Hit Song Collection 2: I Am a Child of the Town* [*Watashi wa machi no ko*]. Columbia, 1954.

———. *Together with This Song* [*Kono uta to tomo ni*]. Columbia, 1961.

Nagai, Frank, and Matsuo Kazuko. *Song for First Love* [*Hatsukoi no uta*]. Victor, 1962.

Three Cats [Sanbiki no neko]. *Yellow Cherry* [*Kiiroi sakuranbo*]. Columbia, 1959.

Wada, Hiroshi, and His Mahina Stars, featuring Matsuo Kazuko. *Party Songs* [*Ozashiki kouta*]. Japan Victor, 1964.

Yamaguchi, Momoe. *A Summer Experience* [*Hitonatsu no keiken*]. CBS Sony, 1974.

Sonnet XVII

I do not love you as if you were salt-rose, or topaz,
or the arrow of carnations the fire shoots off.
I love you as certain dark things are to be loved,
in secret, between the shadow and the soul.

I love you as the plant that never blooms
but carries in itself the light of hidden flowers;
thanks to your love a certain solid fragrance,
risen from the earth, lives darkly in my body.

I love you without knowing how, or when, or from where.
I love you straightforwardly, without complexities or pride;
so I love you because I know no other way

than this: where *I* does not exist, nor *you*,
so close that your hand on my chest is my hand,
so close that your eyes close as I fall asleep.

—PABLO NERUDA

About the Author

Paul Brinkley-Rogers is a veteran war correspondent and Pulitzer Prize–winning journalist. For many years he worked in Asia as a staff member of *Newsweek*, covering the wars in Vietnam and Cambodia, the death of Chairman Mao, and Japan's economic miracle. He also reported from Latin America for the *Miami Herald*, sharing the Pulitzer Prize with a reporting team in 2001 for coverage of the Elián González custody battle. Now retired, he lives in Arizona.